P9-DUG-964

WICKED
WOMEN
OF THE
SCREEN

# WICKED WOMEN OF THE SCREEN

DAVID QUINLAN

ST. MARTIN'S PRESS · NEW YORK

## Acknowledgements

About two-thirds of the photographs in this book are from the author's own collection. The remainder were culled from the files of the Stills Section of the British Film Institute. Almost all of the stills were originally issued to publicize or promote films or TV material made or distributed by the following companies, to whom we gratefully offer acknowledgement: Allied Artists, American-International, Anglo-Amalgamated, Artificial Eye, Associated British-Pathe, ATP, ATV, Avco-Embassy, BIP, Brent-Walker, British and Dominions, British United Artists, Cannon-Classic, Cinerama, Columbia, Dino de Laurentiis, Walt Disney/Buena Vista/Touchstone Films, Eagle-Lion, Ealing Studios, EMI, Enterprise, Entertainment, Filmakers Associated, First Artists, First National, Gainsborough, Gala, Gaumont/Gaumont-British, Goldwyn, Granada TV, Grand National, Hammer, Hemdale, Lippert, London Films, Lorimar, Metro-Goldwyn-Mayer, Miracle, Monogram, New World, Orion, Palace Pictures, Paramount, PRC, The Rank Organization, Rediffusion, Republic, RKO/RKO Radio, Hal Roach, Selznick, Titanus, 20th Century-Fox, UIP, United Artists, Universal/Universal-International, Virgin Films and Warner Brothers.

Especial thanks to Markku Salmi, Lisa Dewson and to the staff of the Information and Stills departments of the British Film Institute.

TO ELLEN AND BILL



*Library of Congress Cataloging-in-Publication Data*
Quinlan, David.
Wicked women of the screen.
Includes filmographies and index.
1. Women in motion pictures. 2. Evil in motion
pictures. 3. Motion picture actors and actresses—
Biography. I. Title.
PN1995.9.W6Q56 1987 791.43'028'088042 88-4499
ISBN 0-312-02048-1

First published in Great Britain by B.T. Batsford Ltd
First U.S. Edition, 1988
10 9 8 7 6 5 4 3 2 1
Typeset by Servis Filmsetting Ltd, Manchester
and printed by Anchor Brendon Ltd, Tiptree, Essex

# CONTENTS

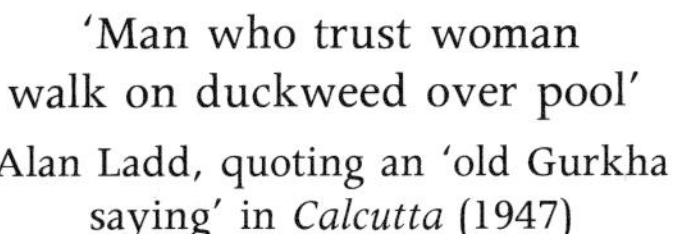

'Man who trust woman
walk on duckweed over pool'

Alan Ladd, quoting an 'old Gurkha saying' in *Calcutta* (1947)

# INTRODUCTION

'I didn't even know I'd fired.
I don't remember anything . . .
just the reports one after another till
there was a funny little click and the
revolver was empty'

Bette Davis in *The Letter* (1940)

They schemed, fought and clawed their way to what they wanted – money, power, men or revenge. They planned, plotted, connived, seduced, blackmailed, double-crossed and even killed for their own ends.

They were the wicked ladies of the screen – liars, temptresses, cheats, schemers and psychos. Men were pawns in their hands. Moths to be incinerated in a flame of danger.

Wicked women have always been among the most striking of cinema's creatures to stalk the screen, and audiences followed their fortunes through 90 minutes of crime and corruption with all the transfixed fascination of a rabbit confronted by a stoat.

Oscars were to be won playing such roles, and the actresses concerned knew it. So let me swing open the spider's parlour door and introduce you to the best of the worst and their catalogues of crimes. Bette Davis, Faye Dunaway, Margaret Lockwood, Joan Collins, Barbara Stanwyck, Gale Sondergaard, Lana Turner, Marlene Dietrich, Brigitte Bardot, Gloria Grahame and many more.

There have been scores of these strong-willed sirens since the cinema first felt the full force of female fury in its early silent days with what became known as vamps. The bad girls nearly always got their just deserts in the last reel. Now I can reward these female predators for some of the pleasure they have given me down the years by raising my glass of hemlock offering them a little of their due on the printed page.

If you don't buy this book, someone, somewhere, may be waiting to scratch your eyes out.

# 1
# THE STARS

'I stayed at a hotel called the Tarantula Arms . . .
That's where I brought my victims'
Vivien Leigh in *A Streetcar Named Desire* (1951)

*Curvaceous cigarette girl. Theda Bara attempts a Spanish stance beside some Californian rocks in a publicity pose for* Carmen *(1915)*

## Theda Bara

She was the silent screen actress who put the vamp in vampire. Also known as 'the love pirate', 'the sex bitch' or (quite often) 'the wickedest woman in the world', Theda Bara, in her relatively short stay near the top of Hollywood's early stars, brought a real flush of anger to the cheeks of many women cinemagoers,who hated her for what she did to men on screen. When Bara herself turned against that image, however, it brought an end to her star career.

Although her studio, Fox, would put out press releases suggesting their sexiest star had been born in France, Egypt, or places even more exotic, Bara was in fact born, (like another sex symbol, Sydne Rome, 50 years later) to a middle-class family from Cincinnati, Ohio. Her name was Theodosia Goodman (Theda was a childhood nickname). Her father came from Poland and her mother, whose own mother's maiden name had been Bara, was Swiss.

Before her sudden stardom in 1914, Theda Bara's life as an actress had been a hard one. There had been a few engagements with a New York road company and some rather undistinguished touring work in England and France but, at 24, and having just cashed an insurance policy to 'stay alive', Theda must have felt her chance of fame had gone.

She had turned down work on films, considering herself a stage actress, but when Frank Powell of Fox Pictures, with whom she had become acquainted, offered her a leading role out of the blue in a melodramatic little number called *A Fool There Was*, Theda decided to accept.

Theda Bara never saw herself as a smouldering lure for men. She once dismissed herself as 'an ordinary woman, a little tall (she was five feet six), a little thin, with big black eyes and a face of shadows'. In fact she was a little on the large side all round for a sinuous seductress (especially by today's standards) with a big round face, generous bust, long feet and a prominent chin that clever cinematographers did their best to disguise.

But she also possessed an intense stare, a good grasp of what was required to put sex appeal

*Theda Bara strikes one of her famous publicity poses, on this occasion as the doomed heroine of* Camille *(1917). Garbo would have blanched at so much flesh . . .*

(ABOVE RIGHT) *Bara, looking anything but 'the wickedest woman in the world', as Cigarette in* Under Two Flags *(1916)*

across and a melodramatic style very suited to the kind of vehicle in which she made her name.

The impact she made as the predatory nymphomaniac in *A Fool There Was* (1914) was so great that it was small wonder she found it impossible to escape the type and retain her popularity at the same time. It also provided her with her most famous line: 'Kiss me, my fool', which quickly passed into American folklore.

Publicity photographs showed Bara crouching over a skeleton, which was about all her character left of the men in the film, including the 'fool' of the title. 'Miss Bara misses no chance for sensuous appeal,' wrote the *New York Dramatic Mirror*. 'She is a horribly fascinating woman, cruel and vicious to the core.'

Unprepared for such notices, Fox had no ready-made follow-up for Theda; so they co-starred her in *The Kreutzer Sonata* (1915) as the spiteful and passionate creature who steals her sister's husband. Theda also stole the honours and was not to concede top billing again during the next hectic five years.

The next in her album of crimes was *The Clemenceau Case* (1915). She plays Iza, whose mission in life is to subject men to humiliation. She is eventually stabbed to death by her cuckolded husband, a fate from which even her pet python cannot save her.

After Bara's next film, *The Devil's Daughter* (1915), an adaptation of D'Annunzio's *La Gioconda*, women started kicking her face in posters, while children fled from her sight. After *The Tiger Woman* (1917), *Variety* wrote that 'the havoc wrought by Theda as a vamp is second only to the European armies'.

Probably no other actress ever made such a stream of films about wicked women. Other titles of Theda's five year reign as Queen Cobra of the screen included *Sin, Carmen, Destruction, Gold and the Woman, The Eternal Sappho, The Vixen, The Rose of Blood, Madame Dubarry, The She Devil, When Men Desire* and *The Siren's Song*.

Roles such as Cigarette in *Under Two Flags* (1916) and the title role in *Camille* (1917) did give her a slight change of pace, but undoubtedly her greatest triumph was back in the old Bara routine as *Cleopatra* (1917). Exotic costumes permitted a barer Bara than ever before and what she did in them – and out of them – caused apoplexy among censors and watch committees everywhere.

Certainly she pours everthing into the part, creating an erotic charge that would look melodramatic a few years later, but still fairly burns out of the screen.

Like many a sex star to follow, Theda Bara would protest that her films were really very moral in their attitudes – to keep girls on the straight and narrow, and to show that the wages of sin were death. Like every player typed in a certain kind of role, she had a yearning to go in exactly the opposite direction. Fox obliged her on several occasions, but always her fans (and

*Theda Bara's rose-covered version of that famous woman of passion* Dubarry *appeared in 1917*

there were millions of them) stayed away in hordes, especially from Theda as a sweet young thing in *Kathleen Mavourneen* (1919).

That was the wrong time for Theda to ask her studio for a $1,000 a week rise and no more vampire roles, but that was what she did. She was also almost 30; the studio contract was terminated by mutual consent.

Theda, who had just married director Charles J. Brabin – they stayed married until her death in 1955 from cancer – made a few more very lukewarm film appearances and did a little stage work, then vanished into seemingly happy retirement.

Many years later, a Hollywood columnist spotted her among a group 'of drab-looking,

*Buxom but beguiling – Bara's 1917* Cleopatra. *'I know,' she told an agog Press, 'that I actually am a reincarnation of Cleopatra. I live Cleopatra. I breathe Cleopatra. I am Cleopatra.'*

middle-aged women. No-one was able to identify these people – except the woman of the eyes . . . Theda Bara.'

### Brigitte Bardot

A wicked woman of the screen? No, Bardot was never anything other than a girl. Not so much a bad cat as a naughty kitten, and indeed the 'Sex Kitten' was a soubriquet by which she became known the world over. With a poutily provocative face and breasts that would have been noticeable in a potato sack, let alone in the tight sweaters and plunging necklines she was called upon to wear, Brigitte set glasses steaming up and temperatures rising the world over for a few heady years in the 1950s.

After 1960, she was no longer the same force and her films grew heavier along with her eye makeup. The wilful child of nature had finally succumbed to stardom.

Following ballet training, she had become a cover girl in leading French magazines before she was 15. From 17 she was playing minor roles in major films and major roles in minor ones. British film-makers spotted her on the verge of success and brought her across the Channel early in 1955 (she was 20) to co-star with Dirk Bogarde in *Doctor at Sea.*

She was merely saucy and piquant in that. It

*We've heard of washing in the sink, but this is ridiculous. No wonder Brigitte Bardot attracts the amorous attentions of a neighbour in* The Light Across the Street *(1955)*

*Bardot, again playing a character called Brigitte, lets fly with a right cross during* Une Parisienne *(1957)*

*As a girl infatuated with her uncle's murderer (Stephen Boyd), Bardot steamed across the screen in* Heaven Fell That Night/The Night Heaven Fell *(1957), one of her greatest international successes. Said Boyd: 'Wonderful girl. She used to chase me all over the set'*

was in French films that she blossomed out as a youthful sex goddess able to drive competing men to desperate measures. The first brick in the wall of this reputation was delivered by *Le lumière d'en face* (in Britain and America *The Light Across the Street*, 1955). A scenario was carefully contrived to make Bardot the bride of a highway café owner (the brooding Raymond Pellegrin) whose health does not permit the consummation of the marriage.

Not surprisingly, he goes round the bend before the film's 100 minutes are over, trying to shoot both his wife and her would-be lover from the garage across the highway before falling under the wheels of a lorry.

The camera prowls after Bardot like a peeping

Tom for virtually the whole film, catching her bending over, washing her legs, standing against the light in a nightdress and generally disrobing in profile. By the end, complained one London critic, 'it is difficult to see the screen for steam'. Bardolatry was born from this clammy piece of cinema and continued unabated for the next five years.

She played lighter roles in her next few films, but when *Et Dieu créa la femme* (1956, directed by her then-husband, Roger Vadim) came along, it became obvious that such flirtatious comedies as *Mam'zelle Pigalle* (1955) and *Mam'selle Striptease* (1956) were mere nine-carat gold, compared to the rich vein of erotica uncovered (!) by this slice of sex and sand.

Called *And Woman . . . Was Created* in Britain, with America plumping for *And God Created Woman*, the film cast Brigitte, then 22, and in the process of changing from brunette to blonde, as an orphan girl who becomes a less than obscure object of desire for several men in a small coastal town. Her oversexed nymphet is drawn to two brothers, marrying the younger, then allowing herself to be seduced by the elder, before fleeing to the mansion of a wealthy shipping magnate (Curt Jurgens).

*Yvette (Bardot) realises that she attracts the elderly lawyer (Jean Gabin) engaged to defend her on a robbery charge in* Love Is My Profession *(1957)*

Ultimately, the worm turns and her husband (Jean-Louis Trintignant) beats up his brother, shoots Jurgens, finds Bardot dancing drunkenly in a club, drags her home and beats her frenziedly, presumably to live happily ever after. Said one British critic: 'She is all the screen vamps rolled into one'.

With this film, Bardot conquered both British and American box-offices. She made two more frothy contract comedies, however, before the next 'sexation', *Heaven Fell That Night* (1957, in America *The Night Heaven Fell*) made her France's most profitable export.

By now divorced from Vadim and into the first (with Trintignant) of numerous well-publicized love affairs (and husbands) Bardot appears as a convent girl caught up in a vaguely *Bonnie and Clyde*-ish situation when she runs off with rough ne'er-do-well Stephen Boyd, who has killed her uncle and seduced her aunt. Following numerous bouts of sado-masochistic sex on the run, the girl is killed by police bullets after they have been hunted down through mountainous countryside. Boyd said he would willingly co-star again with Bardot, despite describing her as 'complicated, impulsive and a little bit off her rocker'.

Meanwhile, Bardot came to another bad end in *Love Is My Profession* (1957). Co-starring with Jean Gabin, still France's top male star at 53, Bardot plays a prostitute who ensnares the ageing lawyer who defends her on a robbery charge, ruining his life and marriage before being stabbed to death by a former lover. Clearly Bardot had grown out of the 'child of nature' stage and the dewy-eyed freshness had totally gone when she tackled her favourite acting role in *La vérité* (1960).

The film also introduced her to Sami Frey, who supplanted her second husband, Jacques Charrier, in her not so private life. At the beginning of the film he is engaged to Bardot's dowdier sister (Marie-José Nat) but eventually falls for the amorous writhings of Bardot as the footloose, amoral, sex-obsessed Dominique.

When he ultimately throws her out, she threatens to shoot herself, then shoots him instead. In prison, unable to cope with the prosecution's demands for her death, and the defence's demolition of her lover's character, she commits suicide by slashing her wrists.

The filming had a bizarre postscript that made world headlines when Bardot herself almost succeeded in committing suicide by cutting her wrists and taking a bottleful of pills. 'I am in despair,' she wrote. Certainly her career could not have driven her to it: *La vérité* contains her best, most fully-realised performance for which both she and director Henri-Georges Clouzot deserved credit. But had been found 20 minutes later, doctors revealed, Bardot would have gone the same way as Marilyn Monroe in 1962.

*La vérité* was certainly the highpoint of a

*Brigitte Bardot's last great international hit. Maria and Maria (Bardot and Jeanne Moreau) go to war in* Viva Maria! *(1965)*

career which now increasingly looked to be functioning on automatic pilot. Of her later films, only *Viva Maria!* (1965), Louis Malle's joyous comedy-adventure which dazzlingly teamed Bardot with Jeanne Moreau, gave rise to anything like the same worldwide queues of her peak years.

In her last film to date to be seen outside France, *Don Juan or: If Don Juan Were a Woman* (1973), she returned to Vadim's direction at the age of 39 as a woman who destroys men – one of whom is forced to agree to his own suicide as the price for possessing her. Her one sympathetic act results in her death in a blazing building.

Time, alas, had caught and passed both star and director and the film was a very pale copy of former erotic glories, with none of the sexual spark that had ignited the screen in the mid 1950s. Strangely, the major preoccupation of the star once dubbed 'Sex Kitten' has, in later years, been the conservation of animals and, like a few other famous stars, she has become something of a recluse as far as the Press has been concerned. But at least she has survived.

*Joan Collins was skimpily clad again in one of her first Hollywood roles, as the scheming and ambitious Nellifer in* Land of the Pharaohs *(1955)*

*Evelyn (Joan Collins) samples the velvet swing in Stanford White's (Ray Milland) observatory, in* The Girl in the Red Velvet Swing *(1955)*

## Joan Collins

There's no doubt that if Oscars were handed out for tenacity and astuteness in the furtherance of a career, and for sheer professionalism, Joan Collins would have no room left on the mantelshelf for anything else.

A stunning London-born brunette with slinky, 'working-class' type looks and a reed-slender but curvy figure, she had a low-lidded, full-lipped challenge about her in the early years that got her cast as sluts, schemers and slum youngsters struggling to go straight.

Her faintly haughty bad-girl qualities were put to good use as the high-class prostitute in *Turn the Key Softly* and the desert-island dish in *Our Girl Friday*. These were both made in 1953 when she was still barely 20 but already a hot box-office bet.

Hollywood swiftly beckoned but, although she worked hard under her Fox contract, the studio gave her too many good girl roles (to which she lent a certain fresh appeal with a hint of wilfulness), only barely realising how much more effective she was at witches and bitches.

She was the scheming second wife of pharaoh Jack Hawkins in her first Hollywood-backed film *Land of the Pharaohs* (1955). When one critic said that 'only Joan Collins has sufficient bouncy enthusiasm to be at home among all this exotic hokum' he might have been describing her performance as Alexis in television's soap opera *Dynasty* 30 years later.

Perhaps the best notices of Joan's Fox years came for her performance as the flighty showgirl Evelyn Nesbit (also a prominent figure in the more recent *Ragtime*) in *The Girl in the Red Velvet Swing*. Nesbit was a real-life turn-of-the-century figure who drove her current lover to murder a former flame – and to the brink of madness. Joan was appropriately coquettish while keeping the audience guessing as to the true malevolence of the character.

It was MGM who calculated her appeal to the nth degree when they cast her as the hard-boiled, husband-snatching Crystal in *The Opposite Sex* (1956) – the role played by Joan Crawford in the original version, *The Women*, in 1939.

Although surrounded by actresses around 15 years her senior, Joan certainly gave as good as she got in the eye-scratching stakes in this bumper bundle of bitchiness, with its impact slightly weakened by having men added to what was originally an all-woman story.

Although physically alluring enough and eager to give comedy a try, Joan proved it wasn't her natural forte when she portrayed the man-hungry femme fatale-next-door opposite Paul Newman in *Rally 'round the Flag, Boys!* (1958) and, of the rest of her Fox vehicles, only *The Wayward Bus* (1957), in which she had some torrid love scenes with Rick Jason, played into her strongest suit.

Joan's Hollywood contract ended in 1960 and, when she played second fiddle to Bob Hope and Bing Crosby in *The Road to Hong Kong* (1962) – a chore that should in any case have gone to Dorothy Lamour, who only got a cameo role – it was clear that Joan's film career was going astray.

There began years of wandering, career-wise, in which Joan appeared, often almost in guest star roles, in Italian and British films, and numerous television series, when she should by rights have been queening it in movie melodrama. Her private life was no more settled. Her second marriage, to actor Anthony Newley, had ended in divorce by the early 1970s, as had her first marriage (1952–57) to Irish-born film star Maxwell Reed.

Although she kept working, Collins must have thought she had hit rock-bottom in *Revenge* (1971, in America, *Inn of the Frightened People*), beating up perverts and eagerly submitting to

*Carol (Collins) is the half-willing victim of rape by her stepson (Tom Marshall) in the overheated 1971 release* Revenge

*Though dominant in this scene with Alan Price as Alfie in* Alfie Darling *(1975), Joan Collins must almost have despaired at this time in her career of regaining centre stage*

'rape' by her husband's son, crying 'I don't know what's come over us'. Not that the rest of the decade involved her in classier fare. In *Fear in the Night* (1972), she was shot by her lover after engineering the death of her husband at the hands of an unbalanced girl, while in *Tales from the Crypt* (1972), she viciously murders her husband before being strangled by a prowler dressed as Santa Claus.

More lurid horror followed, mixed with decoration in such abortive sexual farragos as *Alfie Darling* (1975) and a highwaywoman, Black Bess, in *The Bawdy Adventures of Tom Jones* (1975). When her adventuress was eaten alive in *Empire of the Ants* (1977), few could have blamed her for calling it a day. However, salvation was just around the corner.

Not that *The Stud* (1978) was any better than her previous films from the 1970s, but a great pop soundtrack and a publicity campaign that had more class than the film, made it a great popular success and revived the Collins star career. Based on sister Jackie Collins's novel, it cast Joan as wildly amoral Fontaine Khaled. Her first nude appearance in films did its box-office prospects no harm at all.

It was followed by two other films, *The Bitch* (1979), in the same character, and *Nutcracker* (1982), which were both sold along similar lines, and combined to make Joan a strong marquee name again. 'I don't regret *The Stud*,' she said later, 'because it was a renaissance for me. I did regret *The Bitch*; I hated the script and, quality-wise, it was a disaster. It also saddled me with that goddam label . . .'

No doubt, though, the 'label' stuck in producers' minds – especially when casting for Alexis, the queen bitch in the high-gloss television soap opera *Dynasty*. Though its scripts are not exactly of the real world, Collins makes her character hypnotic to watch.

By 1986, she was appearing in a gigantic television mini-series, *Sins*, doing the kind of role in which Joan Crawford might once have revelled. She suffers, uses people, dominates in the business world, and goes through 30 costume changes.

Said one reviewer: 'Collins announces . . . that the character's chief sin is pride, but there are plenty of transgressions along the way to be totted up – from adultery to blackmail to covetousness, just to start at the ABCs'.

*Sins* put Joan Collins at last into her rightful place – splendidly sinning as the queen of heady melodrama in an all-gloss world.

## Arlene Dahl

An almost too-lovely green-eyed redhead whom Hollywood used largely as decoration in Technicolor escapades, Arlene Dahl also had disturbing qualities that were all too rarely exploited in films, and might, despite her limited acting ability, have made her a much bigger star.

From the beginning, however, all the young Arlene really wanted to do was sing. That really is her singing in *Three Little Words* (1950) but she wasn't bouncy enough to be another Doris Day and her opportunities in the musical field proved extremely sparse.

The Dahl family had originally emigrated to America from Norway, but were well established in Minneapolis, Minnesota, by the time Arlene was born in 1924 (she has always insisted it's 1928, but no reference work seems inclined to believe her).

As she moved from modelling to stage work,

*Fontaine (Joan Collins) toys with her toy-boy (Oliver Tobias) in* The Stud *(1978), a watershed film in the Collins career*

*Fontaine (Joan Collins) is about to hear bad financial news from her business manager Arnold (Kenneth Haigh) in* The Bitch *(1979). But you can't keep a bad girl down for long . . .*

*A gambler and his lady. David Brian with Arlene Dahl in her first really interesting dramatic role, in* Inside Straight *(1951)*

her outstanding beauty soon attracted the attention of Hollywood, and Warner Brothers' chief Jack Warner signed her to a weekly contract. He said he saw her as another Ann Sheridan, detecting her earthy qualities, but missing the demon at the corner of her dimpled smile.

While Warner was away in Europe, MGM's Louis B. Mayer whisked Arlene from under his nose after only two Warners films. But he did little with her for several years beyond photographing her in Technicolor and/or draping her in becoming period costumes.

Only in 1951, ironically her last year at the studio, did Arlene fleetingly look a dramatic force to be reckoned with. Playing a scheming dance-hall hostess in *Inside Straight*, she unexpectedly proved a match for David Brian as the gambler who becomes a ruthless tycoon.

And she was even better in *No Questions Asked*, one of her first real 'bitch' roles. Her rejection of her lawyer boyfriend (Barry Sullivan), for a man who can buy mink, is the trigger which decides him to make a lot of money himself in a legal but highly unethical racket.

In the early 1950s, Arlene Dahl embarked on the other two facets of her life for which she would be remembered: her marriages (which would number six in all) and her syndicated beauty hints, which would make her one of the most widely-read columnists on the subject.

She also became a fashion designer with the formation of Arlene Dahl Enterprises in 1952, the year she divorced first husband Lex Barker. Two years later she married another handsome actor, Fernando Lamas. Unfortunately, during this period she also made several films. They were almost all bad and required her to do no more than look luscious.

Looking back on 1952–55, the time of *Desert Legion, The Diamond Queen* and several more, Arlene said recently: 'Those films are such an embarrassment. Talk about past sins. They keep coming up on television to haunt me.'

The only one of her assignments from this period that was worthwhile from an acting point of view was her role in *Woman's World* (1954), as the self-centred wife trying to push husband Van Heflin to the top of his company. The role wasn't half as interesting, however, as the one that she was asked by RKO to do in the late summer of 1955 for their film *Slightly Scarlet*. The character she plays in this Technicolor *film noir* is quite frankly as nutty as a fruitcake. Not exactly dangerous perhaps, but distinctly unbalanced, as 'hero' John Payne finds out.

*(RIGHT) Dahl in one of her juiciest roles: the smilingly psychotic seducer Dorothy Lyons in* Slightly Scarlet *(1956)*

*Kathy (Dahl) is determined to get to the top – even if it means marrying the boss (Herbert Marshall) in the 1956 film* Wicked As They Come

*The unlikely romantic combination of an insurance investigator and a firebug brought Jack Hawkins and Arlene together in 1956 for* Fortune Is a Woman *(aka* She Played with Fire*)*

Dahl was never the subtlest of actresses, but when she switches on at full beam, the results can be quite disturbing in a part like this. Especially memorable is the scene where she denies stealing Payne's lighter and after being forced to admit it, switches it on to his hand as she gives it back.

An alcoholic, nymphomaniac and kleptomaniac rolled into one, Dorothy (Dahl) is fresh out of prison as the story starts to unfold. Dahl's cropped hairstyle, here at its shortest, helps to emphasize the unbalanced nature of her character, which quickly becomes the most interesting in the film. She does not, however, succeed in seducing Payne (contrary to the original James M. Cain book) and is left whimpering in the dark like a child, in the arms of her (over-)protective sister (Rhonda Fleming) after Payne submits to severe wounding so that the villain may be brought to justice with a gun in his hand.

The success of Dahl's performance in *Slightly Scarlet* caused producers to look again at her screen image and enabled her to complete a trio of roles which make up the most interesting work of her career. Her next two films were made in England for Columbia, beginning with *Wicked As They Come* (1956). In *Slightly Scarlet* she tells John Payne, 'We're two of a kind. Both bad.'

In *Wicked As They Come*, she's Kathy, one of a kind and all bad. The victim of a New York slum upbringing and a gang rape as a teenager, Kathy is determined to make men pay for all this, while crookedly making a success of her own life. The first victim of her seductive charms fixes a beauty contest for her, then she relieves another of his money, wrecking his career as a photographer.

After an affair with her employer, Kathy marries the boss of her company, but accidentally kills him and is charged with murder. When the truth comes out, she's free to go on the prowl for more rich pickings. But she never does get her claws into the man (Phil Carey) she really wants.

Later the same year, Arlene made *Fortune is a Woman*, released in 1957. Hollywood changed the title to the more appropriate (and saleable) *She Played with Fire*, as Arlene portrayed an arsonist who leads insurance assessor Jack Hawkins astray with her lies. Well directed by Sidney Gilliat, it was a polished and satisfying thriller which provided Dahl with the last good role of her career.

She took time out from acting in 1958 to have a son, her first child, Lorenzo Lomas, now a popular television actor. But her marriage to Fernando Lamas ended in divorce in 1960. He later married another actress, Esther Williams. Arlene's career at this time quickly slid into glamorous cameos, and business interests rapidly took over the greater part of her life.

Despite the fact that she never achieved her ambition to be a musical comedy star, Arlene said recently that she still felt she'd been lucky. 'Believe me, in my first screen test I was terrible. I thought they'd never use me. And I've almost always had at least two professions going at the same time, so I've never felt insecure.

'And my films? Let's just say the best productions of my life have been my three children.'

## Bette Davis

Bette Davis lived up to Mae West's famous words. 'When I'm good I'm very, very good. But when I'm bad, I'm better.' Few actors could have failed to flinch at the Davis evil, wilfulness, or lust for power in full force. Although she played many sympathetic roles to great effect, it is undoubtedly for her bitches that Bette Davis will be remembered.

She was born Ruth Elizabeth Davis in 1908 in Massachusetts, the New England state that gave

*Johnny Ramirez (Paul Muni) keeps his boss's predatory wife Marie (Bette Davis) at bay, in* Bordertown *(1934). But one way and another, Marie proves deadly trouble . . .*

her those harsh, clipped tones that so well expressed decision and ruthlessness. Bent on an acting career from an early age, she had already made her Broadway debut before coming to Hollywood, where she failed a screen test with Goldwyn, but succeeded at Universal, despite, or perhaps because of a talent scout who said she 'didn't look like any actress I had ever before seen on the screen.'

She dyed her hair ash-blonde (it suited her), but her early roles before she transferred to Warner Brothers in 1932 were quiet and sympathetic.

It was her man-hungry flapper in *The Rich Are Always With Us* (1932) that allowed the studio to see her more spiteful side, and they cast her as the seductive rich girl in *Cabin in the Cotton* (1932). The film gave out with the first classic Davis quote, when she tells weak-kneed Richard Barthelmess that 'I'd love to kiss ya, but I jest washed ma hay-ur.'

Barthelmess goes back to his sweetheart in the end, but the script leaves no doubt that the Davis character still feels he is hers for the taking.

Her hell-raising Jenny was reformed by George Arliss in *The Working Man* (1933), but there was no reforming the slut Mildred from *Of Human Bondage* (1934). Davis's cockney accent sounds tatty now, but there is no mistaking the venom in her portrait of the illiterate waitress, incapable of genuine affection, who almost ruins the life of embryo doctor Leslie Howard.

Years later she described it as 'the first leading-lady villainess ever played on a screen for real', although Theda Bara and Pola Negri (*qqv*) might well have been justified in asking her exactly what she meant.

Davis's sins catch up with her in the end, as she dies of locomotor ataxia in impoverished circumstances. But the mould had been set. In *Housewife* (1934), she played a career-conscious husband-stealer and moved from bad to worse in *Bordertown* (1934) in which, to try and get her claws into the hero, she kills her husband and arranges the death to look like suicide.

In the end, the hero is arrested for the crime, but Davis's disintegration in the witness box into complete mental breakdown provided a beanfeast for Davis fans and a happy ending for

*Davis, Henry Fonda (between them, Fay Bainter) and the famous red dress in the 1938 film* Jezebel. *Davis and Bainter both won Academy Awards*

*'Oh, it was all instinctive. I didn't even know I'd fired.' Bette Davis filling her lover full of those little round things that kill you, in* The Letter *(1940)*

hero Paul Muni. It's still one of her most startling performances.

That part set her up for her first Oscar in *Dangerous* (1935). Davis' electric performance as the alcoholic actress who blights the lives of all who cross her path caused E. Arnot Robertson to pen the famous lines in *Picture Post* in which she wrote that 'if she had lived two or three hundred years ago, I think Bette Davis would probably have been burned as a witch'. Davis' punishment in this instance resulted from an attempt to put paid to her husband in a crash – a crash which only made him a cripple, whom she would have to look after for life.

*Satan Met a Lady* (1936) was a remake of *The Maltese Falcon* (1931), giving Bette the role (of the murderess) that Mary Astor would play in the classic version of 1941. It was such a bad film, however, that it triggered off Bette's now-famous running battle with the studio for better parts.

Following flight to England, and court action – which she lost – she got them, most notably with *Jezebel* (1938), which won her an Academy Award. By this time back to being brunette, she pre-empted Vivien Leigh by playing a tempestuous Southern belle in 1850. Wilful even by Davis standards, Julie Marston tries to embarrass her fiancé (Henry Fonda) in public for some imagined slight, by wearing a sacrilegious red dress to a ball. But she is hoist with her own petard when he goes off to the North to work and marries on the rebound. Enraged, she encourages an admirer (George Brent) to challenge him to a duel. But Fonda is called away to New Orleans to fight an epidemic there; his younger brother fights in his place and Brent is killed. A contrite Julie elects a probable death with Fonda, who has contracted yellowjack fever, by marching off – headstrong as ever – to nurse him on a quarantine island.

There didn't seem to be a year at that time, and deep into the 1940s, when Bette Davis wasn't being nominated for an Oscar. It was the period of her greatest acclaim. She played the spoiled socialite going blind in *Dark Victory*, the fidgety Elizabeth I half-falling for Errol Flynn in *The Private Lives of Elizabeth and Essex*, and the empress descending into madness in *Juarez* – all in 1939.

The following year brought her skilfully-devised portrait of the cool, calculating Leslie Crosbie, who shoots her lover on a Malayan plantation in *The Letter* (1940). After using her 'distraught' act to manipulate the sympathy of her husband (Herbert Marshall) and defence counsel (James Stephenson), who agrees to buy an incriminating letter she has written to the dead man, from his oriental widow (Gale Sondergaard), Leslie is acquitted. She then shakes her husband's dog-like devotion by declaring that 'With all my heart, I still love the man I killed'.

The Hollywood codes of the time demanded that retribution catch up with her at the hands of a vengeful Sondergaard, but few fans of Davis, or Somerset Maugham, on whose story the film was based, were convinced, nor did it suit the brooding atmosphere director William Wyler had created.

Previously made in 1929 with Jeanne Eagels, *The Letter* was reworked rather than remade as *The Unfaithful* (1947), with Ann Sheridan on trial for the shooting of a 'prowler' who turned out to be her lover, and made more faithfully (but badly) as *East of Elephant Rock* (1973), with Judi Bowker and a Sri Lankan setting.

Davis' deepest-hued villainess of the period was probably her Regina Giddens in 1941's *The Little Foxes*. An entirely self-centred woman, Regina schemes and blackmails her way to power, engineering her husband's death from a heart attack along the way. She ends wealthy, hated and alone.

Playing a much younger role than of late, Bette was up to all her old tricks in *In This Our Life* (1942). As Stanley Timberlake (in a family of girls with boys' names), she steals her sister's husband and drives him to suicide. Returning to the family fold, she tries to win back her former suitor (the hapless George Brent), who has turned to her sister (Olivia de Havilland).

Rejected by him, Stanley drives off blindly and runs down a child, a crime which she tries to wriggle out of, but pays for when she herself is killed in a car crash while fleeing from police.

After *In This Our Life*, Bette took a hard-

*Davis as the heartless Regina Giddens, with Herbert Marshall as her sickly husband, in* The Little Foxes *(1941). By his side: the medicine she is soon to deny him*

*Bette Davis and Baby Jane doll – a macabre duo from her hugely successful 1962 comeback film* What Ever Happened to Baby Jane?

earned break from the highly-coloured wicked ladies who had dotted her career, until the last film under her long Warners contract – *Beyond the Forest* in 1949.

Bette is Rosa Moline, a snarling tigress thrown out by her husband (Joseph Cotten) and determined to net a Chicago industrialist (David Brian), who initially rejects her but eventually succumbs. Shooting a man who threatens to tell Brian she's pregnant, Bette tries without success to get her doctor husband to perform an abortion.

She contrives to lose the baby by jumping from an embankment, but succeeds in contracting peritonitis as well. Rising from her sickbed to catch a train for Chicago, she staggers towards the station, but collapses and dies as the train speeds away. Bette was over the top in more ways than one in this film, which heralded a graduation to more mature roles, the best of which came as the queen bitch actress in *All About Eve* (1950).

Scattered among these, however, were a couple of throwbacks to her heady days as the queen of high melodrama. In *Another Man's Poison* (1951), she poisons her fugitive convict husband and later his fellow-escaper, before accidentally getting a dose herself and dying in bursts of hysterical laughter. In *Dead Ringer* (1964. In Britain: *Dead Image*), she kills her twin sister and takes her place, before being convicted and executed for a murder she did not commit.

There are other Davis demons – the woman who drowns her young charge in *The Nanny* (1965), her silver-haired sibyl in *Where Love Has Gone* (1964) and her master criminal in *Madame Sin* (1971, originally for television). And she did some pretty unkind things to her long-time Warners rival Joan Crawford in *What Ever Happened to Baby Jane?* in 1962. But the foregoing films represent the cream of her catalogue of crimes. When Bette Davis played a wicked woman, she stayed played.

## Faye Dunaway

There's no doubt that when Faye Dunaway is on screen, her fellow cast-members have to be on their toes to keep up with her. Like many of the actresses in this book, she has played fewer wicked ladies than one thinks, yet few actresses were as fierce in the occasional portrayal of irredeemable evil.

The daughter of a regular army officer, the Florida-born Dunaway brought authority to her film roles from the start, jumping straight into movie leads from off-Broadway work. But her smouldering gun-girl Bonnie Parker in *Bonnie and Clyde* (1967) jetted her to top stardom more quickly than even she can have expected.

Perhaps perversely, Faye was more softly feminine in this film than in any other, at the same time exactly catching the sexual aggression of the character and the way breaking the law made her adrenalin flow.

Ultimately, the law catches up with the lawless lovers (their unconventional sex lives were treated somewhat gingerly in the film), riddling them and their car with bullets. It is typical of Dunaway's professionalism that she remembers the set-up with relish rather than disgust.

'A hundred or so tiny charges, together with little packets of blood-like liquid, were attached to my body, and connected to invisible wires that ran behind the camera.

'Then my face was made up in five places to make it look as if a bullet had just gone in. I

*'We rob banks.' Clyde Barrow (Warren Beatty) and Bonnie Parker (Faye Dunaway) proving the truth of their introductory line in* Bonnie and Clyde *(1967)*

remember that especially – black circles each with a red rim. Skin wax was put over them, and the wires were attached. Then they were all set off, and I had to do this St Vitus's Dance, as though it were one impact after another. I thought it was very effective.'

It wouldn't be the last time a Dunaway character would bite the dust (or break the law), even though her next role was the ultra-cool insurance investigator fencing with Steve McQueen in *The Thomas Crown Affair* (1968). By the time it came out, the unexpected success of *Bonnie and Clyde* had made her a star of the first rank. It also won her the first of her Oscar nominations.

Although her disturbed fashion model in *Puzzle of a Downfall Child* and her predatory Mrs Pendrake in *Little Big Man* (both 1970) may have been less than sympathetic characters, Faye eschewed outright villainy until inheriting Lana Turner's larger-than-life role of Milady de Winter in *The Three Musketeers* (1973) and its simultaneously-shot sequel, *The Four Musketeers* (1974).

Faye came into her own in the second of the two films, whether seducing Michael Gothard's jailor into committing assassination, strangling Raquel Welch's Constance, or enthusiastically submitting to Christopher Lee's equally dastardly Rochefort over a bath of blood. She is eventually apprehended by her ex-lover Athos (Oliver Reed).

She played a much more complex woman in her next film *Chinatown* (1974). Both it and her character, Evelyn Mulwray, were throwbacks to the *film noir* of the 1940s. A true-black widow, she draws private eye Jack Nicholson into a complex web of big-business corruption. In the end she wounds her own father (John Huston), the evil power behind the corruption, before fleeing for the state border and being gunned down by police.

Dunaway's performance resulted in her second Academy Award nomination, but she finally won the award for her portrayal in *Network* (1976) as the foul-mouthed TV executive who

*Dunaway as ruthless, tough-talking Diana Christenson, concerned only with the ratings of her shows in the film that finally won her an Oscar,* Network *(1976)*

*At times Dunaway looked uncannily like Joan Crawford when she played her in the controversial 1981 film* Mommie Dearest. *Mara Hobel was excellent as Crawford's adopted daughter Christina as a child*

*Lady Barbara Skelton (Faye Dunaway) with Hogarth (John Gielgud), the servant she tries to poison before finally suffocating him because he knows of her secret life as a highwaywoman, in* The Wicked Lady *(1983)*

lets nothing and nobody – and certainly not scruples – stand in her way.

Having created a star out of a ranting ex-newsman now fired with evangelistic zeal (Peter Finch, also an Oscar-winner), she and fellow-executives have him assassinated when he begins to fall in the ratings, an act of terrorism that will provide the basis for another segment of her popular new programme, *Mao Tse Tung Hour.*

Despite its awards, the film was an overheated and over-caricatured look at life, accusations also levelled against Dunaway's version of Joan Crawford in the controversial *Mommie Dearest* (1981). Here the star was depicted as a tyrant who beat and half-strangled her adopted daughter whom she expected always to be perfect. Although Dunaway looked uncannily like Joan Crawford at times, most critics objected to the biased view of the story – based on the daughter's somewhat hysterical autobiography.

From fictionalized fact, Faye flew to outright fantasy in her two 1983 films *The Wicked Lady* and *Supergirl*. Again Faye trod in the footsteps of another wicked woman of the screen, Margaret Lockwood, in her portrayal of the notorious Lady Barbara Skelton, a character actually based on a true-life adventuress called Lady Kathleen Ferrers, who lived in the seventeenth century in

*Most of Dunaway's recent roles have been unworthy of her, although she still gives them 101%. In 1984 she played the power-hungry witch Selena, menacing Helen Slater's* Supergirl

a house that still stands today, as does the secret passage from her bedroom where she left at night to take up her clandestine career as a highwaywoman, robbing and killing travellers to London.

Faye tore ferociously into her role and did her own stunt riding. Director Michael Winner gave her a duel of whips to fight with a topless opponent and added generous lashings of nudity and other period rudery to spice up the hoary old tale, which refused to look anything but ludicrously out of date.

'Michael asked me to strip too, of course,' she commented. 'Most directors these days do. But...I'm protected by a no-nudity clause that's standard to all my contracts. A long time ago, I decided that wasn't the route I would take.'

She obligingly died off at the end of the film, however, as she did in *Supergirl*, playing another role unworthy of her as Selena, a fairground witch who unsuccessfully tries to dispatch the title character with the help of such forces as 'the Invisible Monster'.

Faye defends these concoctions by saying that she hadn't had such fun in ages. But she hasn't had a meaty film role in quite a while; it was sad to find her as the murder *victim* in the abysmal *Ordeal by Innocence* (1984) and she badly needs a dominant leading character into which to sink her teeth. *Barfly* (1987) may provide it.

In 1983, Faye Dunaway said, 'I love to play these defiant, ambitious females who wind up winning their struggle, even if they don't overcome the scars of their pasts. They're multidimensional characters, with various shades, moralities and conflicting emotions.' And they're what Faye Dunaway should be trying to rediscover.

## Gloria Grahame

Like so many of her characters, sultry Gloria Grahame aimed high but never quite reached the big time. Unlike some of the actresses in this book, who were successful in a wide variety of roles, Gloria Grahame only really came into her own playing bad girls of lighter or darker hue – and often stealing the film.

The end of Hollywood's studio years in the middle and late 1950s found Gloria at an awkward age. She made some poor career decisions at this stage that more or less resulted in the cinema losing one of its most powerful, provocative and personable players at a time when she still had much to offer.

Born Gloria Grahame Hallward in 1924, she was on stage at 16 and signed for films 18 months later. Unaccountably, she kicked her heels around at MGM for two years, not doing very much until director Frank Capra saw her distinctive sulky looks in a screen test and hauled her across to RKO to play town flirt Violet in *It's a Wonderful Life* (1946), who, in the vision of what would have happened had hero James Stewart never lived, descends to prostitution and is hauled off to jail. In reality, Stewart is kind to her and gives her the money to head for New York and a fresh start.

Back at MGM, her tinsel voice, pouting lips and hooded gaze got her cast as a silent screen vamp in *Merton of the Movies* (1947). She was a torch singer bumped off in *Song of the Thin Man* (also 1947), but in the same year crossed again to RKO for the leading female role in the much-praised *Crossfire*. As a soft-hearted trollop, Grahame won her first Oscar nomination at only 22.

She now divorced her first husband, actor Stanley Clements, and married director Nicholas Ray, who helped bolster her stagnating career (the expected flood of offers after *Crossfire* having failed to materialise) by having her cast in one of her few successful sympathetic roles, opposite Humphrey Bogart in Ray's *In a Lonely Place* (1950).

Even in this film, Gloria's character almost gets throttled at the end. Bogart is suspected of a murder of which he is innocent but although she loves him and helps him, Gloria is also afraid of him. When she tries to flee on the day of their wedding, he attacks her in an uncontrollable rage, ruining the future for both of them even as he is proved innocent of the original murder.

Gloria would later joke that it was about the closest she ever got to a happy ending. But she enjoyed working with Bogart more than any other co-star. 'A darling man,' she said. 'So helpful, so nice.'

There was certainly far from a happy ending in *Sudden Fear* (1952), in which she and lover Jack Palance plan to murder his wealthy wife Joan Crawford. As Irene, Gloria is the driving force behind the scheme to poison Joan's heiress Myra. Her character also displays signs of a masochistic sex drive unusual in an early Fifties film.

Retribution is duly wrought when Palance's Lester, trying to run down Myra in his car, kills Irene instead, dying as well when he tries to

*Mary (Jacqueline White) fights to clear her husband's name in a murder investigation, and tries to enlist the help of Ginny (Gloria Grahame, left) in* Crossfire *(1947)*

swerve at the moment he recognizes he has the wrong woman in his headlamps.

Just for a change, she was killed in a plane crash with her lover in *The Bad and the Beautiful* (1952). She won an Academy Award as best supporting actress for her portrayal of the Southern belle tramp Rosemary Barlow.

Even after this accolade, however, Gloria still rarely seemed to be right at the top of cast lists, unless it was in offbeat critical successes such as *The Glass Wall* or such out-and-out rubbish as *Prisoners of the Casbah* (both 1953); the latter was bad even by 'eastern' standards.

The same year, Gloria tackled another subsidiary role, this time in Fritz Lang's *The Big Heat*, although she and Lee Marvin are the best-remembered characters from the film as a gangster and his moll – and particularly for the scene in which he disfigures her with scalding coffee.

*This dangerous duo will eventually sink in its own conspiratorial stew. Gloria Grahame with Jack Palance in* Sudden Fear *(1952)*

(TOP) *Debby (Gloria Grahame) shoots a blackmailing widow in order to bring retribution down on the gangsters who have disfigured her, in* The Big Heat *(1953)*

(CENTRE) *Vicki (Grahame) hopes her lover Jeff (Glenn Ford) will kill her murderously jealous husband Carl (Broderick Crawford), in* Human Desire *(1954). But it is not Carl who dies*

(BOTTOM) *Gloria in the famous 'little black number' from* Naked Alibi *(1954). The drunk at the table is Gene Barry*

She gets her own back, not only by shopping him and his boss to the policeman (Glenn Ford) whose wife's death they caused, but by murdering a woman whose death will ensure the gangsters go down for good. She repays the compliment to Marvin with hot coffee just before he guns her down. She dies hiding the burnt side of her face in a mink coat.

Lang reunited Ford and Grahame in *Human Desire* (1954), an (inferior) remake of the French film *La bête humaine*. Broderick Crawford completed the trio as Carl, who suspects that his wife Vicki (Gloria) has sold her sexual favours to help him keep his job. He forces Vicki to arrange a meeting with the man in question and kills him.

Vicki now starts an affair with Jeff (Ford) and persuades him to murder Carl. Jeff cannot bring himself to do it (although he does retrieve a blackmail letter Carl holds over Vicki) and Vicki is forced to leave town with her husband. As she taunts him with her sexual peccadilloes and her plan to bump him off, Carl loses control and strangles her. In the 1938 Jean Renoir version Jeff dies too, but Hollywood spared him.

By this time, Gloria was divorced from Nicholas Ray and had married another director, Cy Howard. She was back in the hard-boiled routine as the torch-singer girlfriend of clever killer Gene Barry, hunted by persistent cop Sterling Hayden, in *Naked Alibi* (1954). Once again, she was killed off at the end. The film was more admired in Britain and France than America, and Gloria made the covers of several magazines in a slinky black 'petticoat'.

She then cleverly diverted her stereotyped sluttish flirt into the plum musical role of Ado Annie in *Oklahoma!* (1955). Hollywood held its breath in anticipation of a disaster, but Gloria, doing her own singing with *All Er Nuthin'* and *I Cain't Say No* – two songs which summed up almost all her screen characters – was a piquant, provocative delight.

*Oklahoma!* did not lead to better things. The next few years brought only recyclings of roles she had done better the first time around. Her third marriage broke up in 1957 and her film career rapidly followed suit. Perhaps there are fewer parts for a bee-lipped, sloe-eyed lady of 35 with a wheedling temptress's voice, but all the same, one has the feeling that Gloria should have done better with the latter stages of her career.

She was still acting, on the London stage, at 57, when suddenly taken ill. She was flown to New York, where an emergency operation failed to save her from dying of cancer. There hasn't been a shopsoiled siren to match her since.

## Rita Hayworth

Some performers' careers are enhanced by their marriages, but Rita Hayworth's was wrecked by hers. The fiery Latin temperament inherited from her father led her into a series of hasty engagements and marriages, which fragmented and finally shattered the pattern of her career. But, at least until the fateful year of 1948, few if any Hollywood stars were as capable of playing exotic temptresses of such character that they left an indelible imprint on film history.

*It's the beginning of the end for matador Juan Gallardo (Tyrone Power) when he falls under the spell of the seductive Dona Sol (Rita Hayworth), in* Blood and Sand *(1941)*

*Hayworth steps into screen immortality performing* Put the Blame on Mame *from her 1946 classic* Gilda

The pity of her comparatively brief time at the top was that she had started so early. Born Margarita Cansino in 1918, to a Spanish dancer and a Ziegfeld Follies girl and cousin to Ginger Rogers, she was on stage with her parents, as 'The Dancing Cansinos' from childhood. Breaking into films at 16, she made her feature film debut dancing on board a doomed ship in *Dante's Inferno* (1935).

She was soon playing roles in decent second-features, among them *Human Cargo* (1936), as a fiery Mexican called Carmen (her real middle name) who gets mixed up with smugglers and is bumped off for her pains. At this time she was billed as Rita Cansino but in 1937, when stuck as leading lady in very small westerns (and still with her natural black hair), she married salesman Ed Judson, who switched from selling cars to selling Rita, and manoeuvred a move to Columbia that would prove vital to her career.

Here she got a new name (with a 'y' added to her mother's maiden name, Haworth) and a new leading man in Charles Quigley, a virile hero of action movies. They co-starred six times before Quigley's career faltered as Rita's blossomed. The first was *Criminals of the Air* (1937), in which she diverts Quigley's attention from duty before proving to be in the pay of the smugglers he's after.

Becoming tired of getting bumped off as bad girls, or falling into Quigley's arms as good ones, Rita pressed Judson to get her more important roles. The story goes that after macho director Howard Hawks saw her in a slinky gown she had bought for the occasion, the rest was a formality. She got the part she was after in Hawks' *Only Angels Have Wings* (1939). As the straying wife of pilot Richard Barthelmess in a Latin-American 'banana' republic, she tries to rekindle an old affair with Cary Grant, who rewards her by dousing her ardour with a pail of water. The brief but showy role, and the critical applause it gathered, proved that Rita would soon leave 'B' pictures behind.

Hayworth had made 28 feature films by the time she got her first 'A' film lead as a girl accused of murder in *The Lady in Question* (1940). She is cleared by a lawyer (Brian Aherne) who falls in love with her, but ends up with his son, played by Glenn Ford in the first of their five films together.

Hayworth, who had now adopted the flame-red hairstyle for which she is best remembered, was fourth-billed but captivating as *The Strawberry Blonde* (1941). She then got the showiest role in *Blood and Sand* (1941) as the high-born temptress who seduces bullfighter Tyrone Power away from his wife and his career. As his star fades, so does their affair and, by the time Power has taken a fatal goring in the ring, Rita is already casting her eye over another rising young matador, ironically once her lover's best friend (Anthony Quinn).

She had made one minor musical at Columbia, *Music in My Heart* (1940), but now, as she returned to the studio a star (*Blood and Sand* was made at Fox), there followed a magical quartet of exhilarating musicals opposite top dancing

*Hayworth was an obvious choice for the role of Carmen in* The Loves of Carmen *(1948), her last Columbia film for four years. Glenn Ford looks less comfortable*

stars. And what dancers! Two films with Fred Astaire, *You'll Never Get Rich* (1941) and *You Were Never Lovelier* (1942), one with Gene Kelly, *Cover Girl* (1944) and one with the dazzling but forgotten Marc Platt, *Tonight and Every Night* (1944).

Rita has described the Astaire films as 'the only jewels of my life. Fred asked for me in the first place. He knew I was a dancer. He knew what all these dum-dums at Columbia didn't know.'

From musicals, she moved back to femmes fatales and that siren par excellence called *Gilda* (1946). Hayworth's animal magnetism was never used to greater effect than here, as the convergent point of a triangle in which three people constantly play one against the other against a Buenos Aires casino background. The highlight is Hayworth's *Put the Blame on Mame* number as, in a drunken ecstasy of animal abandon, she peels off long black gloves in a high-voltage striptease, stopped only by her ex-lover (Glenn Ford).

She had divorced Judson in 1943 and married actor-director Orson Welles, but this marriage was ending even as Welles was directing a valedictory anthem to their relationship in *The Lady from Shanghai* (1947).

In contrast to Gilda, there are no good points about Elsa Bannister, the twisted, ice-cool schemer of *Shanghai*. Welles had Rita go blonde for the role, a canny move which drains her personality of much of its natural warmth. She seduces an itinerant seaman (Welles himself) into the depths of a lies-within-lies scheme which results in the murder of a participant and Welles' trial for murder, defended by Elsa's crippled husband (Everett Sloane).

Anticipating the verdict, he escapes and hides out in the local Chinatown, where things come to a head in the famous hall-of-mirrors climax in which Elsa is shot to death by her own husband.

*The Loves of Carmen* (1948) isn't Hayworth on top form, even though made by her *Gilda* director Charles Vidor. The familiar story of the fiery gypsy girl who seduces a soldier into loving her then killing for her would be more rewardingly filmed as the musical *Carmen Jones* six years later. The plot ends with Ford plunging a knife into his faithless Carmen, then dying himself, the lovers entwined in death.

Rita then embarked in a disastrous marriage to Prince Aly Khan, millionaire son of the spiritual leader of millions of Moslems, which took her away from Hollywood for four years. On her return in 1952, she was generously reinstated by Columbia, and immediately teamed with her old partner Glenn Ford. The three films she then made, *Affair in Trinidad* (1952), *Salome* and *Miss Sadie Thompson* (both 1953) would have certainly maintained her career momentum had they come straight after *The Loves of Carmen*.

In the early 1950s, however, she is clearly six or seven years too old for all three roles, especially *Salome*, and seems vaguely tired. The willingness is there, but some of the vivacity has gone. *Miss Sadie Thompson*, though, did give some evidence that Rita was adapting to her new age group with her portrait of Somerset Maugham's South Seas sinner. But then another unfortunate marriage, this time to singer Dick Haymes, took her away from the movies for another four years, and this time it really was all over. Her 'other woman' in *Pal Joey* (1957) attracted some attention, but the rest – and there is a lot of it – is a sad and shadowy echo from the past. Especially distressing was her appearance in *The Money Trap* (1965): a couple of short scenes as the alcoholic ex-mistress of former co-star Glenn Ford, before she gets pushed off a rooftop and out of the plot.

Her last appearance, in *Circle* (1976), has not been seen in most parts of the world, and she was increasingly ill in the 1980s with Alzheimer's Disease, which finally killed her in 1987.

Fortunately many of her fans from the 1940s

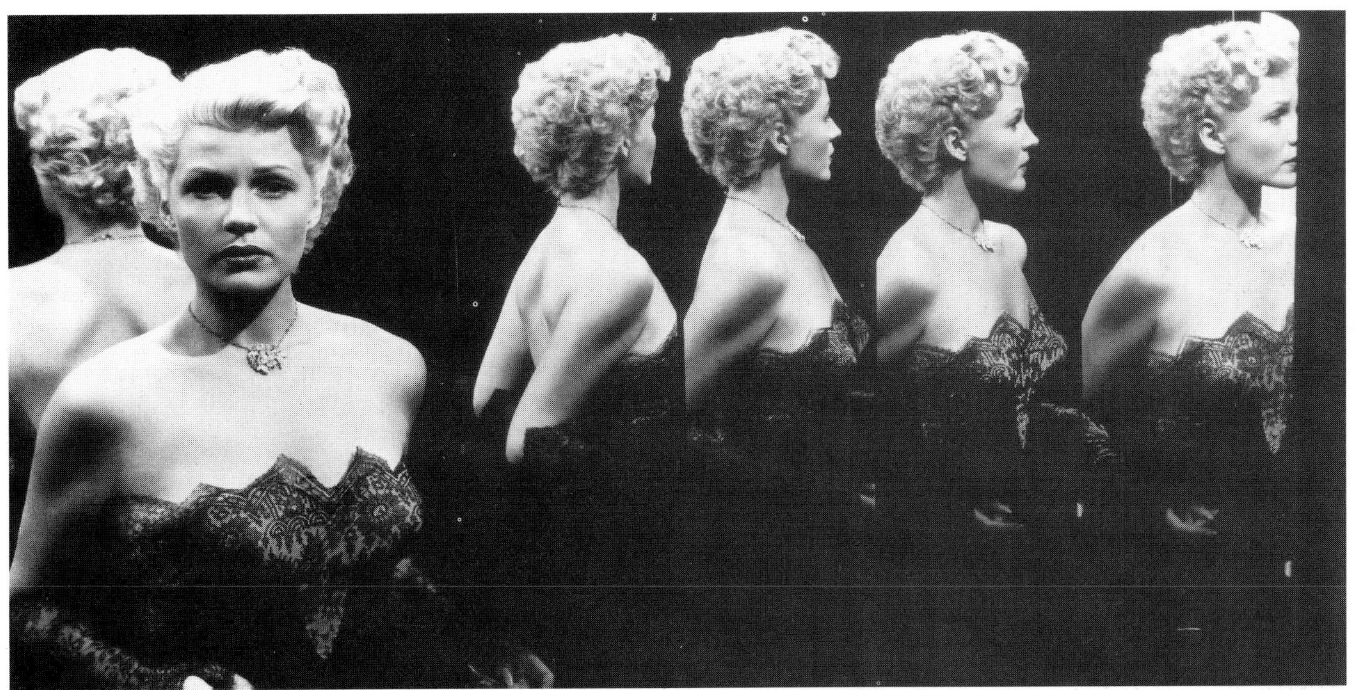

*A blonde Hayworth at the hall-of-mirrors climax to* The Lady from Shanghai *(1947)*

*Hayworth dances up a storm as Somerset Maugham's South Sea sinner* Miss Sadie Thompson *(1953), a film originally due to be released in 3-D!*

*Hayworth was a little past her prime to be an exotic dancer when Columbia cast her in* Salome *(1953). Being the trouper she was, she gave it a good try. The chap in the funny hat is Stewart Granger*

(RIGHT) *A touch of the Rita Hayworths for Jean Kent as the tempestuous gipsy girl of* Caravan *(1946)*

have seen little of her work since the lustre faded. They remember Rita only as the sexiest and most glamorous woman of her time.

## Jean Kent

Spite and malice were qualities that few actresses could express so well as British star Jean Kent. In the end, though, like so many wicked ladies of the screen, she got tired of projecting malice, aforethought or otherwise, and it proved the undoing of her film career.

She was born Joan Summerfield in Brixton, London, in 1921. She lied about her age to get into show business as a dancer at 12, and began in films the following year, playing a small part in *The Rocks of Valpré* (in America: *High Treason*); she was also drafted in to swim in long-shot for a non-swimming star.

She had a thinnish time as Joan Summerfield (and later Jean Carr) before she settled on Jean Kent, and began to command larger roles from 1942. After her performance as the heroine's friend Lucy in *Fanny By Gaslight* (1944, in America: *Man of Evil*), she became one of the 'Gainsborough ladies', appearing in films for Gainsborough and Two Cities through the decade, including *Madonna of the Seven Moons* (1944), *The Wicked Lady* (1945), *Carnival* (1946), *The Magic Bow* (1946) and *Caravan* (1946), the latter her first screen demise playing a fiery gipsy girl.

At this stage, she was still billed below the leading lady, as she was in *The Man Within* (1947, in America: *The Smugglers*) where she played a barrister's mistress who seduces hero Richard Attenborough. Her thin upper lip and the challenging look from under those lidded eyes had already steered her towards conniving shrews; it was a mould she would soon find hard to break.

She was the heroine's spoilt younger sister in *The Loves of Joanna Godden* (1947), an epic farming romance, marrying the man big sister (Googie Withers) loves, but running out on him when his flock gets foot-and-mouth disease.

That set her up for her first *bona fide* lead in *Good Time Girl* (1947), the film that fixed the image by which filmgoers seem to remember her. As Gwen, a teenager at the start of the story, she is sacked by her boss for stealing and beaten by her father. Falling foul of the crooked owner of the nightclub where she next works, she is arrested at the flat of a friend, Red (Dennis Price), for – unwittingly – pawning stolen jewellery, and sent to a reformatory. Escaping to Brighton, she becomes the mistress of a racketeer.

*Jean Kent's first* bona fide *scarlet woman was as the barrister's mistress who seduces cowardly hero Richard Attenborough in the oddball eighteenth-century smuggling yarn* The Man Within *(1947)*

*Keen gent bags Jean Kent. Gwen (Kent) with Red (Dennis Price), her tragic true love, in the film that made her a big name,* Good Time Girl *(1947)*

*Fortune-teller Astra (Kent) toys with the affections of her sister's fiancé (Dirk Bogarde) in the 1950 drama* The Woman in Question

*Crocker-Harris (Michael Redgrave) is overwhelmed by the gift of a book, despite the scornful attitudes of his wife (Jean Kent) and her lover (Nigel Patrick) in* The Browning Version *(1951)*

Involved in a car crash in which a policeman is killed, Gwen leaves the racketeer, but ends up with two GI deserters. In a holdup they shoot a witness – Red. Gwen is sent down for 15 years.

If her characters' morals were little improved in subsequent films, at least Jean was going up in the world, as befitted her natural elegance. She was a model coming to a sticky end in *Bond Street* (1948) and an unscrupulous adventuress in *Sleeping Car to Trieste* (also 1948), a remake (with certain plot alterations) of the 1932 classic *Rome Express*.

Understandably, Jean asked her employers for something lighter, and the result was one of her favourite films, *Trottie True* (1949, in America: *Gay Lady*). A Technicolor romp, it cast her as a talented but flighty entertainer from London's Camden Town who charms her way to the top with the help of a series of sexually susceptible men and ends up marrying into the nobility. A flight with an old flame in a balloon (after a tiff with her husband) ends in a disastrous crash into a stream. A wet Trottie decides it's much safer being a duchess.

From finishing up dead at the fade-out of some of her pictures, Kent was dead at the beginning of *The Woman in Question* (1950, in America: *Five Angles on Murder*). An enigmatic fortune-teller of easy virtue and complex character, she's found strangled. The film adopts the unusual line of five very different views of her from those who knew her, while the police trace her killer.

Kent had all the hypnotic fascination of a spider in the centre of her web in this one. She still played dominating women in her lighter films, but *Her Favourite Husband* (in America: *The Taming of Dorothy*) and *The Reluctant Widow* (both 1950) were less successful.

The Kent eyebrows and top lip were never quite so severe as in *The Browning Version* (1951). Perfectly cast, she hit top gear as the vindictive wife of dowdy teacher Michael Redgrave at a boys' public school. Despising him for the failure he is, she openly carries on an affair with the science master (Nigel Patrick). In the end, the adulterous duo are left with each other when the teacher gains strength from the present of a book from a pupil, endears himself to the school with an impassioned speech about his failings and strikes out on his own for a new life.

In later years, Jean Kent would express regret about only two aspects of her career: firstly that she had never tried Hollywood and secondly that she refused to renew her studio contract in

*1955, and the transformation from siren to shrew is complete. Jean Kent's wicked stepmother seems to have finished off Mona Freeman's April in* Before I Wake

1952 because, 'they had given me this boring, irritating tag of being a bad girl and it had stuck to me'. The result was that, to quote Kent again, 'I virtually stopped doing pictures in the full flood of stardom'.

There was another film, *The Lost Hours* (1952, in America: *The Big Frame*), but it was very minor by Jean's standards. After a gap of three years, she took another independent film, which put her back in the old routine and gave her the last of her strong leading roles.

Called *Before I Wake* (1955, in America: *Shadow of Fear*) and directed by Hollywood veteran Al Rogell, it pitted Jean's wicked stepmother against Mona Freeman's resourceful but much-menaced heroine. At stake: a fortune, for which stepmother has already killed Mona's mother and father. A suspenseful and decidedly lethal battle of wits develops, which stepmother eventually loses only after the girl narrowly escapes death in a cleverly-contrived 'accident'.

At the same time, Jean did a notable television play, *Call on the Widow*, as a murderess who poisons her husband, and then attempts a love affair with the young police detective on the case. A second television production, *Love Her to Death*, was in similar vein. Three years later, she was back in films in another no-better-than-she-ought-to-be role as the music hall singer eventually throttled by Boris Karloff in *Grip of the Strangler* (in America: *The Haunted Strangler*).

In the early Sixties, Jean Kent and her husband, businessman Yusuf Hurst, went to live in Malta, and she made only sporadic stage appearances thereafter on the occasional return to Britain. In 1981, she did a stint on the television soap opera *Crossroads*.

'Looking back,' she said, 'I don't think *The Browning Version* helped as much as I thought. For that part I had to look much older than I was (30 at the time). I suppose when I went independent people felt I had got to the stage where I could only play that sort of part.

'It's rather sad really. I never enjoyed my stardom and never really appreciated the fact that I was a star. When autograph hunters used to come at me with pencils and books, my immediate instinct was to run.'

## Margaret Lockwood

British cinemagoers never really took wicked ladies of the home screen to their hearts until Margaret Lockwood came along. It was perhaps because this most open and hard-working of actresses, having starting as an ingenue of considerable charm, could be just as ingratiating in romantic roles. From 1938 to 1950 she remained a force at the British box-office, while from 1943 to 1948 her films were pure gold.

Born in Karachi, India, either in 1911 or 1916, according to your source of reference, Margaret Lockwood was as dedicated from an early age to a career in show business as she was to her position as top star once she reached the highpoint of her fame. More so than any of her contemporaries, with the possible exception of Anna Neagle, she was every inch a professional working actress.

She had begun at 16 by enrolling simultaneously at acting and dancing schools, having already made her London stage debut. Spotted for films in 1934, she spent most of the decade playing plucky heroines or girls who won the hero in the end from less deserving rivals. Her touching portrayal of the nurse in Carol Reed's *Bank Holiday* (1937, in America: *Three on a Weekend*), followed by the central role in Hitchcock's *The Lady Vanishes* (1938), propelled her to the forefront of the younger British actresses. The believable, sympathetic personality she projected in that film was to stand her in good stead through her years of villainy.

Before these began, however, there was an unhappy foray to Hollywood – 'I was so ill, they had to carry me off the boat on a stretcher' – where she played a couple of minor leads, before returning to England to tackle the watershed role of the shallow, faithless wife of Michael Redgrave (as the idealistic son of a miner) in Reed's *The Stars Look Down* (1939).

Lockwood's ambitious wife soon renews her affair with local sharpie Emlyn Williams after Redgrave takes a teaching job to support her; consequently her husband leaves her. Williams' reopening of an unsafe mine leads to it being flooded, with much loss of life.

With the outbreak of war, Lockwood's career as a bad girl lay dormant for a few years. She worked again for Carol Reed in *Night Train to Munich* (1940, in America: *Night Train*) and *The Girl in the News* (also 1940), before a co-starring role with James Mason in a minor thriller, *Alibi* (1942), led to them re-teaming in the splashy Gainsborough Regency melodrama, *The Man in Grey* (1943)

As Hesther Shaw, an impoverished social climber, she marries and divorces a naval officer before becoming an actress and setting her cap at the saturnine Lord Rohan (Mason). He's married to Hesther's girlhood friend Clarissa (Phyllis Calvert), who employs Hesther as a governess.

The ruthless Hesther soon becomes Rohan's

*Margaret Lockwood's first unsympathetic part was as a spoiled heiress in* Man of the Moment *(1935). Here she and daddy (Peter Gawthorne) learn that she has lost her fiancé to a girl from a lower social order!*

*Like a harbinger of doom, Hesther (Margaret Lockwood) arrives to be governess to her friend's child, in* The Man in Grey *(1943)*

mistress and, looking for an opportunity to usurp Clarissa from the house altogether, finds it when the latter falls ill. She cold bloodedly allows her to die from pneumonia, but does not live to enjoy the spoils of her villainy. Rohan takes a horsewhip and thrashes her to death.

Critics ho-hummed, but audiences queued for miles and with one bound Lockwood had jumped to the top of the British tree. The following year, she made the first of her big Gainsborough weepies, *Love Story* (in America: *A Woman Surrenders*) as a dying composer-pianist who falls for a mining engineer (Stewart Granger) going blind as a result of injuries while serving with the RAF. Like most of the Gainsborough films, it was the purest tosh, but public response made nonsense of critical opinion. And they made its theme music, *The Cornish Rhapsody*, a best-seller.

The gap between critics and public was even more marked with Lockwood's most famous role, as *The Wicked Lady* (1945). Lockwood, now with the left cheek beauty spot that was to become one of her trademarks, rampaged all over the screen as the cunning, amoral Barbara whose marriage to her best friend's rich fiancé proves so dull that she takes to highway robbery to restore excitement to her life.

Barbara is soon well into an affair with fellow-highwayman Jerry Jackson (James Mason), but robbery has turned to murder before she decides to steal her friend's new fiancé as well. Through Barbara's perfidy, Jackson is nearly hanged, but escapes – only to be shot by Barbara. She is badly wounded in return and barely gets back to her room through a secret passage before dying under the eyes of the man she now covets.

There was scarcely a critic willing to give this florid melodrama a kind word, but Gainsborough cried all the way to the bank, as the film's risqué theme and Lockwood's low-cut seventeenth-century dresses caused queues all round wartime cinemas. It was the most successful British box-office film of the year.

Clearly, Lockwood had to go on being bad, and the result was *Bedelia* (1946) in which she plays a lady rather more deadly than Lucrezia Borgia. Having already bumped off three husbands, we meet Bedelia in 1938 going for four in a row, having persuaded her current spouse (Ian Hunter) to insure himself up to the hilt before she poisons him. A detective gets on to her little game, and her attempt to poison him fails. Confronted by her husband with the truth, and the certain prospect of conviction and hanging, she is left alone with the poison.

After playing tempestuous beauties from the wrong side of the tracks in the period sagas *Hungry Hill* (1946) and *Jassy* (1947), Lockwood mistakenly relinquished her role of bad girl of the British cinema, leaving Jean Kent and Googie Withers (*qqv*) to fight over the crown. After a series of foolish tear-jerkers and comedies, her great popularity began to slide.

She had interesting roles in *Laughing Anne* (1953), an adaptation of a Joseph Conrad story set in 1890 Java, in which she plays a singer prone to 'laughing fits' who ultimately dies to save her lover, and in *Cast a Dark Shadow* (1955), in which the *Bedelia* situation is reversed as she survives wife-killer Dirk Bogarde's attempts to put an end to her.

By this time, however, her larger-than-life characters had run the course of their popularity, and the film career of Britain's greatest woman star since Gracie Fields slipped quietly into obscurity. Possibly she had believed too long in the magic of the days when 'people believed anything. We never had any location shooting on *The Man in Grey* or *The Wicked Lady*. A couple of strategically-placed trees and a plant or two, stuck in the studio, made a forest and

nobody asked questions. The public adored the stuff.'

Although those words reveal Margaret Lockwood as an actress with her feet firmly on the ground, it also shows she may have underrated her own contribution to her most successful films, when a flash of the liquid Lockwood eyes could as easily draw a tear as send a shiver of apprehension up the spine.

### Ida Lupino

In a near 50-year film career, the bad girls for which Ida Lupino will be remembered were almost all crammed into the period from 1939 to 1949. Hard-boiled, shop-soiled and in a continual head-to-head battle with life, their single-mindedness was sometimes on their own behalf but often concerned their interest for others too.

Amazingly, not one of her dynamic performances was even nominated for an Academy Award, although she did win the New York Critics' best actress award for *The Hard Way* in 1943, with a typically dominant portrayal.

The beginnings were very different. Born in London in 1914 (some sources insist on 1918), she found herself a member of one of Britain's best-known theatrical families. Most of her cousins and uncles were music-hall stars and her father was film and (mainly) stage farceur Stanley Lupino (1893–1942). Her father built Ida and her sister Rita a small theatre at their home and, immediately after her RADA training, Ida's mother Connie Emerald, also an actress, introduced her to film studios.

She was an extra in *The Love Race* (1931) and a leading lady at 18 the following year. She played a series of little blonde ingénues and her British films are almost as insignificant as those she made on her arrival in Hollywood at the end of 1933.

She was quite notable, though, as the pushy, spoiled socialite who flirts with Gary Cooper in *Peter Ibbetson* (1935) and as the Manhattan gold-digger opposite George Raft in *Yours for the Asking* (1936), but in general was so disap-

*All set to hoist the mask and rob another stagecoach, the adventurous Lady Barbara (Margaret Lockwood) lies in wait in the original version of* The Wicked Lady *(1945)*

*Ian Hunter gets the message – his wife (Lockwood) is out to poison him in* Bedelia *(1946)*

*Ida Lupino in her breakthrough role, as Bessie, the low-class strumpet hauled off the streets by painter Ronald Colman to pose for his portraits in* The Light That Failed *(1940)*

pointed with the quality of her roles that she 'retired' in 1938 following her first marriage, to actor Louis Hayward.

Although Lupino returned to films the following year, with hair grown out to its natural deep auburn, the parts she was handed had, if anything, less bite than before. The turning point came at the end of 1939 with *The Light That Failed*. It was a role she learned in its entirety before confronting director William Wellman and playing a scene which won her the part of Bessie Broke, for which she accepted fourth billing.

It was in some ways similar to the role with which Bette Davis (*qv*) sprang to fame in *Of Human Bondage* five years earlier. Bessie is a tempestuous, selfish, opportunistic cockney tart hauled off the streets to pose as a model at the princely rate (for 1900) of £3 a week for artist Ronald Colman, who is going blind.

Colman drives himself, and Lupino, too hard, taking to drink and mistakenly telling her what her thinks of her. Vengefully, she returns after he goes blind and destroys his masterpiece: the portrait of herself. Colman returns to the Sudan (where he received the wounds that damaged his sight) and dies there.

Most of Ida's Hollywood films had been made at Paramount but, with her new, tougher image, she now signed for Warners, a studio to which she was ideally suited. She soon demonstrated that the ability as a vivid dramatic player she had shown in *The Light That Failed* was no flash in the pan.

As Lana Carlsen in *They Drive by Night* (1940, in Britain: *The Road to Frisco*), she sets her cap at Joe (George Raft), a truck-driver employed by her husband (Alan Hale), whom she impulsively murders one night by leaving him drunk in their car in the locked garage with the engine running. Raft is accused of the crime but, in a startling piece of acting by Lupino, Lana goes out of her mind in the witness-box at the trial.

The performance got her top-billing over Humphrey Bogart in her next film *High Sierra* (1941) as the 'taxi-dancer' moll who's more loyal to Bogart's escaped killer than the cripple girl he helps, and is near him when he is finally gunned down by lawmen. Following two movies opposite John Garfield, Lupino gave one of her most dominating performances – opposite her then-husband Louis Hayward, whom she would divorce in 1945 – in *Ladies in Retirement* (1941).

Although a little young at 27 for the part of Ellen Creed (Flora Robson had played it on

(LEFT) *Almost unrecognizable compared with her peak years: the blonde, teenage Ida Lupino as the girl with two men on a string in the 1933 British film* Money for Speed

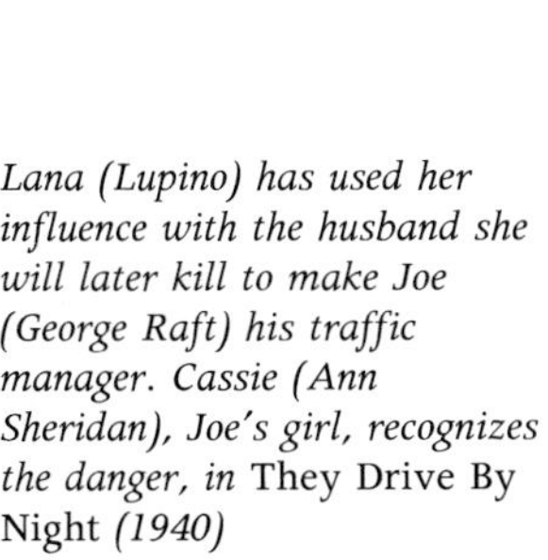

*Lana (Lupino) has used her influence with the husband she will later kill to make Joe (George Raft) his traffic manager. Cassie (Ann Sheridan), Joe's girl, recognizes the danger, in* They Drive By Night *(1940)*

Broadway), Lupino had sufficient steel to carry it off in style. As housekeeper to an elderly actress (Isobel Elsom), Ellen succeeds in foisting her two retarded sisters on the household. When the actress decides they must go, Ellen throttles her with curtain cords and walls up the body in the kitchen bake-oven (the period is the late 1800s).

But the dead woman's rascally nephew (Hayward) cooks up a scheme to crack Ellen involving the 'ghost' of her ex-employer. Ellen, after ensuring her addled sisters will be looked after, walks out into the fog to give herself up.

Lupino switched off the single-minded malevolence she had projected so well in this film for her next few assignments at Warners, but it was back with a vengeance in one of her best (though lesser-known) movies, *The Hard Way* (1942).

As Helen, trapped in a loveless marriage to a labourer in an industrial town, Lupino was again the driving force in an intentionally dislikeable role. She sees her younger sister's (Joan Leslie) small talent as a singer and dancer as her ticket out of poverty and encourages the attentions of Albert, a song-and-dance man (Jack Carson) who marries the girl.

Before long she has replaced his partner Paul (Dennis Morgan) but, as soon as she sees the girl has enough confidence to make it on her own, Helen moves in to break up the marriage. Albert commits suicide, and Helen plays on the alcohol weakness of a fading star (Gladys George) to push her sister to the top. Eventually, when her 'meal-ticket' musters up the gumption to run out on her, Helen, in rather unlikely fashion, throws herself in the river. It is uncharacteristic of a Lupino character to give in like that.

The remainder of Ida's Warners films were not of the same calibre, and she refused to sign a new contract in 1947, leaving the studio and making *Road House* (1948) at Fox, as a shopsoiled torch singer at a rural Illinois roadhouse who ends up shooting the manager (Richard Widmark) when he refuses to accept her decision to go for Cornel Wilde instead. She did her own singing in this film, in an attractively husky voice that perhaps owed something of its quality to her years as a heavy smoker.

For Columbia, she made *Lust for Gold* (1949), her last really first-rate film, about greed and treachery in 1870s' Arizona. Ida plays Julia, only too willing to desert her ineffectual husband (Gig Young) to share possession of a gold mine discovered by Jacob (a rare unsympathetic role for Glenn Ford), who has already murdered for it.

The situation leads to much cross and double-cross. Julia at last manages to convince Jacob of her love by stabbing her husband to death. But it is too late; an earthquake buries them both – and the mine.

As the Lupino looks hardened, and the public seemed slightly to tire of her feline schemers, her attentions turned more to the other side of the camera. Besides writing, producing and acting, she directed five films (and co-directed one more) between 1949 and1953. She also married her third husband Howard Duff (her co-star from 1949's *Woman in Hiding*) in 1951.

Her films from this period as director are ambitious co-features whose subjects and treatment were too downbeat to attract a wide section of the paying public on their own merits.

Lupino did her own singing again and co-scripted *Private Hell 36* (1954), but handed the direction to Don Siegel, who turned in a good job on this suspenseful crime drama which again contains no happy ending for nightclub singer Ida, whose lover, crooked detective Steve Cochran, is gunned down by police after appropriating robbery money.

Ida entered Joan Crawford country in *Women's Prison* (1955) as the sadistic prison superin-

*About to be buried by an avalanche, Lupino and Glenn Ford argue over a gold mine in* Lust for Gold *(1949)*

*(*ABOVE RIGHT*) In later years, Lupino reprised her 1955* Women's Prison *role in a 1971 film made for television,* Women in Chains, *as a harsh jail matron*

tendent whose inhuman treatment of the inmates provokes a riot and lands her in a padded cell, babbling incoherently, after being charged with manslaughter. She more or less repeated the performance, after directing hundreds of episodes of drama series for television in the 1950s, 1960s and 1970s, in a 1971 television film called *Women in Chains*, where she played a prison matron who arranges 'death contracts' on those who stand in her way. In the end she is brought to book by an undercover parole officer investigating the death of a friend.

Lupino, who was divorced from Howard Duff in 1968, has been in poor health in recent times. A pity. Films could still do with the disciplined professionalism of the woman who 'never wanted to be an actress'.

## Pola Negri

'Tempestuous' has been an adjective applied inappropriately to many international actresses, but Hollywood's Polish-born Twenties' import Pola Negri, otherwise known as 'The Wildcat', earned it to the full.

Tall, dark, flashing-eyed and chubbily attractive Pola played most of her more infamous ladies of fortune before she came to Hollywood in 1922. Although she was soon living the film-star image to the hilt in America, the film capital never quite found the vehicle in which Pola, or Polita as she liked to refer to herself, could prove herself the great actress all Poland and Germany believed her to be.

Instead, she became notorious for her affairs with famous men, most of them ending in the tragedies forecast for her love life by her Hungarian father, who fancied he had gipsy blood and was very fond of such prognostications.

Her two husbands, both of whom she divorced, each met a sudden end soon after – one drowned, the other was kicked to death by a polo pony. Of her famous suitors, only Charlie Chaplin, the object of her first big Hollywood love affair, seems to have escaped unscathed. Rudolf Valentino, 'the one great love of my existence', was felled by a perforated ulcer which developed into peritonitis and killed him; bandleader Russ Columbo accidentally shot

*The role that made Pola Negri's name on stage and screen. With fiendish glee, she portrays the Slave of Fatal Enchantment in* Sumurun/One Arabian Night *(1920)*

himself while examining a Civil War pistol; English millionaire Glen Kidston crashed his aircraft into a mountain while trying to break a long-distance flying record.

Later, Pola would admit that her first fiancé in Poland, a painter, had died from tuberculosis at 25. It had been there, in 1914, that she had made her film debut in a low-budget picture she had directed herself at the age of 19 in 1914 (Hollywood publicists for years gave her year of birth as 1898, although she was on fact born Apollonia Chalupec on the last day of 1894).

*Pola strikes an exotic pose as various minions prepare her for her oriential lover in* Bella Donna *(1923)*

Not many people saw Pola's (she had changed her name to Negri after her favourite poetess; the Pola was a typically flamboyant patriotic gesture) initial film. But she had better luck on the stage. At the Imperial Theatre in Warsaw, she made her name as the Slave of Fatal Enchantment in the Arabian Nights fantasy *Sumurun*.

Her early Polish films, though, were of little account, and it was not until she reached Germany, and came under the auspices of such directors as Ernst Lubitsch, that she began to build up a big European following.

Pola played many of the roles at the UFA studios in Berlin that Theda Bara (*qv*) had rampaged through a couple of years earlier in Hollywood. She starred as *Camille*, while Lubitsch directed her in *Carmen*, *Die Augen der Mumie Mâ*, *Madame DuBarry* and her stage success *Sumurun*. These played in America (and Britain) as, respectively, *Gypsy Blood*, *The Eyes of the Mummy*, *Passion* and *One Arabian Night*.

All were world-wide box-office successes. But it was the first to reach America, *Madame DuBarry/Passion*, that brought La Negri to the attention of Adolph Zukor, boss of Paramount Studios. When *Carmen/Gypsy Blood* also turned in a fat Stateside profit, Zukor decided to take the plunge, and invited Pola to Hollywood.

Here, Pola quickly fitted in with the idea of film stars living in luxury. She rented Mary Pickford's former mansion and acquired a white Rolls Royce and a tiger cub. However, when it came to making films, she soon found that

*Forbidden Paradise* (1924) was Pola Negri's version of Catherine the Great. Here she takes the measure of leading man Rod la Rocque

working conditions and artistic freedom were not quite those she had enjoyed in Berlin.

Paramount insisted on Pola toning down her mask-like black-and-white make-up, and also her voracious acting style, which made her villainesses too vicious for the studio's liking. In Berlin, Lubitsch had allowed her full-bloodied emoting a free rein, since it was a proven audience-puller, but Lubitsch had not yet arrived in America (he was to do so a few weeks later), though their last film together, *Die Flamme*, was being shown country-wide as *Montmartre*.

Only in her first American film, *Bella Donna* (1923), was Pola anything like the 'evil force' she had been elsewhere. In it, she plays a heartless schemer who marries a young man (Conrad Nagel) who stands to inherit wealth and a title.

She soon tires of their tennis club existence, however, and throws in her lot with an earthy oriental. In the end, her attempt to dispatch her unwanted husband with a dose of poison is foiled in the nick of time by his doctor friend. When we last see Bella Donna, she is adrift in a desert where, if an impending sandstorm doesn't finish her off, prowling beasts of prey will.

From then onwards, however, Pola found herself increasingly at odds with her directors and their studio. A familiar shriek of 'In Poland we kill!' would herald Pola's tempestuous departure from yet another set, unable to interpret a role as she felt best.

She was a wayward wife in *The Cheat* and an Apache dance queen in *Shadows of Paris* (both 1923), but her most successful American film was the one that reunited her with Lubitsch, now installed at Paramount. Pola was cast as Catherine the Great of Russia in *Forbidden Paradise* (1924), and made mincemeat of leading man Rod la Rocque.

Other roles had her as a master-spy and a tattooed countess, but the great roles she sought always eluded her, even when her arch-rival at Paramount, Gloria Swanson, quit the studio in 1926. In 1929, Pola Negri followed her out of Paramount and went to Europe, returning to Hollywood only in 1932 to make *A Woman Commands*, the story of the tragic Maria Draga of Serbia. Sound revealed that her harshly accented English was not nearly as attractive as that of the then-current continental Hollywood queens, Greta Garbo and Marlene Dietrich.

Pola made films in France, Austria and Germany before settling in France late in 1938. There had been rumours of an affair with Adolf

Hitler, who was certainly very keen on Pola's films. Her long-time confidante Agnes Grunstrom doubted it. 'They could not get along ten minutes together,' she commented, 'unless Pola is very much changed.' Staying in France, Pola only escaped to Portugal at the last possible moment when the Nazis invaded, fleeing on to America in 1941.

Here she made another film, *Hi Diddle Diddle* (1943) and, 20 years later, there was a courtesy appearance for Walt Disney in *The Moon-Spinners* in an exotic role as a mysterious fortune-teller with a cheetah for a pet. Said Pola at the time: 'I could go on for ever'. But in August, 1987, she died at 92.

### Lizabeth Scott

Billed initially by her studio, Paramount, as 'The Threat', in the days when every new female star had to have a tagline, Lizabeth Scott was a glamorous but taciturn blonde who played 'tough tomatoes' whose suspicious glare could be either a come-on or a 'hands off'. They were characters determined to have their own way, even if the result was tragedy for the hero.

Her real name was Emma Matzo, as harsh and down-to-earth as some of her characters, but lacking their sultry surface attraction. A good girl opposite Barbara Stanwyck's bad in *The Strange Love of Martha Ivers* (1946), she became a classic *femme fatale* later the same year in *Dead Reckoning*, pulling the wool over Humphrey Bogart's eyes, much as Mary Astor had done in *The Maltese Falcon*.

She made full use of her deadpan charm as nightclub singer Coral Chandler, for whose love Bogart's murdered friend is alleged to have killed her husband. Bogart, as Rip Murdock, investigates the nightclub, whose owner, Mar-

*The indomitable Pola at 69, as the eccentric jewel-fancier and fortune teller Madame Habib, in* The Moon-Spinners *(1964)*

*Coral (Lizabeth Scott) switches on the appealing look when stopped by a motorcycle cop (Ray Teal) in* Dead Reckoning *(1946). In the passenger seat: Humphrey Bogart*

*Corrupt detective Fuller (Dan Duryea) and avaricious killer Jane (Scott) play cat and mouse with each other in* Too Late for Tears *(1949)*

tinelli (Morris Carnovsky), seems to hold the key.

Already suspecting the duplicitous Coral of killing her own husband, Rip compels Martinelli to hand over the murder gun. Martinelli makes a break and Coral, waiting outside the club, shoots him dead. Driving to the police, Rip finally puts two and two together and Coral, after trying the moist eyes technique, demands he give her the gun she used to shoot her first husband – Martinelli having been her second. When Rip refuses, she shoots him and the car crashes. But it is Rip who survives and Coral who dies.

*Dead Reckoning* is a film that has never really received its due, yet it is on a par with all but the best of Bogart's work at his other studio, Warners (this was for Columbia).

Lizabeth was in love with criminals both in *I Walk Alone* (1947), with going-straight Burt Lancaster, and in *Desert Fury* (1947), with murderous John Hodiak. Though she suffered nobly, it was clear she would be more usefully employed expressing ruthless self-interest and United Artists wisely put her in one of her best films, *Pitfall* (1948), which confirmed her as a quintessential denizen of the post-war *film noir* world.

Scott, who had provided as interesting a partner for Bogart as the slightly similar Lauren Bacall, was now paired with screen tough guy and ex-musical star Dick Powell, as an insurance claims adjuster who becomes involved with Mona (Scott), a free-living model, when he has to repossess gifts bought for her with stolen money by a bank robber now in jail.

Despite Powell's solid married life, he begins an affair with the siren, who is also fancied by an oily detective (Raymond Burr) on the case. Powell goes back to his wife, but the detective has already arranged to bail the robber, whom Powell is forced to shoot in self-defence. The detective runs off with Mona but she kills him, and is taken by police.

Having bumped off two husbands in *Dead Reckoning*, Lizabeth did it again in *Too Late for Tears* (1949). She has already disposed of husband number one as the plot gets under way, and Jane (Scott) and number two (Arthur Kennedy) accidentally come into possession of a fortune in stolen money. A corrupt detective (Dan Duryea) forces Jane to agree to share the money, but she kills her husband, knowing he will never agree to keeping the loot, and poisons the detective before making off with it.

But she has been watched by her first husband's brother and second husband's sister. They trail her to Mexico and call the police. Trying to escape, Jane falls from the balcony of her motel room and the money showers down after her.

She played the spoiled, ambitious wife of Victor Mature in *Easy Living* (1949) and had a more sympathetic, if still doomed role in *Paid in Full* (1950), as a girl accidentally responsible for the death of her sister's baby. When the sister dies, Jane (Scott) marries her husband and deliberately has a child, knowing it will kill her, but determined to make amends.

A soulful Lizabeth was less popular, however, than the icy variety, and she was back in her strongest vein in Columbia's 1951 offering, *Two of a Kind*. Lizabeth is a money-grabbing blonde involved with Edmond O'Brien and Alexander Knox in a scheme to pass off O'Brien as the long-lost son of an elderly couple worth ten million dollars. The highlight of the doomed scheme comes when Lizabeth crushes O'Brien's finger in a car door to complete the physical resemblance to the heir.

As the *film noir* cycle declined in the early 1950s, so did Lizabeth Scott's career. She came to Britain to make a film that promised a combination of both good and bad facets of her film characters, called *Stolen Face* (1952). Another fading Hollywood name, Paul Henreid, played opposite her as Ritter, a plastic surgeon who falls for Alice (Scott), a pianist.

She is engaged to someone else and, by the time she is free to come to him, finds he has married a girl criminal after remodelling her face to look exactly like Alice's. The unregenerate lady crook makes life tough all round before

*Scott played a girl who resorts to inordinate lengths to make up for a tragic mistake in* Paid in Full *(1950). Diana Lynn and Robert Cummings co-starred*

falling from a speeding train and putting everyone out of their misery – not least the minimal audiences who were unfortunate enough to see this turgid drama.

Returning to America, Lizabeth went into *Bad for Each Other* (1953) with Charlton Heston, her co-star in the earlier *Dark City* (1950). There were faint echoes of *The Citadel* in a drama which cast Lizabeth as a calculating divorcee who seduces doctor Heston away from his coal-mining hometown and into a high-society clientele. A mine explosion brings him back to his senses and Lizabeth is left out in the cold.

Scott herself was rapidly being left out in the cold by Hollywood. In 1954, her already faltering career was dealt irreparable damage by a scandalous 'smear' story in the magazine *Confidential*, alleging that she preferred women to men in her love life. Scott sued for two-and-a-half million dollars and the case was settled out of court.

*Champagne, an available divorcee (Lizabeth Scott) and money seduce returning serviceman Charlton Heston away from his roots in* Bad for Each Other *(1953)*

Lizabeth Scott was unlucky in that the role in which she specialized – the amoral, bewitching, double-crossing broad-with-class – went out of style in just a few years, and that the parts subsequently offered to her were not of sufficient quality to enable her to widen her range. But, unlike some brief-flowering stars, she invested her earnings wisely and had no need to take parts she did not want as she grew older.

She once told an interviewer that, 'there's no point putting your heart and soul into a part when you know it isn't worth it. And enthusiasm and hard work are prerequisites for the success of any role. I'd rather starve than perform in a picture just for the money.' Thanks to her business sense, Lizabeth Scott has never done either.

### Gale Sondergaard

Open any creaking door from a Hollywood film of the 1940s, and the odds were that you would find Gale Sondergaard lurking behind it. Dark-haired (tightly piled), gimlet-eyed and impassive in full-length, high-buttoned housekeeper's dress, 'Welcome!' would be the last word on her lips. Indeed her grim demeanour more often implied an attitude of 'Abandon hope, all ye who enter here'.

Yet her figures of fate were also impeccably groomed. Not a hair of the Sondergaard head was ever seen to be out of place. There was a ladylike and almost regal quality about her that caused her to be cast in aristocratic roles as well as cruel chatelaines.

And, although she could send a shiver down your spine by her mere sudden presence in a scene, Gale Sondergaard could also project a softer side, two of the latter performances winning her an Oscar (in her first film) and an Oscar nomination.

Yet she never wanted to be in pictures. Sondergaard only went to Hollywood because her second husband, Herbert Biberman, a modestly successful writer-director, was called to work there. 'I never felt I belonged in pictures,' she said. That is, until some years later, when she tried a return to the theatre.

Edith Holm Sondergaard was born in 1899, one of three daughters of an English professor from Minnesota. Her first role at high school was prophetic – that of a cantankerous old woman in a rocking chair.

She had wanted the ingénue lead in the play, but her drama teacher – the same teacher who was so moved by her rendition of a passage from *Ivanhoe* that she insisted Gale's parents enrol her for a course in dramatic art after high school – told her, 'You'll find you can't be an ordinary girl in plays. But don't worry. You have something much more interesting to offer. And you should pursue that course.'

Pursue it she did, through 17 years of stage

*Gale Sondergaard's screen debut as Faith, scheming to steal an inheritance in* Anthony Adverse *(1936), won her an Oscar. With her here: Claude Rains as Don Luis*

*The ubiquitous Miss Lu (Gale Sondergaard) startles the harassed heroine (Paulette Goddard) of* The Cat and the Canary *(1939)*

*The jaws that bite, the claws that snatch . . . Mytyl (Shirley Temple) is harangued by the blandishments of a dog (Eddie Collins) and betrayed by a cat (Gale Sondergaard) in* The Blue Bird *(1940)*

work with stock and repertory companies, and in Broadway plays. Then came Hollywood.

The Bibermans had already been in Hollywood a year before Gale was offered her first role there. Bette Davis had been mentioned in connection with both leading roles in *Anthony Adverse* (1936). But she lost the lead to Olivia de Havilland, and declined the supporting role of the conniving Faith, which won Sondergaard her Academy Award.

A deeper-dyed villainess followed in *Seventh Heaven* (1937), but the film that set the pattern for the remainder of her film career was undoubtedly *The Cat and the Canary* (1939), the ghost comedy that made a top star of Bob Hope. As the inscrutable Eurasian housekeeper Miss Lu, Sondergaard seemed (when not in touch with the spirit world or looming behind lace curtains) interchangeable with a black cat, which may have given someone an idea for her role in *The Blue Bird* (1940).

Ironically, she played the treacherous Cat in the latter film, burnt to death all too soon in a forest fire. That role came immediately after she was almost cast as the witch in *The Wizard of Oz* (1939), in which *Blue Bird* star Shirley Temple would have played Dorothy if her studio had let her.

'They had me fitted for high pointed hats and long flowing gowns,' Sondergaard remembered, 'then decided it was too glamorous an interpretation of the role and cast Margaret Hamilton instead.'

It was in 1940 that Gale Sondergaard was seen in another of her best-remembered roles, as Mrs Hammond, oriental widow of the white man shot by Bette Davis (with whom he has been having an affair) at the beginning of *The Letter*.

The prevailing Hays Code, which demanded retribution for Davis's conniving Leslie Crosbie, did give Gale a chance for some emotive close-up facial acting as as she exacted revenge by plunging a dagger into Davis at the end.

Sondergaard did four pictures with Bob Hope, all in villainous roles – 'You would go home hurting from laughing all day on the set' – and also menaced Abbott and Costello in *The Time of Their Lives* (1946). This is the film in which Sondergaard answers the door of the old mansion, and Binnie Barnes asks her 'Didn't I see you in *Rebecca*?'

The role of the housekeeper in *Rebecca*, the antagonistic Mrs Danvers, was actually played by Judith Anderson, although for years Gale Sondergaard was beset by real-life fans who thought she'd played the part. Such class assignments escaped her for a while in the early 1940s, especially after she played *Spider Woman* (also known as *Sherlock Holmes and Spider Woman*) in 1943. 'Really fun. I had a wonderful time.'

But she hated the 1946 sequel, *Spider Woman Strikes Back*. It cast her as a seemingly blind woman who, with her deaf mute helper (the acromegalic Rondo Hatton), drugs heroine Brenda Joyce with a view to using the girl in her sinister nocturnal experiments with insects and plants. It was real Z-grade horror, with Sondergaard forced to rasp out such dialogue as: 'You're going to die, Jean, just like the others. But it won't be really dying, because you're going to live on in this beautiful plant.'

The same year, though, did bring her a first-rate role when she played Lady Thiang in *Anna and the King of Siam*. 'Such a noble, wise, far-seeing woman,' she said, and the part brought her an Academy Award nomination.

Gale was back menacing Hope (and Bing Crosby) again in *Road to Rio* (1947) – the one in which she keeps hypnotising Dorothy Lamour – but, after *East Side, West Side* (1949), she joined her husband in refusing to testify before the House Un-American Activities Committee about Communist affiliations, and was blacklisted by the industry. She didn't return until 1965, when she did a one-woman show on Broadway. There were a few more films, plus a television movie called *The Cat Creature* and a stint in the television daytime soap opera *The Best of Everything*, before her death in 1985.

There was something about the combination of her dark hair and blue eyes, together with the set of the mouth that could curl into what one always suspected was a crocodile smile, that made Gale Sondergaard one of Hollywood's most effective female frighteners, able to chill with a few words, or even with none.

Despite the unhappy, long-suffered episode of the blacklisting – her husband served a six-month prison sentence and became known as one of 'The Hollywood Ten' – Gale Sondergaard had few regrets about her life when interviewed in later years. One of the few was not getting the leading role in *The Good Earth* (1937), which won Luise Rainer an Oscar, and might have netted Gale two Oscars in consecutive years.

'Luise was a very good friend of mine,' she commented, 'so I can't say I'm sorry she did get it. But I just felt I could have given the part an extra dimension, an inner strength of character that would have made the woman even more interesting.' With her glacial gaze too, who would offer odds that Gale Sondergaard couldn't make even a plague of locusts turn and flee?

*Phyllis (Barbara Stanwyck) and Walter (Fred MacMurray) discuss their plans for murdering her husband for his insurance money, in* Double Indemnity *(1944)*

## Barbara Stanwyck

With a mother who was the victim of drunken manslaughter and a father who ran away from home and died at sea, Barbara Stanwyck was a school leaver at 13 and a chorus girl at 15. Small wonder that she wore a twisted smile and seemed so suited to sultry, world-weary, yet ambitious ladies from the wrong side of the tracks – parts that somehow seemed more suited

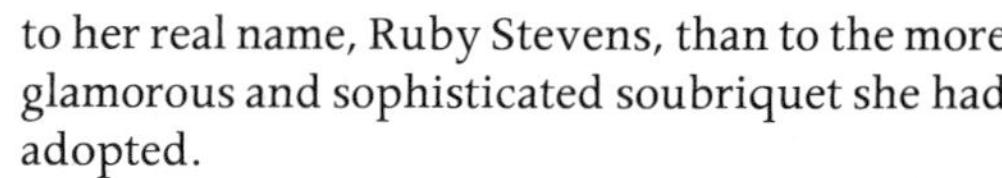

to her real name, Ruby Stevens, than to the more glamorous and sophisticated soubriquet she had adopted.

Despite (or perhaps because of) this rugged apprenticeship, she was a Broadway star at 19, 'the discovery of the year (1926)' as one critic put it, after she had exchanged her dancing shoes for acting brogues. 'I was going to be a great dancer,' she said in later years. 'I simply wasn't.'

In her third film, *Mexicali Rose* (1929), she was already being cast as the updated equivalent of The Vamp. In the title role, she marries Happy (Sam Hardy) but then seduces his best friend. In the end, she is killed by her husband. Although this was a familiar story pattern in such films, Stanwyck soon proved too good an actress to be typed in these roles.

It was her favourite director, Frank Capra, who helped her demonstrate her versatility, in such films as *The Miracle Woman* (1931), in which she plays a fake faith healer, *The Bitter Tea of General Yen* (1933), as a missionary matching wits with a Chinese warlord, and the neglected *Forbidden* (1932) as the rich man's mistress who marries a reporter, then kills him when he threatens to reveal her past.

During this early 1930s' period, mention should also be made of *Baby Face* (1933). Stanwyck had been building an image of a woman well able to take care of herself, and this is perhaps the supreme example of the type in her earlier films. Climbing over man after man (including John Wayne and George Brent) to get from the bottom of a company to the top, her reformation at the end was only brought about by America's Hays Code – the film being refused a certificate in its original form.

The best-remembered Stanwyck wicked women, however, really didn't begin to appear until much later in her career. And it was her lip-licking portrayal of bitch-in-heat, murder-in-mind Phyllis Dietrichson opposite Fred MacMurray in *Double Indemnity* (1944) that set the cycle in motion.

After such light fare as *Ball of Fire* and *The Lady Eve*, plus a final reunion with Frank Capra in *Meet John Doe* (all in 1941), Barbara had to be persuaded by director Billy Wilder that she was right for the part of the Beverly Hills bombshell whose sensual aura seduces insurance man Fred MacMurray into a complicated plot to bump off her husband and collect the insurance.

Wearing a blonde wig and caressed by the camera, Stanwyck spells out a combination of evil and allure with every calculated body movement – *Body Heat*, not used until the 1981 film, could be just as good a title for *Double Indemnity* – before ending up shot by her lover as mutual distrust grows between them.

Stanwyck signed with Warners at this stage, but it was Paramount, who had made *Double Indemnity* (it brought her a third Oscar nomination) who continued to give her, on loan-out, the best roles. Next of these brought some real thunder-and-lightening melodrama in the gloom-and-doom *The Strange Love of Martha Ivers* (1946).

As a teenager, Martha accidentally slays a rich

*Martha Ivers (Barbara Stanwyck) tries to entrap gambler Sam Masterson (Van Heflin), who knows her guilty secret, in* The Strange Love of Martha Ivers *(1946)*

*Spoiled, rich Leona (Stanwyck) argues with her father (Ed Begley) over her husband's future in* Sorry, Wrong Number *(1948). Later, her husband plans to murder her*

*Assistant District Attorney Scott (Wendell Corey) hits the bottle as his relationship with an accused murderess (Stanwyck) causes him to lose his self-respect in* The File on Thelma Jordon *(1949)*

aunt, from whose inherited money she emerges as a powerful figure in her home town, where she has married the boy who witnessed the killing. But her ex-boyfriend returns to expose the misdeeds of the past and, ultimately, after her husband has fallen to his death, Martha is forced to shoot herself.

She was rich, neurotic and selfish again in *Sorry, Wrong Number* (1948), a film which brought her another Academy Award nomination and in which she spends virtually the entire movie on the phone, realising that she is falling victim to husband Burt Lancaster's plan to murder her for her money. Bedridden, she succumbs, despite her frantic efforts to escape.

The character, however, was nowhere near as complicated as her title role in *Thelma Jordon* (*aka The File on Thelma Jordon*), made in 1949. Stanwyck is a gangster's moll on trial for the killing of an elderly woman. The district attorney (Wendell Corey), falling for her, manoeuvres her acquittal, only to find she has been guilty all along. Since Hollywood in the late 1940s still demanded moral endings, a repentant Thelma dies spectacularly in a car crash.

There were few smiles in Stanwyck films in the years that followed. She was an unmarried mother who steals another woman's identity in *No Man of Her Own* (1950), a housekeeper scheming to kill her master in the period melodrama *The Man with a Cloak* (1951), a faithless wife in *Clash By Night* (1952) and a scarlet woman returning to the scene of her misdeeds in *All I Desire* (1953).

Her career moved into a lower key in this period, a time – actually 1951 – when her near 12-year (second) marriage to Robert Taylor broke up. But there was nothing low-key about her role in *Blowing Wild* (1953), torrid stuff in which she pushes husband Anthony Quinn down an oil-well and then goes out of her mind when hero Gary Cooper rejects her.

In the mid 1950s, Barbara made several westerns to add to *Annie Oakley* (1935), *Union Pacific* (1939), *California* (1946) and *The Furies* (1950). Once nervous of horses, she became one of Hollywood's best horsewomen, had her own ranch and confessed that westerns were her favourite films – to watch or make. She was rarely, however, given sympathetic characters to play in them. She survived *Cattle Queen of Montana* (1954), but was gunned down at the ends of *The Maverick Queen* (1956) and *Forty Guns* (1957); in the latter she was the outlaw boss of the title characters!

By far the most interesting character in this group of films is her Martha Wilkison in *The Violent Men* (1954, shown in Britain as *Rough Company*). Swaggering through the film with blonde wig and contemptuous smile, Stanwyck is the embittered wife of crippled rancher Edward G. Robinson, with whose younger brother (Brian Keith) she is having her latest adulterous fling. Glenn Ford also comes into the picture, before Barbara tries to trap Edward G. in their blazing ranchhouse by stealing his crutches. But he survives and she is shot by Keith's vengeful mistress.

*John Parrish (Glenn Ford) recognizes the predatory approach of Martha Wilkison (Stanwyck) in the 1954 western* The Violent Men

Stanwyck continued acting, in diminished roles, although she had a hit television series in the late 1960s with *The Big Valley*. Just about the most popular actress in Hollywood among behind-the-camera staff in her heyday, she was always the complete professional, called a spade a spade, did most of her stunts in action films and, as one technician once put it 'don't take no guff from nobody'. Said director Mervyn LeRoy, who worked with her in *East Side, West Side* (1949): 'If you took a vote among Hollywood crews for the most popular star, she would win by a landslide'.

Stanwyck, always an earthy and direct person in real life, has said that she will go on acting 'until they have to carry me off the set. Just give me five minutes in a film, and I'll take it in those five minutes.' Those who witnessed her short appearance as the lascivious granny in the television mini-series *The Thorn Birds*, as late as 1983, could see exactly what 'Stany' meant.

*Barbara Steele turns on the fright as a princess entombed inside an 'iron captain' in her first horror film triumph,* Black Sunday *(1960)*

## Barbara Steele

It was really by accident, Barbara Steele insists, that she became known in the mid 1960s as queen of the horror film. 'I did it in a panic,' she says of her breakthrough movie, *Black Sunday* (*aka Mask of the Demon*, 1960). 'After not working for two years, you take anything.' But no-one ever panicked into a genre to which they were better suited.

With her huge dark eyes, lovely full lips that could curl into something close to a sneer, perfect nose, raven hair and slightly unsettling on-screen presence, Barbara Steele's haunting beauty made her a perfect 'heroine' of the horrors, able to attract you and scare you within the same film.

She had begun inauspiciously enough. Born in the last few days of 1937, on a ship that had just left Dublin bound for Birkenhead, her earliest ambition was to be a painter. Instead she found herself 'doing rep. on Brighton pier' at 20, making enough of an impression to be the last actress to be signed to a Rank contract (in 1958) in the dying days of the great studio stranglehold.

She had featured roles in four or five Rank films (her debut was in 1958's *Bachelor of Hearts*) before the studio sold her contract to an interested American giant: 20th Century-Fox.

What happened then was that, as Steele puts it, 'I went to Hollywood and sat on a beach for two years. The very few things they did offer were no good at all. I was trying to get out of it all the time.'

After a few days's shooting *Flaming Star* with Elvis Presley, Barbara Steele walked out on a blonde-bewigged part (Barbara Eden took over) and fled to Italy, 'where, out of the blue, this film turned up and they offered me the lead.'

'This film' turned out to be Mario Bava's *Black Sunday* (alias *Mask of the Demon*, but first shown in Britain as *Revenge of the Vampire*) and, for all its multiplicity of titles, a classic of its genre – the genre in which its star was to win huge international fame. In it, she plays a dual role, the first being a seventeenth-century princess, Asa, entombed in a crypt after a supernatural storm puts out the flames which were burning her as a witch.

Two hundred years on, her corpse is reactivated by blood from the cut of someone examining the tomb, and she sets out to wreak vengeance on her descendant (and double), Princess Katia. Vampirising the doctor accidentally responsible for her return, she tells him: 'Come to me. Kiss me. You will die, but you will know bliss beyond the reach of mortals.' She's foiled in the end though, when Katia's brother, about to kill his sister thinking she is the vampire witch, notices his 'victim' wearing a cross. He destroys Asa instead.

Director Roger Corman saw Steele in *Black Sunday* and asked her to play Elizabeth, the wife who plots to drive her husband insane by having him believe she has been buried alive, in *The Pit and the Pendulum*. Her ultimate reward is to be left to rot inside an 'iron maiden' in her father-in-law's torture chamber, placed there by

*Robert Flemyng and Steele playing a deadly husband-and-wife game of cat-and-mouse in* The Terror of Dr Hichcock *(1962)*

*Having killed her husband with drugs, Margaret (Steele) is plagued by blood-boltered visions of his ghost, in* The Spectre/The Ghost *(1963)*

her husband, who has indeed gone out of his mind before plunging to his death in the chamber's pit. No-one is aware of Elizabeth's whereabouts and her imaginary doom now comes home to roost.

After that, it was a return to Italy and an escape from horror films – but she could never make the same impact outside the genre. 'From my second horror film to my last, it was always: "Now this is definitely it. This is goodbye." And then someone would come along with another horror movie and a lot of money. One doesn't have control over one's own destiny at all.'

Barbara next combined with director Riccardo Freda on two of the most frightening chillers of the Italian cycle. Once again she is buried alive in *The Terror of Dr Hichcock* (1962, in America: *The Horrible Dr Hitchcock*), but as the victimised heroine. In *The Spectre* (1963, in America: *The Ghost*) Dr Hichcock and his wife Margaret seem to have escaped the fire that engulfed them in London and pop up 25 years later in Scotland, with Steele switching to the role of Margaret.

Inducing her lover to kill her husband with drugs, Margaret is besieged by spectral visions of the corpse. From it, she learns that the jewels she seeks are under his coffin, but a visit to his tomb proves this to be false. When the housekeeper tells Margaret that her lover has stolen the jewels, she goes berserk, slashes him to death with a razor and burns the remains in the cellar.

Pouring herself poison, Margaret is shattered by the reappearance of Hichcock, who had plotted against her with the housekeeper, whom he now shoots. As Margaret becomes paralysed by curare entering the hand she cut in the razor murder, Hichcock covers the gun with her fingerprints, then drinks to her lingering death – with the poison he believes to be gin. Steele's eye-opening performance is thus climaxed by her final, maniacal, dying laugh as she realises what has happened.

In *The Long Hair of Death* (1964), she rises from the grave again to wreak vengeance, while in *Danse Macabre* (in Britain *Castle of Blood*, also 1964), she is a woman with no heartbeat who turns out to be a deadly ghost. Next she became a multi-murderess meeting a grisly fate in *Terror-Creatures from Beyond the Grave* (1965). By this time, she had been discovered by international critics, one of whom wrote, on seeing her latest offering, that 'Barbara Steele is her usual extraordinary self'.

She was too tied up to do Corman's *The Tomb of Ligeia* (1964), in which she would have been perfect in a good/evil dual role. But she played something similar in *The Faceless Monster* (1965). Another Italian film, it cast her as Muriel, an adulterous wife whose scientist husband burns her and her lover with acid before electrocuting them.

Her (blonde) unbalanced heiress sister (also Steele) is pursued by the scientist, who marries her, plotting to drive her insane and collect the money. But he has hidden the hearts of his victims in an urn and, when they are unearthed by an investigating doctor, Muriel and her lover return in spectral form to burn the scientist alive.

Apart from *L'armata Brancaleone* (1965), Barbara was not permitted to hold centre stage in quite the same fashion in her remaining Italian films and her teaming (again as a long-dead witch) with Boris Karloff and Christopher Lee in *Curse of the Crimson Altar* (1968, in America: *Crimson Cult*) gave her little to do.

In 1968, she married writer James Poe and left Italy vowing, 'I'm never going to climb out of another coffin as long as I live'. The few roles she has played since, however, have been mostly on the sinister side, including *The Parasite Murders*

*Muriel and her lover (Rik Battaglia) are burned with acid before being electrocuted by her scientist husband in the Steele shocker* The Faceless Monster/Nightmare Castle *(1965). But they return to wreak vengeance from beyond the grave*

(1974, in Britain: *Shivers*), *Caged Heat* (1974, as a crippled prison wardress who comes to a sticky end), *Piranha* (1977) and *The Silent Scream* (1979, as a homicidal schizophrenic recluse).

Of the horror films, she now says: 'I had a marvellous time making them, but I only saw a few. I thought *Danse Macabre* and *The Spectre* were my best work; I rather liked those.'

*Meryl Streep and Woody Allen seem an unlikely combination, but they were together in* Manhattan *(1979) as a husband and wife split by her conversion to radical Lesbian feminist causes*

## Meryl Streep

Meryl Streep and Bette Davis are worlds apart in looks and acting styles. Yet Streep is one of the strongest actresses the screen has known in years, stamping her personal mark on every role she plays. Such Davis classics as *The Letter*, *Jezebel*, *The Little Foxes* and *All About Eve* would be tailor-made for the Streep of the near future.

Both stars, too, have the same slightly sour prettiness, even though their facial structures are so different. But Streep is a more enigmatic actress, preferring women of mystery and unexpected depths. With Bette Davis, you knew where you stood. It was small wonder that Streep, on the other hand, was cast in *Still of the Night* (1982) as a character who may or may not be a killer – even though it was one of her few unsuccessful films. With Streep, you are never quite sure where you are; the element of danger is ever-present.

Although christened Mary Louise Streep after her mother, the budding superstar was never, from her birth in 1949, called anything but Meryl. She was an honours student in drama at Vassar College, where a sensational, if slightly over-the-top performance by Meryl as Strindberg's *Miss Julie*, convinced her drama teachers that she was destined for big things.

After graduating with honours, she joined little theatre groups around New England, but it wasn't until 1976 that she began to make inroads into a cinema career, wasted film years that she would attempt to claw back by playing youthful parts well into her thirties.

It was the role of Linda, in *The Deer Hunter* (1978) that got her an Oscar nomination, set her up for a Hollywood career and introduced her to Robert De Niro, one of her favourites among co-stars. She played a smaller role in *Manhattan* (1979) as the wife who leaves Woody Allen to become a radical Lesbian feminist.

*Alan Alda and Meryl Streep celebrate infidelity in* The Seduction of Joe Tynan *(1979)*

(ABOVE RIGHT) *Streep as the tormented Sarah Woodruff, abandoned by her lover and scorned by her neighbours, in* The French Lieutenant's Woman *(1981)*

*The tragic Sophie (Streep) and Nathan (Kevin Kline) near the end of their dance with death in* Sophie's Choice *(1982), which won Streep her second Oscar*

*After World War II, resistance worker Susan (Streep) befriends the young diplomat (Charles Dance) whom, after a stormy relationship, she will eventually marry, in* Plenty *(1985)*

Things were now under way, and she was resolutely dislikeable as the career-minded attorney seducing Alan Alda away from his wife in *The Seduction of Joe Tynan* (1979), a film made at a difficult time for her, as her live-in lover, actor John Cazale, had just died from bone cancer at the age of 42.

She was equally unsympathetic in *Kramer vs. Kramer* (1979), in which she won her first Academy Award. Audience identification is clearly aligned from the start with the husband and son she deserts in order to forge a life and career for herself. For all her principles, Joanna Kramer comes across as cold, edgy and self-interested – a backlash, if you like, against women's lib.

Streep was now obviously ready to hold centre stage, and she did it spectacularly in *The French Lieutenant's Woman* (1981) in which, as the 'scarlet woman' of the title and swathed in black, she stares gloomily at the tossing waves of Lyme Regis, Dorset, where she is known as the French lieutenant's whore. A complex figure afflicted by 'obscure melancholia', she is eventually allowed what amounts to a happy ending. Streep gave the role such bite, however, that something darker might in this instance have seemed more appropriate.

The tragic central figure in *Sophie's Choice* (1982) brought Meryl her fourth Oscar nomination out of six to date, and her second win. It remains her favourite role of those she has so far played.

Sophie is a free-living, over-bright Polish girl living in 1947 New York, vacillating between two men. Her 'secret', as revealed during the film, concerns her war experiences when, as the daughter of a fanatical anti-Semite, she tried to ingratiate herself with Auschwitz commandant Rudolf Hess to save her son, then was forced to choose between her two children, one of whom (her daughter) had to die. In the end, Sophie herself chooses to die, committing suicide with one of her lovers.

Meryl's Polish accent was faultless and, almost as if to demonstrate her versatility, she next tackled the part of a tough-talking, chain-smoking, working-class Texan in *Silkwood* (1983) about a plutonium worker who undergoes horrendous 'cleansing' treatment after being contaminated with radiation, becomes involved in efforts to expose her plant and finally dies in a mysterious car accident. The star even grew her hair out to its natural mouse-brown for the part.

After a reunion with her *Deer Hunter* co-star, Robert De Niro, in the not-too-successful *Falling in Love* (1984), Meryl returned to central dominance in 1985's *Plenty*. She plays Susan, a selfish and manipulative English girl, dissatisfied with everything and everyone in comparison to the war and the lover (Sam Neill) within it, who blights the lives she touches, while slowly but surely coming apart at the seams herself.

Marrying a diplomat of whom she tires, she deliberately sets about having a child by a working-class lover then, when he pursues her, tries to shoot him just before suffering a nervous breakdown.

Responsible for the decline of her husband's career through tactless outbursts against the establishment, Susan, in between bouts of having to be sedated, threatens suicide if he is not reinstated. Again, she is thinking only of herself and they part. A reunion with her wartime lover provides her with a final disillusionment and she is left alone.

Susan was as complicated a woman as Meryl Streep has ever portrayed, but there seems little reason to believe she will stop there. After her immaculate Polish (*Sophie's Choice*), English (*Plenty*) and Danish (*Out of Africa*), perhaps Streep could be persuaded to play a manipulative Southern belle.

She has expressed her fascination with the ideas that women who do good things can be unsavoury and that acts of heroism can equally be performed by basically unsympathetic characters.

## Claire Trevor

Claire Trevor had a touch more glamour than most of Hollywood's 'fading blondes' from the wrong side of the tracks. There was also more steel and more ice to her make-up, the ice only occasionally melting to reveal redeeming qualities. On several of the occasions when it did, this strongest of the cinema's 'tough girls' found herself nominated for an Academy Award. And, unlike most of the actresses in this book, Trevor stayed near the top for 30 years.

She was born Claire Wemlinger in New York City, 1909, and always wanted to be an actress. Her early training at the American Academy of Dramatic Arts, ingénue work in stock companies and a Broadway debut in 1932 gave little intimation of a career that would be most gainfully

*Already looking much as she would for the next 15 years, Claire Trevor took her first Oscar nomination for* Dead End *(1937). Here Baby Face (Humphrey Bogart) finds out that his childhood sweetheart Francey (Trevor) has become a streetwalker*

*Amnesiac Burgess Meredith discovers he has another life – with a 'fiancée' (Claire Trevor) who claims he has killed her employer, in* Street of Chance *(1942)*

spent as molls, schemers, killers, blackmailers, showgirls, adulterous wives and saloon-owners.

In fact, if there was one woman you couldn't trust in films, it was Claire Trevor. No wonder the townsfolk ran her out of town in *Stagecoach* (1939), even if she did turn out on this occasion not to deserve it. For, if there was a morals-loosening saloon in town in westerns from the late 1930s to the mid 1950s, the odds were that Claire had a hand in it.

She was in leading roles through most of the 1930s, but without catching the public eye until cast as Francey, the childhood sweetheart of Baby Face (Humphrey Bogart), now a killer in *Dead End* (1937). He finds she has become a prostitute in their old neighbourhood.

Trevor was nominated for an Oscar for the first time in this role, and found herself with Bogart again in an Edward G. Robinson vehicle *The Amazing Dr Clitterhouse* (1938). She plays a fence working for Bogart's gang of safecrackers. Her play for Robinson angers Bogart and dooms him to death at the hands of the good doctor.

She made an early appearance as a saloon gal at the same studio, Warners, in *Valley of the Giants* (1938), then with George Raft, made a rare appearance for Universal in an intriguing, hard-cored semi-B movie, *I Stole a Million* (1939).

She plays a worldly-wise blonde who marries Joe (Raft), who has become a king-sized criminal following the loss of his life savings in a fraud. When she is jailed for complicity in shielding a criminal, Raft goes on a crime rampage, pulling off a million-dollar theft before almost thankfully accepting his end in a hail of police bullets.

After *Stagecoach*, she made two more westerns with John Wayne, then appeared as perhaps her classic bar-room broad, Gold Dust Nelson, opposite Clark Gable in *Honky Tonk* (1941).

*Street of Chance* (1942) gave the straight-staring Trevor an early experience of the worlds of death, darkness and double-dealing she was to inhabit so convincingly through the decade. Murdering her employer, she nearly succeeds in throwing the blame for the crime on to amnesiac Burgess Meredith. But, through an 'eye code' with the victim's invalid mother, Meredith learns the truth. Trevor, forced to try to dispatch him too, is shot by a detective, and another of Meredith's ruses extracts a dying confession.

It was on with the stars and garters again for her roles in two 1943 westerns, *The Desperadoes* and *Woman of the Town* (the title role of course). But then came another of her most memorable roles: Mrs Grayle in the Dick Powell version of *Murder, My Sweet* (in Britain: *Farewell, My Lovely*), copyrighted 1945 but first shown in December 1944.

The upswept blonde hair, the shoulder pads and vertically striped silver blouses that became part of the Trevor *film noir* persona, were well in evidence, whether she is sensually examining the hero's biceps or menacing him with a gun when he discovers she is the key to the whole puzzle, the missing Velma, involved in murder, drugs and stolen jewels. In the end she is finished off by her incredible hulk of an ex-boyfriend (Mike Mazurki), who has been trailing her all along.

Claire's next film reunited her with George Raft. In *Johnny Angel* (1945), Raft is a ship's captain whose investigation of his father's murder reveals that he was involved in gold-smuggling, one of the smugglers being his killer. The brains behind the operation is, of course, Claire, who browbeat her husband into the killings, but is now turned over to the police, Astor-fashion, by the hero.

*Born to Kill* (1946) was very grim and violent for its time. Lawrence Tierney is the psychotic who kills at the first spark of jealousy, but Trevor provides the hub of the film (sensibly

*Trevor in her Oscar-winning role as gangster's moll Gaye Dawn, with Humphrey Bogart and Lauren Bacall in* Key Largo *(1948)*

*Still heading up a saloon – and keeping her grip on a man. Claire Trevor, with Kirk Douglas as the wandering gunfighter in* Man Without a Star *(1955)*

retitled by the British *Lady of Deceit*) as the ruthlessly self-seeking woman who discovers the bodies of two of his victims, does not report it to the police, and is later driven by what the film calls her 'bad blood' into the killer's arms.

She's the adopted sister of an heiress (Audrey Long), whom the killer marries. A few murders later, the long, complex and well-written plot finds Trevor still determined to break them up. She compels Long to witness Tierney's adulterous longings to try to convince him to shoot the girl. But with the arrival of the police (ironically called by Trevor for an entirely different reason), Tierney turns his gun on her before being shot down himself.

Claire found a slightly more sympathetic role in *Raw Deal* (1948), again at the RKO studio that had become her second home. She was a gangster's girl who, after helping him escape from prison, loses him to a girl kidnap victim. Since the gangster is killed at the end, everyone loses anyway.

The same year found her finally winning her long-deserved Oscar, as the alcoholic mistress of gangland dinosaur Edward G. Robinson in *Key Largo*. When he ditches her to make his getaway, she slips hero Humphrey Bogart the gun that will see the end of the hoodlum.

Although Claire had passed 40, tough leading roles were still offered to her and a western dancehall could always use her behind its counter, or even on its stage. After *Best of the Badmen* (1951), *The Stranger Wore a Gun* (1953), *Man Without a Star* (1955) and *Lucy Gallant* (1955), she hung up her garters for good, appropriately selling her saloon in the last film to Jane Wyman.

There were a few character roles after that, though not as many as her fans would have wished. She was Edward G. Robinson's 'lawful

*Starlets sipping sodas through straws in* They Won't Forget *(1937). Lana Turner (left) went blonde, and on to stardom. But little more was heard from Linda Perry*

*Cora (Lana Turner) prepares to duck the blood and glass as her lover Frank (John Garfield) prepares to bump off her husband Nick (Cecil Kellaway) in the 1946 version of* The Postman Always Rings Twice

wedded nightmare' in *Two Weeks in Another Town* (1962) and the woman who sells underworld information to the police at a price – the old Thelma Ritter role from *Pickup on South Street* (1952) – in *The Cape Town Affair* (1967). Finally the price is her own life.

Towards the end of her long career, Claire Trevor told an interviewer that, 'there are certain parts in your career that command attention. *Dead End* and *Key Largo* were mine. *Stagecoach* was too subtle.' What she didn't say, of course, was that, whatever the role, attention was something she *always* commanded.

## Lana Turner

She was Jean Harlow without the laughs, an American Brigitte Bardot. Her characters were forever trying to escape their poor origins and climb upwards with the help of that shimmering blonde smoulder and a man or two. MGM and Universal kept her elegant, stiff-backed and suffering in mink. Perhaps at Warners or Paramount, she would have discovered, to her audiences' advantage, that, as Barbara Stanwyck says in *The File on Thelma Jordon*: 'Maybe I'm just a dame and didn't know it'. A dame Lana Turner was, and didn't we know it.

She was born Julia Turner in 1920, but always called Judy by her parents. Following a tough childhood – her father was murdered in 1930 after a gambling session – she was spotted by the *Hollywood Reporter* while still a pupil at Hollywood High School in 1936 and sent by its editor to see an agent.

Her looks were so stunning that small decorative roles had begun to come her way by the following year, one of them not only jetting her into the public eye, but tagging her with a soubriquet she would come to hate.

Director Mervyn LeRoy, who would later do her something of a disservice by taking her from Warners to Metro with him, gave her the small key role of Mary Clay, a teenage temptress who gets raped, murdered and thrown down a liftshaft in *They Won't Forget* (1937). Turner did a long walk in a tight jumper that set eyes popping and led the studio to dub her 'The Sweater Girl'.

*Turner schemes as the glacially evil Milady de Winter in* The Three Musketeers *(1948). Gene Kelly's D'Artagnan seems to have sat on something painful*

Over at MGM they hardly knew what to do with her, but did change her hair from auburn to blonde, presumably in an attempt to give her more class. But they let her seduce the title character in *Calling Dr Kildare* (1939), causing Lionel Barrymore's wise old Gillespie to chide Lew Ayres' Kildare with, 'She's a bad little girl and you should have known it'. Needless to say, Lana does not keep her man. Around this time, she also developed the Turner trademark of taking one puff at a cigarette, then stubbing it out. It was typical of her breakneck approach to acting – and life.

The first of her seven husbands, bandleader Artie Shaw, came along in 1940, but they were already divorced by the time Lana appeared in her first important role at MGM, in *Ziegfeld Girl* (1941).

She plays a small-town girl who ruins her life in her attempts to become a star of the Follies and eventually, ill and forgotten, tries to attend the opening of what would have been her show, but crashes down an ornate stairway to her death. In perhaps her most memorable line, she says: 'I'm two people – neither of them any good'.

She was now a star and made two films with Clark Gable, *Honky Tonk* (1941) and *Somewhere I'll Find You* (1942), in which he seemed to humanize her icy glamour. Later teamings between the two, though, were less successful and, meanwhile, Turner marked time in some poor vehicles until *The Postman Always Rings Twice* (1946) came along.

This is the Turner equivalent of Barbara Stanwyck's *Double Indemnity*. The man who will eventually murder her husband for her (in this case John Garfield) is hooked from the moment he sets eyes on her. Hypnotic in white, the eyebrows (shaved off for an earlier exotic role, they never grew back) arched to match the sweep of a turban, she looks like an angel of death – or goddess of destruction.

In the end, the destruction is her own, in a car smash which leaves her lover appropriately facing execution for murder – but one he did not commit.

Turner never quite equalled the impact of that role, although she was extremely well cast as the deadly Milady de Winter in *The Three Musketeers* (1948), the epitome of bejewelled, inscrutable evil. Says one character: 'That woman will destroy you'.

But there were few decent roles left for her in her eight remaining years at MGM, only heartlessly glamorous musicals and silly costume epics. Just about the lone exception was *The Bad and the Beautiful* (1952). Turner plays an alcoholic, washed-up actress who is rescued from the gutter by a ruthless Hollywood producer (Kirk Douglas) – although she wishes she hadn't been by the time he has remoulded her into a star. The film is flawed, but not so Turner's performance, which is possibly her most intelligently considered.

Perhaps the nadir of her MGM tenure was *The Prodigal* (1955) in which she plays the wicked Samarra, high priestess of Astarte, with chorus girl costumes and such lines as, 'I never belong to any one man – I belong to all men' (appropriate perhaps for her male fans). To top it off, she jumps to her death from a tower into a flaming cauldron far below. In real life, Turner had had enough of the cauldron and quit MGM in 1955.

Turner's career was in trouble, but it received a shot in the arm with *Peyton Place* (1957), in which her role as the unwed mother Constance MacKenzie won her her only Oscar nomination. It led to a brief revival in her career with such glossy weepy-dramas at Universal as *Imitation of Life* (1959), *Portrait in Black* (1960, as Anthony Quinn's murderous co-conspirator) and *Madame X* (1966); the latter, another version of the story of an adulterous lady whose fortunes vary from rotten to worse, contains one of her four best film performances.

Turner's private life has blazed with the passion sometimes (understandably) missing in her lesser film roles. She has married eight times and was involved in unsavoury headlines in 1958 when her daughter Cheryl stabbed Lana's gangster lover Johnny Stompanato, to protect her mother from his threats. After a period of

*Lana prepares to go into action as Samarra, high priestess of evil, in* The Prodigal *(1955). Louis Calhern and Edmund Purdom look worried, as well they might: the film was a flop, and Turner's last under her M-G-M contract*

*Lana's Sheila Cabot doesn't seem to be trying too hard to stop her lover (Anthony Quinn) from throttling O'Brien (Ray Walston) in* Portrait in Black *(1960)*

internment in juvenile prison for manslaughter, Cheryl eventually became a successful businesswoman.

Lana's films have been few in recent times and although she did get to bump off another unwanted husband in *Persecution* (1974) – she is eventually done to death by his son, whose life she has also tried to wreck – the film, like all the others since *Madame X*, were pale shadows of her platinum past.

She still crops up in the occasional movie and Broadway revivals for, as she says, 'I have to work. My life has been a series of emergencies. But the past is the past. At least I have never let it destroy me.'

## Mae West

Mae West is not like any of the other wicked women in this book or, come to that, any other wicked woman you ever met. She played her vamps for wicked comedy and wrote streams of masterly innuendos that have passed into screen legend.

And, unlike nearly every other shady lady of the cinema, Mae West really did have a scarlet past of sorts. She had scandalized – and delighted – vaudeville's paying customers from her early twenties with suggestive dances, splendidly vulgar songs and crudely effective acting performances that left little to the imagination.

Just to add to her notoriety, she was thrown

*Mae West finally fulfilled her ambition to appear as a lion-tamer when she played Tira, the carnival vamp, in her first solo success* I'm No Angel *(1933)*

into jail (for a few days) after her play *Sex* was raided by police in 1927. One can't really see Mae getting time off for good behaviour, but she did.

There seems little doubt that Mae's early plays, *Sex, The Drag, The Wicked Age* and *Pleasure Man* (said one reviewer of the latter: 'They don't come any dirtier'), held little more than sensation value. But *Diamond Lil*, first produced in 1928, was a definite improvement and even grudgingly praised by West's most biased critics. It was also to provide the basis for one of her greatest Hollywood triumphs.

Hollywood and Mae were tremendously good for each other – for a few films at least. Theatre critics had constantly advised her to tone down the crassness of her sexual ruderies or find herself back in the bump and grind of burlesque (which, for a while in the early 1920s, she did). Now, Hollywood forced her to seek further subtlety in her amorous banter.

Both as a writer and performer, Mae West responded superbly to the challenge. Until, alas, the demands of the Hays Code's censors took their toll and she was forced to tone down her material too much for it to be side-splittingly funny any more.

She was just two months short of her fortieth birthday when she arrived in Hollywood in June 1932. But her age was never a handicap. Fourth-billed in her first film, *Night After Night*, she sashayed on to the screen as Maudie, owner of a string of beauty parlours (and men).

The double-chin that had marred her Broadway allure had been eliminated by Paramount's beauticians (and cinematographers) and she now looked, at five feet five, what your grandmother and mine might have thought 'a fine figure of a woman'.

The first classic West line was not long in coming. 'Goodness, what beautiful diamonds,' says the hatcheck girl. Drawls Mae: 'Goodness had nothing to do with it dearie.' She does bridle, however, when another character (the treasurable Alison Skipworth) clearly thinks she's the madame of a brothel. 'Hey, what kinda business do you think I'm in?' she demands.

Not throughout the decade (until her famous duel with W.C. Fields in *My Little Chickadee*) would Mae have to share centre spotlight again in a film. Her next, *She Done Him Wrong* (1933) was an adaptation of her play *Diamond Lil*, still set in the Bowery of the 1890s, but with the central character changed from Lil to Lady Lou, 'one of the finest women who ever walked the streets'.

Cary Grant, Mae's personal choice for co-star, was a different kind of leading man if not quite the match for her he would have been a few years on. Playing a missioner thinking of reforming Mae's saloon queen (he's really a federal agent after bigger fish), he gives rise to her aside 'Aw, you can be had' before she offers the famous invitation to 'come up sometime and see me'.

Lady Lou accidentally kills a spitfire Russian rival (Rafaela Ottiano) before Cary rounds up the crooks and approaches her, too, with handcuffs. 'Are those absolutely necessary?' she husks. 'You know, I wasn't born with them.' Says Cary: 'A lot of men would have been safer if you had,' to which Mae muses 'I don't know. Hands ain't everything.' He not only lets her go but threatens to marry her. 'You bad girl,' he admonishes. 'You'll find out,' murmurs Mae.

Grant was also her leading man in *I'm No Angel* (1933) which finds her as a sideshow vamp in cahoots with a pickpocket. Once again Mae proves, to borrow another quote from *She Done Him Wrong*, that 'when women go wrong, men go right after 'em'. 'If only I could trust you,' Grant tells her. Mae gives him an under-the-lashes look and replies: 'Hundreds have.'

As Tira, who later becomes a lion-tamer (fulfilling one of Mae's personal ambitions), Mae's motto is 'Find 'em, fool 'em and forget 'em'. Currently she has found Grant's cousin (Kent Taylor). 'I like sophisticated men to take me out,' she tells him. 'I'm not really sophisticated,' stammers a besotted Taylor. 'Hmm,' says Mae, 'You're not really out yet either.'

Her attentions soon turn to Grant when he asks her if she minds him getting personal. 'I don't mind,' she tells him, 'if you get familiar.' In the end she wins a breach of promise trial against him at the expense of any reputation she might have had left. 'Why did you admit to knowing so many men?' twitters a reporter. Mae takes her measure in an instant. 'It's not the men in my life,' she tells her, 'but the life in my men.'

In *Belle of the Nineties* (1934), the strain of staying within the new demands of the Hays Code was already beginning to show. 'It's better to be looked over than overlooked', for example, is a nice line, but clearly less likely to cause offence than some of the dialogue from her earlier films. 'You're a dangerous woman,' Paul

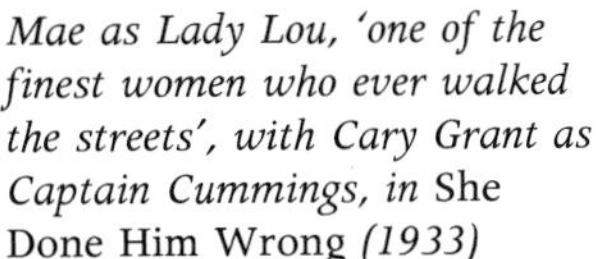

*Mae as Lady Lou, 'one of the finest women who ever walked the streets', with Cary Grant as Captain Cummings, in* She Done Him Wrong *(1933)*

*(*ABOVE RIGHT*) Peaches (Mae West) who sells Brooklyn Bridge to suckers, entrances honest cop McCarey (Edmund Lowe) in* Every Day's a Holiday *(1937)*

*(*RIGHT*) In 1970, Mae made a rather ill-advised comeback in* Myra Breckinridge. *The more liberal censorship attitudes of the day didn't necessarily make for a funnier vehicle*

Cavanagh tells her bar-room blonde in *Goin' to Town* (1935). 'Thanks,' says Mae typically, but she was becoming less dangerous on screen and at the box-office.

When slices of her semi-serious venture *Klondike Annie* (1935) were cut out by a front office scared of scenes of prostitution and death, the writing was clearly on the wall for the major part of Mae's film career. She popped in and out of films until the war years, and made a couple of vaguely distasteful comeback appearances in the 1970s. None of them had the suggestive subtlety of the days when Mae sidled up to her victims with the air of a predatory lobster.

It was what she said when she got there that counted. For this particular wicked woman, who eventually lived to almost 90, words spoke louder than actions.

*One of Marie Windsor's earliest and most striking publicity poses: as a fearsome femme fatale called Edna in the 1948 thriller* Force of Evil

## Marie Windsor

Some of the actresses dealt with individually in this book played just a few bad girl roles, even if, in several instances, they proved to be the best of their career. Such is hardly the case with Marie Windsor, who probably played more wicked women of the screen than any other post-war actress.

A fierce, full-lipped, strong-looking woman, she often proved a match for her male co-stars in more ways than one. Although coming to a sticky end in many of her films, Marie could also generate surprising warmth in her occasional more sympathetic (if never ingenuous) characters. It has been said many times of others, but rarely as truly, she seldom got the roles she deserved.

Born Emily Marie Bertelson in Utah in 1922, she was beauty queen of her native state at 18, although she always felt that her statuesque build: 38-26-37 and five feet nine, was a disadvantage to her career.

After studying acting under the famous Russian star Maria Ouspenskaya, Marie picked up a few film roles in the early war years but, feeling she was getting nowhere, turned to stage and radio until MGM offered her a contract in 1947. Although at first cast in tiny parts, she soon began to make her mark with the studio, first as a gun moll in *Song of the Thin Man* (1947), then as the traitorous lady-in-waiting to Angela Lansbury's Queen Anne in *The Three Musketeers* (1948).

In *Force of Evil* (1948), she looked for the first time the malevolent *noir* protagonist so highly regarded by fans of that post-war genre of violence and alienation. Playing the predatory wife of a syndicate king, it is she whose femme fatale attraction forces hero John Garfield into knuckling under to the organization on the matter of the destruction of his own brother's small-time numbers racket.

MGM rather bafflingly let Marie go in 1949 and, after the leading role in an independent charade called *Outpost in Morocco*, she hitched up with a smaller outfit, Republic. They gave her the second female lead in John Wayne's *The Fighting Kentuckian* and studio boss Herbert J. Yates might have regretted it, as she easily scooped the acting honours from Vera Ralston, Yates' future wife and the star of the film.

Marie played a schemer up to her neck in a plot to cheat French settlers out of their Kentucky land grant. She gets shot for her pains – no unusual fate for a Windsor heavy.

There were some good class 'A' westerns being made at Republic at the time, often in colour, and one of them was *Hellfire* (1949), the first of Windsor's two films opposite strong, silent William Elliott, who had risen to second place after Wayne in the studio's western pecking order.

The outlaw Doll Brown from this film remains Marie's favourite screen character. A cheat, a liar, a thief and a killer, but tragic too, she dies in the arms of the preacher who has tried to save her. 'I dearly loved that role,' Marie recalls. 'It gave me a chance to ride and shoot and be tough, but softly feminine and pathetic too. I used memories of my own emotional experiences to build up the character.'

*The Showdown* (1950), with its gambling-house setting, was even better, 'although the producer decided I was such a bad girl that the hero shouldn't be seen kissing me. So they took out the kiss!'

*At least Marie found a leading man the right height in* Hellfire *(1949), as Forrest Tucker was six feet four inches tall. Here she clearly has him at a disadvantage*

(BELOW) *Keeping her fighting gear under wraps, Marie played a ferocious lady pirate in the highly-coloured 1951 adventure film* Hurricane Island

(FAR RIGHT) *As with Jean Kent in* The Woman in Question, *Marie's ruthless double-crosser in* No Man's Woman *(1955) remained the central character even though she was bumped off early on*

Republic, however, was beginning to run into trouble with its chief's obsession with his protegée and, with Ralston getting the pick of the female roles there, Windsor was freelancing by 1951.

She had a memorable fight with Shelley Winters in *Frenchie* (1950). Marie, a good athlete and expert ,rider, never used stunt doubles. Then she played a small-time criminal in *Two-Dollar Bettor* (1951, in Britain: *Beginner's Luck*) and one of the screen's most fearsome lady pirates in *Hurricane Island* (1951).

Her role in *The Narrow Margin* (1951) caused one critic to exclaim that she 'looked capable of halving a railroad spike with her teeth'. She plays a 'gangster's widow' who turns out to be a policewoman after she has been shot by assassins out to stop her from testifying to a grand jury on organized crime.

This abrasive character is Marie's second

*Racecourse employee George (Elisha Cook Jr) tells his spoiled and ambitious wife Sherry (Windsor) that they are moving into the bigtime, via a massive robbery, in* The Killing *(1956)*

favourite role, not least because for a change she had some excellent dialogue written by Earl Fenton. The film was a hugely successful sleeper and deserved to promote Windsor and co-star Charles McGraw to top roles. But it never happened.

Although Marie's leading roles grew no less forceful, even violent, they were now largely in poor-quality movies, while her occasional supporting roles proved to be much more worthwhile. She was a gang leader called Iron Mae in *Outlaw Women* (1952) before hitting probably her all-time low as another sort of bad-girl leader in *Cat Women of the Moon* (1953).

Fortunately, she was back to her best in *City That Never Sleeps* (1953). An exciting crime thriller with a string of second-line stars, it was a sort of Chicago equivalent of *The Naked City*. Windsor plays treacherous Lydia, who not only betrays her lawyer husband (Edward Arnold), but also her criminal lover (William Talman), who eventually shoots her down.

If you aren't reading many ends of plotlines in these paragraphs, that's because Marie Windsor's characters all too often failed to survive to the end of the film. She was blasted by gunfire again in *No Man's Woman* (1955), in which she played a vindictive art-lover, and murdered by her screen husband, Elisha Cook Jr, in the third of her three favourite films, *The Killing* (1956).

It was also the only film that won her an award of any kind, albeit only a nod as best supporting actress of the year in the opinion of the American magazine *Look*. She plays Sherry, the wife of one of a group of once-in-a-lifetime racetrack robbers. Learning of their plans, she squeals to her lover, a small-time crook who, with a confederate, attempts to relieve the successful robbers of their fortune in banknotes.

The ensuing shootout leaves Sherry's husband fatally wounded, but he finds the strength to reach home and put paid to his faithless wife. Although some have described the character of Sherry as 'whining, lying and licentious', Marie, as always, could find shades of grey in a seemingly black-and-white character, thinking her 'not just vicious, but rather sad too, and very mixed-up about what she wants'.

After that, it was back to tough gun-girls for Marie, in such epics as *Swamp Women* (1956) and *Island Women* (1958). On television, she was a frontier-style Ma Barker in a 1965 episode of *Bonanza*, in which she played an embittered widow with several outlaw sons. In the television movie *Wild Women* (1970), she was prominent among a group of women stockade prisoners who help to fight off an Indian attack.

'Sometimes,' she once said, 'I think I was cast in all those rough roles because I could take it or no-one else was prepared to tackle them. I was sad that I never became a great star, or played many classic roles, but I did keep working and

*1944, and Googie Withers starts to blossom as a more cutting kind of actress with her dominant widow in* On Approval. *Clive Brook looks as elegant as ever*

(RIGHT) *Googie's first really evil role was as Pearl, the seaside landlady who poisons her husband, in the period melodrama* Pink String and Sealing Wax *(1945)*

felt that, with the odds against me, I did accomplish a few things that were worthwhile.'

What a Cleopatra Marie Windsor might have made – one to swallow Antony and Caesar whole and spit out the pieces.

## Googie Withers

Although one's image of Googie Withers remains as severe and scheming, she did not spend the majority of her career playing bad girls. Those she did play bore such force and – often – bitterness that they have erased the memory of all her lighter roles.

There were a great many of these latter parts – more than 30 of them before promotion to dramatic starring roles. That apprenticeship, and the power she subsequently brought to her acting, made her relatively short stay as a top film actress all the more surprising. People have cited her departure for Australia in 1959 as a turning point, but her slide in status had begun a long while before that.

Born in Karachi, India (now Pakistan) – also the birthplace of Margaret Lockwood – in 1917, where she acquired the babyhood nickname that stuck (her real Christian name is Georgette) she was dancing in London stage shows at 12. Five years later she was still earning a living as a dancer, but her first stage speaking role in May 1934 whetted her ambitions for a career as a dramatic actress.

Given a very tiny film role in a 1934 low-budget British comedy *The Girl in the Crowd*, she was promoted to second lead by director Michael Powell, who was to become a major force in the British cinema. It did not, however, lead to instant stardom, perhaps because producers saw Googie's slightly sulky blonde (in those days) prettiness as more suitable to flighty other women or character roles.

She had the lead in her next film, *All at Sea* (1935), as a glamour girl who turns out to be a humble typist, appearing opposite another embryo star, Rex Harrison. But after that the treadmill of British film-making in the 'quota' years of the 1930s reached out and gripped her in its tentacles. Like many working actresses of the period who had not quite reached the top of the ladder, she could be found in fourth place in one cast list and 20th in the next.

Michael Powell used her a couple of times in featured roles in *Her Last Affaire* (1935) and *Crown V Stevens* (1936) and she did service as female foil for most of the contemporary British film comics, such as Will Hay in *Convict 99* (1938), George Formby in *Trouble Brewing* (1939), Jack Buchanan in *The Gang's All Here* (1939, in America: *The Amazing Mr Forrest*) and Arthur Askey in *Back Room Boy* (1942).

She enjoyed her first top billing in *You're the Doctor* (1938) as a headstrong heiress who bags the doctor of her choice, and followed this up with a tricky spy in *Strange Boarders*. But she was away down the cast again in Hitchcock's *The Lady Vanishes* (1938) and played very much second fiddle to Barbara Mullen in *Jeannie* (1941, in America: *Lady in Distress*).

The breakthrough coincided with a reunion with Michael Powell, and Googie's decision to grow her hair out to its natural titian (dark red-brown) colour, which photographed as brunette in black and white. After her strong performance as the Dutch patriot Jo de Vries in Powell's *One of Our Aircraft is Missing* (1942), she landed the part of Ralph Richardson's wife in the Powell-produced *The Silver Fleet* (1943), in which Richardson (who also co-produced) plays a Dutch shipbuilder who pretends to collaborate with the Nazis to further his guerilla activities.

After playing the dominant widow pursued by fortune-hunters in *On Approval* (1944) in which she proved herself more at ease with such sophisticated comedy than with farce, Googie moved to Ealing Studios and it was here, in the next few years, that she went profitably to the bad.

There was an uncertain beginning (as the waitress) in the allegorical – and unpopular – *They Came to a City* (1944), but she moved on to the 'haunted mirror' segment of *Dead of Night* (1945), Ealing's classic chiller compendium. Playing the woman whose fiancé is possessed by an old mirror that has witnessed murder and suicide, Googie looked about as normal as Dracula's daughter, so her unease filled the audience with rightful apprehension. She prevents her own murder in the episode's climax by smashing the mirror and the past's hold on her fiancé (Ralph Michael).

Withers was the whole show in *Pink String and Sealing Wax* (1945). The faithless, ambitious wife of a publican in 1880 Brighton, she is slowly poisoning him with strychnine obtained from the premises of besotted chemist's son David

*Skeletons rattle in Rose Sandigate's cupboard, to the horror of her family. Edward Chapman, Patricia Punkett, Googie Withers and Susan Shaw in* It Always Rains on Sunday *(1947)*

*A more sympathetic role came in* White Corridors *(1951). But who could trust Googie Withers with that set expression on her face and a hypodermic in her hand?*

(Gordon Jackson). The loutish, alcoholic landlord (Garry Marsh) duly dies, but David's father refuses to withhold evidence and the murderess throws herself into the sea.

She paused for a while there, before making her second best-remembered film of the period, *It Always Rains on Sunday* (1947). She was equally forbidding of mien here, as another woman looking for an opportunity to escape an environment in which she feels imprisoned.

As Rose, she is trapped both in London's East End and a loveless marriage, when her ex-lover (John McCallum) suddenly reappears, now a convict on the run. He and Rose soon resume their feverish affair, and she hides him in her bedroom, taking out her tension on her daughters, until a snoopy reporter makes some deductions and the convict has to make a run for it. As Rose tries to commit suicide by putting her head in the gas oven, her lover makes a break for freedom through the railway yards. Both bids fail.

Withers eventually married McCallum and they made several more films together, including *The Loves of Joanna Godden* (1947), in which Googie does a sort of British Barbara Stanwyck as the indomitable owner of a sheep farm on Romney Marshes. 'I'd like to meet the man who wouldn't take orders from me,' she declares, and who can doubt her as she ploughs her way through foot-and-mouth and other natural disasters to finish with the neighbouring farmer (McCallum) who has loved her all along.

After this, Googie's film career decisions seemed ill-advised. After all, what was one of Britain's strongest actresses doing playing second banana to Glynis Johns in *Miranda* (1948), to Gene Tierney in *Night and the City* (1950) and to Anna Neagle in *Derby Day* (1952, in America: *Four Against Fate*)?

In between, there were some silly comedies in which the McCallums were only too plainly ill-at-ease, and Googie was only her old dominant self again in *White Corridors* (1951) as a single-minded doctor working to perfect a vital serum. At least in *Derby Day* she was back on home ground, on the run again with McCallum after he has killed her husband, although she is captured at the climax.

The film was the end of the line for the famous Anna Neagle-Michael Wilding partnership and near it for Withers and McCallum. Their next, *Devil on Horseback* (1954), played the lower half of double-bills, while *Port of Escape* (1955), with McCallum again on the run after killing a man, was an out-and-out second feature. Three years later, the McCallums took their own escape when they went to live and work in his native Australia.

In more recent times, Googie Withers has made return visits to Britain, most notably to play the prison governess in the long-running television series *Within These Walls*. One writer described it as 'an enterprise which Miss Withers dominates as though it had been poured around her and allowed to set'.

Googie Withers always put family before her own career. 'Although I love a role with some bite,' she says, 'I have never been a terribly ambitious person.' Thereby lies the secret of her professional decline – and her personal and private happiness.

# 2
# OTHER WICKED WOMEN

'You thought I loved Rebecca? I hated her....
She was incapable of love, or tenderness, or decency'
Laurence Olivier to Joan Fontaine in *Rebecca* (1940)

Some actresses have built up a reputation in the mind's eye for wickedness on screen with just a few roles in a possibly sporadic screen career. Others, such as Anne Baxter, have excelled as evil characters, but created a more wholesome image overall.

Then again there are actresses with whom one associates unpleasant and unsavoury characters with very little actual justification when it comes to looking at all their films. Foremost in this category must be **Joan Crawford**.

During the writing of this book, friends would naturally suggest their own lists of classic wicked ladies of the screen. Joan Crawford was always near the top. Just one more injustice for the woman whose characters seemed to suffer so many of them on screen.

Born Lucille LeSueur in 1904, she was renamed Billie Cassin as a baby by her mother's second husband. But it was as Joan Crawford that she began to win attention in 1925 at Metro-Goldwyn-Mayer, the studio at which she was to remain as starlet, star and finally discard for almost 20 years.

*Described in the screenplay as 'thick as thieves', the gossipy Sylvia (Rosalind Russell) and the catty Crystal (Joan Crawford) provided roles that boosted the stars' standing, in* The Women *(1939)*

In the 1920s, Joan played flappers, dancers and showgirls. Her first tough role came in 1928 as the gun moll of *Four Walls* who has no compunction about taking up with the second-in-command when her kingpin lover (John Gilbert) goes down for a prison stretch.

This might have thrust Crawford into a career of hard-hearted Hannahs, had her next film not been *Our Dancing Daughters*, which gave the image of a jazz baby. She felt it was the turning point in her ever ambitious career.

Two years later, in 1930, there was a hint of Crawford melodramas to come in *Paid* (1930), with Joan as the wrongfully imprisoned woman bent on an ingeniously-extracted revenge on her release. She fought the studio for the role, but afterwards they put her back to playing working girls for whom the path of true love ran rougher and rougher.

She was over made-up and over-melodramatic as Sadie Thompson in *Rain* (1932), a role also played by Gloria Swanson and Rita Hayworth, but attempted by Joan too early in her career. That was it for heavy drama for the rest of Joan's tenure at MGM. She did get the title role in *The Gorgeous Hussy* (1936), but she was wilful rather than wicked as the low-bred charmer who scandalizes Washington society at the time of Andrew Jackson.

Crawford's catty Crystal in *The Women* (1939) was her last nasty piece of work until *Possessed* (1947) in which, Oscar-nominated, she was unlucky not to win a second Academy Award to go with her 1945 Oscar for *Mildred Pierce*.

By this time she had finally left MGM and found herself at Warner Brothers, where gloom and suffering set in for virtually her entire tenure with the studio. In *Possessed*, she is found wandering the streets of Los Angeles in a catatonic state after killing Van Heflin, the climax of a tale of unrequited love in which her character's mental control gradually disintegrates to the point where she imagines killing the woman Heflin really loves.

*Mask of malice as Eva (Joan Crawford) steers her sister-in-law (Betsy Palmer) towards suicide in* Queen Bee *(1955)*

She killed at the end of *Flamingo Road* (1949) too, though any wickedness in her character is forced on her by the man she eventually bumps off, southern political boss Sydney Greenstreet, who has her sent to prison on a frame-up, a move which forces her into prostitution. The same semi-happy ending ground was trodden by *The Damned Don't Cry* (1950), while *Harriet Craig* (1950), a remake of the 1936 film *Craig's Wife*, saw Joan as the wife whose obsession with fastidiousness and possessions alienates everyone in her life.

Her move from Warners was definitely a wise one after *This Woman is Dangerous* (1952), which found her yet again as the reformed sinner (murderer's mistress) whose true love will still be waiting for her after a prison sentence. And it was at Columbia that Joan played what was perhaps her only truly wicked woman in films, Eva Phillips in *Queen Bee* (1955).

Eva is a ruthless, wealthy bitch who dominates everyone about her. Her husband (Barry Sullivan) has long since taken to drink, and the girl he should have married (Fay Wray) has gone genteely potty through Eva's manstealing. Eva's sister-in-law (Betsy Palmer) commits suicide after Eva lets her know that her fiancé (John Ireland) is another of Eva's conquests.

The character's a bit like a whodunnit murder victim. Said one critic: 'Miss Crawford plays her role with such silky villainy that we long to see her dispatched.' Sullivan plans to bump her off in a car 'accident', but it's Ireland who gets her in the end, although he crashes to death with her.

Roles were reversed in the British-made *The Story of Esther Costello* (1957, in America: *Golden Virgin*), in which Joan eventually drives herself and her husband (Rossano Brazzi) to their deaths after he has raped the deaf, dumb and blind girl (Heather Sears) who has been the focus of Joan's charity work.

After her film career was over, Crawford once confessed that she would liked to have played more of the kind of parts that her sometime Warner rival, Bette Davis, was getting. 'I love playing bitches,' she told an interviewer. 'There's a lot of bitch in every woman – and a lot in every man.' She died in 1977.

Another much-maligned lady was the American-born oriental star **Anna May Wong**. My mother always insisted that Anna May was the finest film villainess she knew, yet whenever I saw her early sound films, poor Anna May always seemed to be committing a noble suicide.

Fine-boned and pretty, with an unnerving stare, she was born Wong Liu Tsong in Los Angeles' Chinatown in 1907, to Chinese parents. By the time she left school, in 1922, she had already won bit parts in films and would now attain an unprecedented status for an oriental girl. Her first suicide scene came that same year, at 15, in *The Toll of the Sea*, in which she drowns at the end of this experimental colour film.

Her main villainess parts in the silent era were in *The Thief of Bagdad* (1924), as the Mongol slave girl, and *Old San Francisco* (1927). But she was dissatisfied with the range of her work in Hollywood and, from 1928, went abroad in search of more interesting acting parts.

In Germany and England she made herself a brilliant reputation on stage, also filming in both countries, finding herself a leading lady, a status somehow barred from most orientals in Hollywood. She was up to her old tricks, however, in the multi-lingual release *The Flame of Love* (1930), poisoning herself in pre-revolutionary

*At 17, Anna May Wong gained international recognition as a sinuous Mongol slave girl in* The Thief of Bagdad *(1924)*

Russia to save her brother from death.

On a trip back to Hollywood, she played the evil daughter of Fu Manchu in *Daughter of the Dragon* (1931) and also squeezed in the role of Hui Fei, the Chinese prostitute who stabs Warner Oland at the end of *Shanghai Express* (1932). Back in England it was suicide time again in the second-rate *Tiger Bay* (1933), but she did have a fine old time as the sinister Mrs Pike in the Sherlock Holmes thriller *A Study in Scarlet* (also 1933). Perhaps her most tragic suicide scene came the next year in *Java Head* (1934) as the pathetic Chinese bride Tao Yuen whom hero John Loder brings back to England, where she soon realises he is still in love with his childhood sweetheart.

After a successful stage tour of European countries, it was suicide as usual on her now-permanent return to America in *Dangerous to Know* (1938). With the coming of the war years, Anna May found herself in demand for a few minor slit-eyed villainesses, such as her Lois Ling in *Ellery Queen's Penthouse Mystery* in 1941.

Although her talents warranted a far wider range of roles in her screen career than she received, Anna May, though saddened by this, was never really bothered. 'Life is too serious,' she once said enigmatically, 'to be taken seriously.' The actress who always seemed to be administering or taking poison on screen died from a heart attack in her sleep in 1961. She was only 54.

Although only occasionally a woman who was wicked through and through, Britain's own post-war blonde bombshell, plumply tempting **Diana Dors**, was almost always the smiling vamp who, with an eye to ermine and pearls, would be the lure to make the good (if often ineffectual) guy step over to the wrong side of the fence.

Born Diana Fluck in 1931, her bold, overt sexuality was being used in films when she was 15 and, although she must have tired of being the girl good boys were warned about, she became a familiar face – and figure – in a fistful of British films, although only good for a walk-on laugh in most.

A great publicity seeker, especially at film festivals, where she once sported a famous 'mink' bikini which she later confessed had been made of rabbit, she somehow occupied a unique position in the British cinema of post-war times.

And, although she had showed up well as a Dickensian lowlife character in David Lean's *Oliver Twist* (1948), it wasn't until late in 1953 that she began to show signs of taking dramatic acting seriously when she played a 'good time girl' (a familiar Dors character description) taking the rap for a boyfriend in *The Weak and the Wicked*. One of Britain's first stabs at portraying life in a women's prison, it was a rose-

*Fu Manchu's daughter Ling Moy (Anna May Wong) seems to have the advantage of a harassed Bramwell Fletcher in* Daughter of the Dragon *(1931)*

coloured view in comparison with a second Dors vehicle to follow.

Before this, though, she gave further evidence of dramatic talent with a quieter, and partially deglamourized performance as an East Londoner in Carol Reed's fantasy *A Kid for Two Farthings* (1955)

Although *Yield to the Night* (1956, in America: *Blonde Sinner*) was based on another book by Joan Henry, who had been responsible for the source material for *The Weak and the Wicked*, it was an altogether grimmer treatment, loosely based on the case of Ruth Ellis, the last woman in Britain to hang.

Here called Mary Hilton, she falls for a nightclub pianist for whom she leaves her husband. He in turn falls for another woman and, when she rejects him, kills himself. Consumed by a desire for vengeance, Mary guns down her rival and is condemned to death for the crime. After an agonizing time in jail, she learns there is to be no reprieve.

Playing the prison scenes as a shadow of her glamorous self, Diana won the applause of critics and public alike and was offered work in Hollywood. In America, however, her riotous lifestyle won more headlines than the two films she made. The first, *I Married a Woman* (1956), was a mild comedy that teamed her with 'nervous' comedian George Gobel. The second,

*Mary (Diana Dors) contemplates her past life and future death from the grim corner of a prison cell in* Yield to the Night *(1956)*

*Planning to kill her husband 'in mistake' for a prowler, Diana Dors as* The Unholy Wife *(1957) bandies words with the hated mother-in-law (Beulah Bondi) who will eventually be her downfall*

*Dors the character star – here as the raddled, malevolent housekeeper in* The Amazing Mr Blunden *(1972). She appears to have nagged David Lodge to death*

*The Unholy Wife* (1957), found her back in the death cell as the faithless wife of hard-working Rod Steiger.

Intending to replace him with her current beau (Tom Tryon), a rodeo rider, she tries to shoot Steiger, hoping to claim she thought he was a prowler. But, in the dark, she shoots his friend by mistake. Steiger takes the blame and is sentenced to death. Justice catches up with the 'unholy wife', however, and she takes her husband's place in the death cell, for the murder of his invalid mother who, ironically, had poisoned herself.

Unfortunately, this quite promising *film noir* material was cheaply handled and, together with unfavourable publicity garnered from her Hollywood visit, it heralded Diana's return to Britain. Here she played a succession of seductresses and call-girls in such films as *The Long Haul* (1957), *Tread Softly Stranger* (1958) and *Passport to Shame* (1959).

As the 1960s progressed, Diana gradually put on weight and moved into predatory character roles, the most successful of which was her evil, wart-ridden housekeeper menacing the children in *The Amazing Mr Blunden* (1972). She also played in a great many unworthy comedies before cancer struck her down in the early 1980s. A trouper to the end, she made one last film, Joseph Losey's *Steaming*, just before her death in 1984. Her third husband, actor Alan Lake, unable to live without her, shot himself a few months later.

Diana once said, 'The figure was fabulous. But my face was never much – little eyes and lips like rubber tyres. I did well because I was the first and only British blonde bombshell.'

It was too bad that in her case the image too often ruled the actress.

As with Joan Crawford, one thinks of the great **Marlene Dietrich** as a consistently wicked woman of the screen without any real justification. Undoubtedly, she was a spider who wove a web in which to entangle her male victims – but not always for totally evil reasons!

Born in Berlin in 1901, her stage name is a

*Falling in love again . . . Marlene Dietrich's startling breakthrough to world fame as the heartless bierkeller singer in* The Blue Angel *(1930). Some of those chorus girls look a bit long in the tooth*

*A rather different Dietrich, distantly desirable, appeared in Hollywood. Here she is as Catherine 'Empress of all the Russias' in* The Scarlet Empress *(1934)*

contraction of her two Christian names, Maria and Magdalene. Although her twice-widowed mother was against her pursuing an acting career, Marlene got her way and, after one early bit part, landed the good role of the floozy who becomes a high court judge's mistress in *Tragödie Der Liebe* (1923).

'Retirement' after her marriage in 1923 caused her virtually to start from scratch on her return to the screen in 1925 and it wasn't until after stage successes that she got another juicy film role, this time in *Café Electric* (1927), the first of two films in which her lowlife characters would be seduced by gigolos played by Willi Forst, then a top German matinee idol.

These roles, plus certain vampish stage performances, encouraged top director Josef von Sternberg to sign Marlene as the erotic bierkeller singer Lola-Lola in *The Blue Angel* (1930), the film which was to make her name with Anglo-American audiences and start a Dietrich-Von Sternberg partnership that would continue in Hollywood for years to come. Her co-star, Emil Jannings, having forgotten their association seven years before in *Tragödie der Liebe*, frowned on such a little-known actress getting the role.

Marlene's interpretation of the part, however, was scandalously successful. The centre of attention in the smoke-filled cabaret in her silk top hat, dark stockings with suspenders showing, and world-weary throwaway pose, she enslaves the middle-aged professor (Jannings) with such songs as 'Falling in Love Again', the English lyrics of which would sum up her film characters for another 20 years: 'Men cluster round me, like moths around the flame. If they get their wings burned, how am I to blame?'

Jannings certainly gets his wings burned. Married to his Lola-Lola, he gradually loses all self-respect. In the end, he finishes back where he began – at his classroom desk, where he dies.

It was Marlene's character, Amy Jolly, who got her wings singed in her first Hollywood film *Morocco* (1930). Again she was cast as a 'decadent' cabaret singer (dressing in a man's suit and kissing a woman on the lips was certainly very daring even in the early Thirties before Will Hays and his censors clamped down on Hollywood), but this time in Morocco, where she falls for legionnaire Gary Cooper, and ends the film trudging off into a sandstorm to follow him as he embarks on a fresh mission.

In *Dishonored* (1931), she was a prostitute turned spy who finally faces a firing squad after a change of heart, while her fourth film with Von Sternberg, *Shanghai Express* (1932), gave her another of her most famous roles – and lines: 'It took more than one man to change my name to Shanghai Lily'!

There was another caberet singer in *Blonde Venus* (1932) and a stunningly stylish interpretation of Catherine the Great in *The Scarlet Empress* (1934), before she was allowed another femme fatale in 1935 with *The Devil is a Woman*.

Marlene's heartless Concha Perez operates in late nineteenth-century Spain, where men duel over her and generally wreck their lives. Sumptuous to look at, the film was a financial failure, partially because of the Spanish government's objections; not so much to Marlene's character, as to the 'insult to the Spanish armed forces' who were shown wenching and drinking.

Marlene was forced to reassess her career, but her later 1930s' adventuresses were not too popular with the public, and it was only as the saloon queen in *Destry Rides Again* (1939) that she regained some of her former standing. A warm-blooded painted woman, as opposed to her glacial vamps of earlier years, she has a terrific fight with Una Merkel, sings *See What the Boys in the Backroom Will Have* and steps in the way of a bullet meant for hero James Stewart, dying in his arms.

She more or less reprised the role in *Seven Sinners* (1940), as the infamous Bijou Blanche (Dietrich dames have probably the most colourful set of names in movie history), ensnaring naval officer John Wayne somewhere in the South Sea islands. Dietrich continued to be the singing siren strong men fought for through the war years, and it was not until 1952 that she landed another dominant role: Altar Keane, the outlaw queen of *Rancho Notorious*.

Altar runs a haven for wanted men at the Chuck-a-Luck ranch, but revenge-seeking Arthur Kennedy is the catalyst who ends all that and everything climaxes in a blaze of gunfire, with Marlene once again stopping a bullet, this time meant for her ex-lover (Mel Ferrer).

Most of Marlene's ensuing showbusiness years have been filled by her one-woman shows. Said Marlene once, enigmatically: 'I never had

*The taut-skinned, exotic image of later years had already set in alabaster by the time Marlene appeared as Jamilla in the 1944 version of* Kismet

*Strands of destiny. Arthur Kennedy, Marlene Dietrich (in her last dominant role), Mel Ferrer and the chuck-a-luck wheel in* Rancho Notorious *(1952)*

any ambition to be a film star, even though I enjoyed Von Sternberg's creation of my 'legend'. But then I am not an actress. Perhaps that is the secret.'

One of the saloon queen roles that Marlene turned down in the latter stages of her career was Charlie in *Station West* (1948) at RKO. The role was inherited by **Jane Greer**, perhaps the best of the studio's duplicitous femmes fatales, whose cool, calculating, butter-innocent act drove many a man to murder.

In 1951, Jane broke from RKO in search of more varied roles. 'I didn't want my children to grow up and, when asked what their mother did, say: "Oh, mom's a gun moll in the movies",' she said, somewhat illogically, at the time. Whatever she really felt, the move was fatal to her career. An actor's longing for variety springs eternal – and is usually their undoing.

Born Bettejane Greer in 1924 to an itinerant inventor, her future career was dramatically endangered in 1940 by an attack of Bell's palsy that paralysed the left side of her face. It took her months of arduous physiotherapy requiring immense patience, but she finally recovered, the attack giving her face a quizzical, enigmatic look and 'Mona Lisa' smile that added a fascinating further dimension to her film femmes fatales.

A model at 12, president of the school drama club and band singer at 17, Jane was eager to break into film acting, and a successful test led to a contract with RKO in 1943 (the year she married bandleader Rudy Vallee), although she didn't make a film for a year. The movie, *Two O'Clock Courage*, was released in March 1945 (by which time Jane had divorced Vallee) and Greer's small role had set her on a treadmill of minor, but almost all unsympathetic parts in black-and-white thrillers.

From junior bad girls, Jane was promoted to fourth billing in *The Falcon's Alibi* (1946), a good entry in a low-budget detective series. She played the double-crossing wife of homicidal disc-jockey Elisha Cook Jr and also gets to sing a couple of songs before he bumps her off.

A more sympathetic role in *They Won't Believe Me* (1947) promoted Jane to stardom, and she was handed the best role of her career as the poisonous Kathie Moffett in *Out of the Past* (1947), based on Daniel Mainwaring's famous crime novel *Build My Gallows High* (also the film's British title).

Kathie is a classic example of a ruthless woman who uses her sexual allure to escape justice. A private detective (Robert Mitchum) is hired to find her after she has shot and wounded her lover (Kirk Douglas) and made off with $40,000 of his money. He too falls for her deadly charm, and they hide out in Mexico until traced by Mitchum's partner, who is unceremoniously gunned down by Greer. Finding out that she had lied about not taking the money, Mitchum walks away, but is dragged back into his own past by Douglas, who intends using him, via blackmail, as the fall-guy for a well-planned murder.

Mitchum meets Greer again, back in business as Douglas' mistress. Hunted by the police, he

*The enigmatic Jane Greer (centre) look is already evident in her first film,* Two O'Clock Courage *(1945), here apparently playing gooseberry to Ann Rutherford and Tom Conway*

turns the tables on Douglas, who, at last discovering Jane's true nature, agrees to turn her in. She stabs him (this time dead) and makes a getaway with an apparently infatuated Mitchum, who has in fact alerted the police. On to him, she puts a bullet in him too just before they and their car are riddled with bullets at a police road block. Told by one character that Jane 'can't be all bad: no-one is', Mitchum replies laconically 'She comes the closest'.

*Greer's best role came as the double-crossing Kathie of* Out of the Past *(1947). Here she's for once not trying to put a bullet into Kirk Douglas but to pull the wool over his eyes*

Jane was equally double-dyed in *Station West* (1948), a sort of western *film noir*. Playing a character described by the *Hollywood Reporter* as 'a luscious-looking lady heavy', Jane is a casino hostess making up to undercover agent Dick Powell, who is unaware that she's the head of the gang of gold robbers he's after.

The film, in which Jane again 'gets hers' at the end, contains stretches of dialogue that might have been written by Mae West. 'Have you ever made love to a woman?' Jane asks. 'Only from the doorway,' he replies cryptically. 'You haven't made love to me,' she purrs, to which he responds 'Come over to the doorway'.

Jane was behind the barrel of a gun again in *The Big Steal* (1949), which was shot around star Robert Mitchum's 60-day sentence for possession of marijuana. It was hard to tell the good-bad guys from the bad-good guys in this complex, fast-moving (all done in 72 minutes!) thriller in which army captain William Bendix turns out to be the biggest bad guy of all.

In her last RKO film, *The Company She Keeps* (1950), Jane was fresh out of jail after two years for cheque forgery. Parole officer Lizabeth Scott, in an unsuitable good-girl role, has a tough task keeping her on the straight and narrow. Ultimately, she not only saves Greer from a return visit to jail for helping a lawbreaker, but is willing to let her go off with the man they both love. *New York Times*' Bosley Crowther got thoroughly fed up with all this. 'Things might have been better,' he grumbled, 'if Miss Scott had sent Miss Greer back to jail.'

On the brink of the big-time, Jane made the switch to MGM. But they wasted her and, in a different sense, her career, with minor comedies and dramas. Her only bad-girl part was as Antoinette de Mauban in *The Prisoner of Zenda* (1952), but it was a subsidiary role and she was fifth-billed. In later times, critics applied such adjectives as 'listless' and 'passive' to some of her performances. Listless and passive? Not the

*Greer as the outlaw queen who entices undercover agent Dick Powell to 'come over to the doorway' in* Station West *(1948)*

Jane Greer who played Kathie Moffett in *Out of the Past.*

Although these are some personal favourites in the annals of wicked women of the screen, there were many more who gave films distinctive bite by being the girls you loved to hate. One of Jane Greer's rivals at RKO was Faith Domergue, originally drafted in by studio boss Howard Hughes to provide competition for Jane Russell.

Domergue had Russell's sultry, almost insolent stare, but otherwise the two were miles apart as performers.

Russell showed up best in comedy or moodily romantic thrillers, but Domergue was truly a creature of the night. Her speciality was bad girls with whom good men become obsessed, often leading to their mutual destruction.

Beverly Michaels and Cleo Moore, two big blondes, were equally destructive, but in much lower budget fare. Both were protegées of the stubby Czech actor-writer-director Hugo Haas, who normally cast himself as the hapless victim of their treacherous advances. Beverly starred in the first of these tawdry melodramas, *Pickup*, in 1951. Later, the buxom Cleo took over for seven more.

Greece's Melina Mercouri was usually a wicked woman of some kind or another, whether as the Regency gipsy, sending the girl who stands between her and a fortune to an asylum before drowning as her coach crashes into a river in *The Gypsy and the Gentleman* (1957); as the earthy prostitute in *Never On Sunday* (1960); as the all-devouring *Phaedra* (1961); or as the criminal mastermind planning the perfect robbery in Istanbul in *Topkapi* (1963).

Mercouri's performances were full-blooded

*Angelic little devil Patty McCormack dispatches her victims by thought transference in* The Bad Seed *(1956)*

as well as full-throated. Her characters let danger, and sometimes tragedy, into your life.

Carroll Baker was petulant rather than poisonous, as demonstrated in her screen breakthrough as the thumb-sucking *Baby Doll* (1956). Later, she went to Britain and the Continent to play temptresses, witches and schemers in such films as *Station Six Sahara* (1963), *The Sweet Body of Deborah* (1968), *Baba Yaga – Devil Witch* (1973) and (back in America) *Andy Warhol's Bad* (1976). In most of her outings, especially the European ones, a display of skin seemed to take preference over a display of venom.

Like Baker, most Hollywood sex symbols were cast as evil schemers at some stage of their career. In consecutive films (*Don't Bother to Knock* and *Niagara*) in 1952, Marilyn Monroe played a psychotic babysitter and a woman planning to have her husband killed (he gets her first).

In her earlier films, Kim Novak lured Fred MacMurray away from the straight and narrow in *Pushover* (1954) much as Barbara Stanwyck had done ten years earlier in *Double Indemnity*, and planned to rob a casino the following year in *Five Against the House*.

Although not exactly evil in *Vertigo* (1958), Novak certainly led James Stewart up the bell-tower to near-destruction, before getting in over her head with the Bette Davis role (as had Eleanor Parker in 1946) in *Of Human Bondage* (1964).

The tawny, tigerish Ursula Andress was usually dangerous as well as desirable, no more so than as the ageless evil in *She* (1964) or the sexy bank-robber mastermind in *Perfect Friday* (1970).

Dark-haired, flashing-eyed Yvonne de Carlo could have been the best of the sex symbol bad-girls, as she proved with her entirely self-centred Anna in the unseen-for-many-years *Criss Cross* (1948), but she was afterwards restricted to wilful adventuresses in colourful escapades of the old west, or east. Only her comic villainess in *Happy Ever After* (1954) endowed her with the right streak of malice.

Down the social scale were the tawdry blondes who had seen better times and, although they sometimes had hearts of gold, were more likely to betray the hero at the spin of a dollar. These included Veda Ann Borg, Gladys George, Ann Savage, Mary Beth Hughes, Isabel Jewell, Iris Adrian and Robin Raymond.

Further up the cast list from these tough tomatoes, but gold-digging in the same vein was Hillary Brooke, notably when throwing her injured husband overboard in *The House Across the Lake* (1954). And no-one was as catty or scheming as Miriam Hopkins, particularly when trying to do Bette Davis out of what was rightfully hers in one of their Warner weepies together.

British blonde Christine Norden weighed in with a few minor-league blonde schemers, notably plotting to murder the husband she thought was dead, in the 1951 thriller *Black Widow*.

These wicked ladies in top supporting roles were generally of a slightly older type, and frequently dominated the film, whether as sinister housekeepers, treacherous discarded mistresses, harridan wives or repressed spinsters.

Chief among these chilling 'charmers' were stone-faced Gale Sondergaard (who has a chapter to herself elsewhere), haughty, strong Judith Anderson, sharp-tongued Agnes Moorehead, and frighteningly evil Eily Malyon.

In Britain there was the raucous Freda Jackson, an arch-portrayer of dominant harridans, who always seemed to be pushing people downstairs, the often psychotic blonde Kathleen Byron, darkly gloomy Rosalie Crutchley, the first face you were likely to encounter behind a creaking door, and, fiercest of all, the tight-lipped, merciless Sonia Dresdel.

Besides memorably portraying Ralph Richardson's hateful wife in *The Fallen Idol* (1948), in which sheer malice drives her to destroy a small boy's pet snake, the demonic Dresdel really got a grip on such films as *The World Owes Me a Living* (1944), *While I Live* (1947) and *This Was a Woman* (1948).

She had the leading role in this last film, as a

*Before she burst through to world fame in* Never on Sunday, *Melina Mercouri played a wild, malevolent gypsy in the British melodrama* The Gypsy and the Gentleman *(1957). Here she persuades drunken husband Keith Michell to sign some vital papers, while lover Patrick McGoohan hovers in the background*

power-crazed wife who tries to poison her husband and ruin her daughter's marriage. By and large, though, Dresdel and her ilk were too ferocious for supporting roles, but hadn't quite the leading lady charisma that led such stars as Bette Davis to get away with so many wicked women without damaging their careers.

In later years, they, like Davis and Joan Crawford, might well have been dragged into horror films – indeed, Jackson and Sondergaard did make one or two. It's sad today that there are no new female frighteners on the horizon to replace them, or such heroines (?) of the horrors as the smouldering Ingrid Pitt, the sveltly dangerous Barbara Shelley, or the frighteningly wide-eyed Barbara Steele (*qv*), all of whom expressed evil with such fierce emotion in the 1960s and 1970s.

At the other end of the scale to the older women were the evil children. Sybil Jason, Virginia Weidler and Jane Withers could be brattish – sometimes even malicious – with the best of them, although none of them could hold a candle to the scandal-mongering all-bad Bonita Granville (ironically an actress often found in 'sweet' roles) in *These Three* (1933).

In the fantasy and horror field, outstanding examples of evil-eyed girls were etched by Patty McCormack, killing by thought transference in *The Bad Seed* (1956) and Chloë Franks, sticking pins in dolls of her victims, in *The House That Dripped Blood* (1971).

But even these are only the tip of the iceberg – just a platoon in the legion of flint-hearted females that have marched across the screen, to their own and others' destruction, for the past 75 years. Many more of these deadly Delilahs can be found in the pages that follow.

# 3
# MURDERESSES OF FACT AND FICTION

'I saw him lying there, drunk,
and I heard the motor running.
Then I saw the doors and I heard the motor.
I saw the doors. The doors made me do it.
Yes, the doors made me do it.'

Ida Lupino in *They Drive By Night* (1940)

One suspects this chapter will give away a few secrets. Perhaps if you're a fan of screen whodunnits, you shouldn't read it at all. Crime writers, however, seem often to think that a woman will be the least likely killer – so they make her the villain of the piece, only to be revealed in the last reel.

There have been some bizarre castings as lady killers, too, possibly because the actress in question is fighting to avoid type-casting as a do-gooder. I mean, would you believe Rachel Ward (in 1980's *Terror Eyes*), Hayley Mills (in 1974's *Deadly Strangers*), Mia Farrow (in 1979's *Death on the Nile*) or June Allyson (in 1972's *They Only Kill Their Masters*)? If the answer is no, then I'm sure they, and their writers, can go home satisfied, because they all Did It.

Certainly a change of pace must have been what Joan Fontaine had in mind when she made *Ivy* (1947), who plans to poison her way clear of husband Richard Ney and lover Patrick Knowles in Edwardian times, and into the arms of rich Herbert Marshall. Unfortunately for her schemes, production codes of the time demanded that she, like Margaret Lockwood on the other side of the Atlantic in *Bedelia* (1946), should get an illogical come-uppance at the end.

*Contemplating the rewards of adultery and murder in Edwardian times, Joan Fontaine prepares to poison another victim in the title role of* Ivy *(1947)*

The trouble with 'nice-girl' actresses taking a break as wicked ladies was that, much as one admired the attempt to break from type-casting, they all too often weren't very convincing at it. Happy as one was for Joan Crawford that she proved not to be doing the axe-murders in *Strait-Jacket* (1964) or the grisly circus killings in *Berserk!* (1967), Diane Baker and Judy Geeson as the real killers still took some swallowing.

And what can one say about limpid, dolefully beautiful Gail Russell as the arch-baddie in *Calcutta* (1947 – actually completed in 1945)? One reviewer said it all. 'It's quite a job,' commented *Cue* magazine, 'trying to palm off this wide-eyed bobby-soxer as a cold-blooded killer and brains of a giant international smuggling ring, and Paramount doesn't quite manage it.'

A pity, since *Calcutta* has some honourable-man/wicked-woman exchanges worthy to set alongside *The Maltese Falcon*. 'You counted on your beauty with guys,' Alan Ladd tells Gail, 'even ones you were killing in cold blood.' It's just a shame he's not saying it to Hedy Lamarr or Donna Reed. Miss Russell herself was at the killing business again in 1957, when she shot down her treacherous lover (Jack Carson) in *The Tattered Dress*. But the circumstances were somewhat different.

No, a screen murderess had at least to *look* capable of such duplicity. Thus the successful casting of Olivia de Havilland as good and evil twins (much later nicely duplicated by Jane Seymour in a television movie version) in *The Dark Mirror* (1946).

Jean Peters certainly looked capable of poisoning her way to a fortune in *A Blueprint for Murder* (1952). But it was easier to accept baby-faced blonde sexpot Stella Stevens as an axe-murderess in comedic vein in *The Secret of My Success* (1965) than as the real thing in *The Mad Room* (1969).

Anne Baxter had a certain underlying hardness in her make-up that allowed her to be quite

*No prizes for guessing which of the Olivia de Havilland twins is the evil one in this trick photography set-up from* Dark Mirror *(1946)*

*Butter wouldn't melt in her mouth. So what's that piece of glass that Ellen (Stella Stevens) is brandishing in* The Mad Room *(1969)?*

startling as the homicidal hussy of *The Come-On* (1956), a film whose violence and amoral attitudes offended contemporary censors. Further calculating charmers from the multi-faceted Baxter can be found elsewhere in this book.

It's notable that women as killers are quite thin on the ground – Bette Davis seems almost to have cornered the market – before the World War II years. The subject was played for comedy by Ginger Rogers in the popular *Roxie Hart* (1942) but, alas, she hadn't shot her lover after all. The killer was her husband; all Ginger was after was the publicity and a new career in vaudeville.

But with the gradual emergence during the 1930s of laconic, *Black Mask*-type crime writers such as Raymond Chandler, James M. Cain, Dashiell Hammett, Cornell Woolrich, W.R. Burnett and, slightly later, Mickey Spillane, the idea of a woman as an angel of death began to be accepted in films as well as pulp fiction.

Mary Astor was probably responsible for starting the whole cycle with her Brigid O'Shaughnessy in Hammett's *The Maltese Falcon* (1941), despite the fact that hers was the third reincarnation of the role, after Bebe Daniels (1931, same title) and Bette Davis in *Satan Met a Lady* (1936). But Davis, in particular, was always likely to make an audience suspicious of such a character, whereas Astor had a kind of vulnerability that kept the viewer guessing both ways.

Hollywood now began to swoop on these writers, at first buying books and bastardizing them to fit the detective characters in minor series. Thus Chandler's *Farewell, My Lovely* became *The Falcon Takes Over* (1942) and *The High Window* re-emerged squeezed into 60 minutes as *Time to Kill* (1942), with Philip Marlowe transmuted into Lloyd Nolan's Michael Shayne character and Ethel Griffies as the deadly dowager eventually identified as pushing her wealthy husband out of the window in the book's title. The part was later played by gorgonic Florence Bates when the book was 'properly' filmed as *The Brasher Doubloon* (in Britain *The High Window*) in 1947, although in some respects the Nolan version is more faithful in spirit to the original – the murderess is seen in a photograph rather than a film.

Most of the misogynistic Chandler's killers turned out to be women, as was the case with the first proper adaptation of one of his books *Murder, My Sweet* (in Britain *Farewell, My Lovely*) in 1945. It turned out to be Claire Trevor (*qv*) as the mysterious Velma everyone is looking for, in a role later played by Charlotte Rampling in the 1975 remake.

*Paula (Janis Carter) finally gets her hands on the $250,000 she has schemed for, but all it buys her is a one-way ticket to the gas chamber, thanks to the lover (Glenn Ford) that she double-crossed, in* Framed *(1947)*

These dark dramas were first cousins of the *film noir*, a genre of treachery, alienation, despair and death (to say nothing of complex plots) in which lethal women often played a key part.

Many was the poor sap, for example, who fell for the glacial blonde exterior calm of Janis Carter, an actress who was almost totally ineffective in submissive heroine roles, and only came alive as a femme fatale, often injecting disturbing qualities into the role not to be found in the script. In 1947's *Framed* (Britain rightly called the film *Paula*, since Carter's character completely dominates it), Glenn Ford is the patsy Carter and her lover plan to frame for their planned $250,000 bank robbery.

Falling for Ford, she dispatches the (ex-)lover instead by pushing him off a cliff in his car. Equally coolly, she poisons Ford's coffee when she thinks he might betray her, but he survives and Paula is taken by the law.

Sweet-faced Bonita Granville, who had hardly played a mean character since her sensational early success as the monstrously vindictive teenager in *These Three* (1936) went to the bad again in the long and tortuous *Suspense* (1946), as the rejected mistress who sees that ambitious murderer Barry Sullivan gets his just deserts in the end as she fills him full of holes in a deserted night-time street – one of the favourite locations for directors of *noir* films.

Some stars, though customarily seen in lighter roles, proved equally suited to the darker side of fiction. Rosalind Russell, for example, had a murderous year in 1947, firstly in the thoroughly gloomy *Mourning Becomes Electra*, which was a bit like *Hamlet* without the action. Russell is cold-blooded Lavinia Mannon, who brings about the suicides of her mother and brother after conspiring to murder her mother's lover, the mother herself having killed her own husband. We leave Lavinia psychotically content to 'live alone with the dead...until the curse is paid out and the last Mannon is let die'.

*Katina Paxinou and Rosalind Russell indulge in a mother-and-daughter staring competition, from which Russell will emerge the winner, in* Mourning Becomes Electra *(1947)*

*Gregory Peck's barrister has that lapdog look, as he interviews Valli's enigmatic Mrs Paradine in Alfred Hitchcock's* The Paradine Case *(1947)*

Pretty bleak stuff and the public stayed away in hordes, but Russell created a sensation by losing the Best Actress Oscar to Loretta Young after being four to one on to win, still the biggest upset in the history of the awards.

She took it out on co-star Leon Ames in her next, *The Velvet Touch*, displaying far from the title finesse when smashing him over the head with a statuette. Detective Sydney Greenstreet finally bags Rosalind on behalf of the law after she nearly commits suicide on stage.

Russell may not have fooled the policeman Greenstreet any more than Humphrey Bogart had in *Conflict* (1945), but the impassive Valli, she of the shining hair, pulled the wool right over defence attorney Gregory Peck's eyes as the murderess on trial in Hitchcock's *The Paradine Case* (1947).

'I will tell you about Mrs Paradine,' Louis Jourdan, as the lover for whom she commits murder, says to the smitten Peck. 'She's bad, bad to the bone. If ever there was an evil woman, she is one.' Peck won't listen, but, after Jourdan's suicide, Valli confesses in the witness box.

Joan Crawford takes the opposite tack in *Mildred Pierce* (1945), trying to convince police she has shot sneering lothario Zachary Scott. Despite the first word in the film – Scott croaks 'Mildred' as he lurches forward, dying, before the camera – few members of the audience were deceived into thinking Crawford was doing anything other than cover up for her spoiled minx of a daughter (Ann Blyth, effectively cast against type with evident enthusiasm) who had really plugged the man who had called her a 'rotten little tramp' which was just what she was.

Crawford collected a Oscar, while Blyth took the drop (and an Oscar nomination). She was considerably more convincing than a miscast Maureen O'Hara (killing perennial bad girl Gloria Grahame) in *A Woman's Secret* (1949) or that great non-actress Vera Ralston in *I Jane Doe* (1948) who might both have stood trial for more than murder on their performances. But the usually diffident Jane Wyatt successfully brought off reverse casting in *The Man Who Cheated Himself* (1951), as the bored socialite who shoots her husband with his own gun.

Miss Blyth herself was again involved in a mysterious murder in *A Woman's Vengeance* (1947), an adaptation of Aldous Huxley's intriguing story *The Gioconda Smile*. But it turned out in the end that repressed spinster Jessica Tandy had poisoned Charles Boyer's wife.

Ms Tandy was one of a brigade of older killers who were, on the whole, more sinister and menacing than their younger counterparts. Geraldine Page murdered her housekeepers and buried them in her garden in *Whatever Happened to Aunt Alice?* (1969), simply so she could appropriate their savings and live in the style to which she had became accustomed.

Servants struck back with Jean Cadell helping her mistress to commit suicide by administering poison in 1951's *The Late Edwina Black* (in America, *Obsessed*). Again suspicion fell on the dead woman's husband (David Farrar), but he was cleared in the end, as was Margaret Lockwood in *Jassy* (1947), in which little Esma Cannon, playing her devoted maid, enjoyed her finest acting hour collapsing and dying in court in the midst of confessing to poisoning beastly Basil Sydney in this Regency melodrama.

Again in Britain, a number of actresses got to grips with playing suspect nurses in *Green for Danger* (1946), a marvellously creepy comedy-thriller in which people seemed to be forever getting gassed or bumped off in dark corners. Not for the nervous – who included the superb Alistair Sim as the inspector who at the end wrests a hypodermic from the hand of surgeon Trevor Howard – who had been trying to administer an antidote to the suicide-bent killer, Nurse Rosamund John.

Older woman killers in America tended to be in the Florence Bates mould of *The Brasher Doubloon* – strong-willed and merciless. Certainly there were few redeeming features about the character played by the normally gracious Selena Royle in *Murder is My Beat* (1955), casually bumping off a blackmailer in this fatalistic, Chandler-like thriller directed by the cult-rated Edgar G. Ulmer.

The Chandler villainesses themselves plotted on, none more ingeniously than little-known actress Jayne Meadows in *The Lady in the Lake* (1946), a fiendishly complicated mystery about a missing woman. The plot takes some summarizing but here goes: Philip Marlowe (Robert Montgomery) visits the vanished Crystal's lover, Lavery, who knocks him cold. A corpse found in the lake is identified as Muriel, wife of Crystal's husband's caretaker. Returning to question Lavery, Marlowe meets his faintly eccentric landlady, then discovers Lavery's body. Police Lt Degarmo seems to suspect Marlowe, and later tries to frame him for drunk driving. Crystal's husband tells Marlowe that Crystal wants $5,000 delivered to her.

When Marlowe reaches her, he finds she is not Crystal at all, but Mildred Haviland, Degarmo's mistress, alias Muriel Chess, alias the landlady. She has killed not only Lavery, but Crystal as well, switching identities after she dumped her body in the lake. In a climactic shootout as the police arrive, Mildred/Muriel and Degarmo are killed.

In some much later, and weakly distilled doses of Chandler, stripper Rita Moreno turns out to be the killer in *Marlowe* (1969), an adaptation of *The Little Sister*, while you may think Nina van Pallandt's hands not entirely clean at the end of the near-disastrous *The Long Goodbye* (1973). In the book, Van Pallandt's character is an out-and-out murderess, but the film, perhaps unwisely, is more enigmatic.

Robert Mitchum, who played Marlowe in the two most recent film adaptations of Chandler, *Farewell, My Lovely* (1975) and *The Big Sleep* (1978), seemed doomed to tangle with deadly damsels at almost every stage of his career.

After being lured to destruction by Jane Greer (*qv*)in *Out of the Past* (1947), Mitchum was ensnared by psychotic Faith Domergue, an ideal sultry villainess, in *Where Danger Lives* (1950). Not suspecting her mental state, Mitchum fights with her husband (Claude Rains) and knocks him out. While he is outside, Domergue smothers Rains with a pillow.

Heading for Mexico with her, Mitchum (who is supposed to be a doctor!) finally latches on, which is when Domergue tries to kill him too. He pursues her to the border, where she shoots him but is in turn shot by the police. Mitchum somehow recovers to return to his old girlfriend.

There was no escape for Mitchum, however, in *Angel Face* (1952). This time an ambulance driver, he encounters homicidal nutcase Jean Simmons (a much underrated performance in her Hollywood debut) just after she has almost succeeded in gassing her stepmother in her bedroom. Despite his suspicions, Mitchum becomes infatuated with this angel of death, who finally succeeds in killing both her stepmother and (incidentally) her father by tampering with their car.

Indicted with her, Mitchum is forced by his lawyers to marry her to play for jury sympathy. When they get off, he tells Simmons he is leaving. Too late, poor fool. She backs their car off the edge of a cliff and kills them both.

Apart from Mitchum's mishaps, we will leave psychotics, deadly or otherwise, to another chapter. Nothing but straightforward evil dripped from that strongest of actresses, Agnes Moorehead, in *Dark Passage* (1947), framing Humphrey Bogart for the murder of his wife, which she has committed.

*Monte's (Zachary Scott) rejection of Vida (Ann Blyth) is about to get him a bullet at the climax (and beginning) of* Mildred Pierce *(1945)*

*Robert Mitchum seems to have the measure of man-killer Faith Domergue in this scene from* Where Danger Lives *(1950). But he'd better keep his wits about him . . .*

Escaping from prison and getting a new face through plastic surgery, Bogart accidentally gets on to Moorehead, who has by now carried out a second killing, through dialogue with a would-be blackmailer. Moorehead robs him of justice by jumping from a high window and Bogart, with his new love, inevitably played by his real-life wife, Lauren Bacall, is forced to opt for a new life in South America.

Equally eager to pass the buck for her capital crime was another sharp-voiced bad girl, Audrey Totter, in *Tension* (1950). Ironically, husband Richard Basehart had planned to bump off both faithless Audrey and her new lover, before himself falling for the sweet charms of a non-dancing Cyd Charisse.

Totter, who seems to go through the film with a perpetual scowl, kills her lover herself and is happy to see Basehart hunted down for the crime. But a deep-thinking policeman (Barry Sullivan) traps her into revealing that she is the killer.

As the 1940s ended, Hollywood's tougher attitudes enabled them to begin to look at the pulp-fiction thrillers of Mickey Spillane. First up for filming was *I, The Jury* (1953), in which Spillane's detective Mike Hammer (Biff Elliot) falls over corpse after corpse trying to find the murderer of an amputee friend. He finally suspects to his horror that the culprit is the woman he loves, psychiatrist Charlotte (Peggie Castle) out to take over a narcotics racket.

Embracing Hammer in a clutch of death, she attempts to shoot him, but he shoots her first. 'How could you?' she gasps, dying. 'It was easy,' he replies in typical Spillane fashion, the dialogue being repeated word for word in the 1982 remake with Armand Assante and Barbara Carrera.

A rather better film was made from Spillane's *Kiss Me Deadly* (1955) – not surprisingly as the director was Robert Aldrich and the plot was more suitable for filming, derived as it was from various elements to be found in classic detective thrillers of previous years.

As in *Farewell, My Lovely*, there's a mysterious evil doctor who fills our hero to the gills with drugs, and a dual identity female mastermind (Gaby Rodgers), supposedly the 'frightened flatmate' of the murder victim, who shoots the doctor (and Hammer, though naturally not fatally) to lay her hands on the film's 'McGuffin', a box containing rare radioactive material.

Fortunately for the film's climax, she can't resist opening the box, which sets light to her and the doctor's beach-house, leaving Hammer (Ralph Meeker) and the heroine to stagger to freedom in a tableau more often seen in a horror film.

Like Spillane, although at the more genteel end of the scale, Agatha Christie has rarely filmed well except in the hands of such master directors as Billy Wilder (1957's *Witness for the Prosecution*) or René Clair (1945's *And Then There Were None* – known in Britain under its original title of *Ten Little Niggers*)

Nonetheless, some highpowered actresses have tried their hands at Christie villains, including a hatpin-wielding Flora Robson in *Murder at the Gallop* (1963), practically half the cast of *Murder on the Orient Express* (1974), Mia Farrow in *Death on the Nile* (1979), Elizabeth Taylor in *The Mirror Crack'd* (1980) and Jane Birkin in *Evil Under the Sun* (1982), all of them, and many more, eventually unmasked by Ms Christie's legendary detectives Hercule Poirot and Jane Marple.

Whodunnits had not been so popular in Hollywood since the demise of the series detectives, Charlie Chan, Mr Wong, Philo Vance and many more. But Anne Bancroft turned out to be the perpetrator of an unexpectedly good minor mystery called *The Girl in Black Stockings* (1957),

*British critics were horrified by the 'Hollywoodization' of Jean Simmons in* Angel Face *(1952). But it was one of the meatiest roles the film capital gave her. Here she looks right through Robert Mitchum*

just as she had in *Gorilla at Large* (1954), in which she ended up in the lethal embrace of the title character. Other 1950s' Hollywood whodunnits in which the wrong character nearly goes to the wall resulted in the trapping of murderesses Ruth Storey in Fritz Lang's *The Blue Gardenia* (1953) and Jaclynne Greene in Samuel Fuller's *The Crimson Kimono* (1959).

Death-dealing females have been thinner on the ground in recent times, although macho cop heroes Clint Eastwood and Charles Bronson both tangled with one. Eastwood ultimately let Sondra Locke (avenging her sister's rape) go, in the repulsive *Sudden Impact* (1983), but Bronson dispatched seemingly invincible Carrie Snodgress from a great height in *Murphy's Law* (1986). In the latter film, Snodgress's psychotic avenger proved equally lethal with gun, crossbow or garrotter's cord!

The French, too, had enough grim-faced actresses to enable them to trade wicked women with the best of them, especially in the 1950s, when Simone Signoret plotted to drive Vera Clouzot round the bend and beyond in *Les Diaboliques/The Fiends* (1954), Jeanne Moreau took a *Lift to the Scaffold* (*Ascenseur pour l'echafaud*. In America: *Frantic*) in 1957, and Mylène Demongeot plotted to do away with a rival in love in *Une manche et la belle* (In Britain: *The Evil That is Eve*. In America: *What Price Murder?*), also in 1957.

Later, in a lighter vein, the statuesque Bernadette Lafont played the multiple would-be murderess whose victims are forever being rescued in the nick of time by the men she has seduced. She finally does get to bump off the

*Ingrid Bergman, in an Academy Award-winning performance as a humble missionary, was only one of many murderers in* Murder on the Orient Express *(1974)*

*Joan Freeman (Carrie Snodgress) gets the information she needs from a private detective (Lawrence Tierney) – before killing him, in* Murphy's Law *(1985)*

people she hates most, leaving her latest victim, the researcher of a book on criminal women, to carry the can – especially as she has seduced his lawyer, who is now acting as manager for her new singing career. The film, *Une belle fille comme moi* (1972) was based on Henry Farrell's black novel, *Such a Gorgeous Kid Like Me*, also the film's American title.

The cinema's most recent murderess, Theresa Russell in *Black Widow* (1987), has got rid of a number of victims before the film even starts. Russell, the blonde bombshell from *Insignificance* (1985), here plays a granite-hard modern Bluebeard who lives in luxury by the simple expedient of marrying wealthy men, murdering them, then collecting the settlements from their wills.

Her method of dispatch is normally poison, but she is unusually careful in that she poisons some item of favourite food, then makes sure she gets out of town until the 'tragedy' occurs. The film's twist is that the Justice Department agent who gets on her trail (Debra Winger) finds herself envious of the murderess's lifestyle and becomes almost fatally fascinated by her.

One cannot leave the subject without a salute to two girls who were not murderesses so much as executioners. So let's hear it for Wynne Gibson of *City Streets* (1931) and Cathy Downs of *The Dark Corner* (1946). They blasted down two of the slimiest slugs ever to stalk the corridors of crime in Paul Lukas and Clifton Webb. In the words of the song from the stage musical *Chicago*: 'They Had It Coming'.

Real-life cases of murder committed by women have received scant treatment in the cinema, probably on account of their downbeat nature, not a good omen for box-office returns.

One of the earliest attempts, set appropriately far back in time, was David Lean's *Madeleine* (1949), a record of the case of Madeleine Smith in 1857, as a vehicle for his then-wife Ann Todd. Madeleine, a Glasgow merchant's daughter, was accused of poisoning her blackmailing lover (Ivan Desny) with arsenic.

Thanks to a brilliant defence, the verdict (acceptable in Scottish law) was Not Proven. Miss Todd, however, made Madeleine such a cold fish it was difficult to identify with her, and you may think the final scene, with Madeleine permitting herself a small smile as she is driven away to freedom, implies that she has got away with it.

Not so lucky was Barbara Graham (Susan Hayward), found guilty of murder and sent to the gas chamber in *I Want to Live*! (1958) even though she protested her innocence to the end. The role finally won Hayward an Oscar after four unsuccessful nominations.

Certainly guilty of a *crime passionel* was Ruth Ellis, the last woman to be hanged in Britain. Her story was (sort of) told in *Yield to the Night* (1956. In America: *Blonde Sinner*) with Diana Dors, and with some (although not much) greater accuracy in 1984 as *Dance with a Stranger*, with Miranda Richardson offering an interpretation as brittle as Dors' had been full-blown.

For the French, Isabelle Huppert weighed in with *Violette Nozière* (1978), an award-winning film by Claude Chabrol about a 14-year-old girl in the 1930s who led a double life and poisoned her mother and stepfather-to-be.

But probably the most repulsive of real-life killers was depicted by heavyweight actress Shirley Stoler who, with Tony Lo Bianco as her partner, formed *The Honeymoon Killers* (1969). These deranged characters, actually executed in 1951, stripped lonely women of their savings and, in one especially horrific (all the more so for being off-screen) sequence, drowned a small girl in a bucket of water.

American television movies took their slice of real-life with *The Legend of Lizzie Borden* (1975), an account of the axe-murderess (played by Elizabeth Montgomery) who 'took an axe and gave her mother forty whacks. When she saw what she had done, she gave her father forty-one.' But did she really do it? Like so many maybe-murderesses, Miss Montgomery keeps you guessing.

# 4
# PSYCHOS, DANGEROUS NYMPHOMANIACS AND ALL POINTS TO THE ASYLUM

'She tried to sit on my lap while I was standing up'

Humphrey Bogart of Martha Vickers in *The Big Sleep* (1946)

*Pretty as a picture, but poisonous to the touch . . . that's Tuesday Weld as Sue Ann Stepanek in the 1968 film* Pretty Poison

The characters under these categories offered even more scope to an actress than straightforward killers. But their performances also had to be more skilfully pitched, so as never to appear over the top. Chills rather than laughs were what most of these ladies were after.

Chills were asssuredly the order of the day when Tuesday Weld, one of the great underrated Hollywood actresses, was *Pretty Poison* in 1968. At the beginning of the story, it's Anthony Perkins (would his mother in *Psycho* qualify for this chapter?) who looks bound once more for the padded cell. Having burned down his home (with his aunt in it), it seems somewhat inadvisable for Dennis (Perkins) to be found a job in a chemical factory on his release from an institution, but there you are.

Living a fantasy life, he tells Sue Ann (Tuesday Weld), a wide-eyed blonde who chats him up about her repressed life at home, that he's a government agent out to foil a plot to pollute the town's water with chemical effluent. Out on a mission to 'sabotage the factory' they are surprised by a watchman. Dennis is disconcerted, to say the least, when Sue Ann thrashes the man over the head with a spanner, then gleefully drowns him in a stream by sitting on him.

With Dennis under suspicion, they plan to run away to Mexico. Suprised by her mother, Sue Ann pulls a gun (which she has taken from the watchman) and blasts her into eternity. Now even Dennis has had enough, and calls the police, confessing to the crimes when Sue Ann denounces him, knowing that no-one will believe him.

He does, however, talk with his probation officer, who spies on Sue Ann, and eventually homes in on her chatting to another young man about her restricted home life...

Before encountering the deadly females listed in the chapter on murderesses, poor Robert Mitchum really suffered in his early cinema years. Having nearly lost Katherine Hepburn to emotionally disturbed Robert Taylor in *Undercurrent* (1946), he ran straight into no-less-disturbed kleptomaniac Nancy (surprisingly well played by the normally passive Laraine Day) in *The Locket* (1946).

*Ellen (Gene Tierney) plans to kill herself with poison in such a way as to point a murder finger at two other people, in* Leave Her to Heaven *(1945)*

*Susan Anspach is at the end of the line . . . and of her mental tether in Dusan Makaveyev's* Montenegro *(1980) a film which, as the Boulting Brothers once said of something else, contains something to offend everyone*

The character is more destructive than the one played many years later by Tippi Hedren in Hitchcock's *Marnie* (1964), as Mitchum ends by killing himself, though not before convincing Nancy's first husband (Brian Aherne) of her true nature. The film, which has an unusual and quite successful flashback-within-flashback structure, begins with Nancy making preparations to marry again, and ends when the locket of the title, which she coveted and stole as a child, is passed to her, causing the past to break through to the surface. She suffers a complete mental breakdown and is committed to an asylum.

Madness in films may come in many forms. In *Leave Her to Heaven* (1945), which might be described as the first Technicolor *film noir*, Ellen (Gene Tierney) suffers from an irrational possessiveness that unhinges her mind. It may seem a trifle extreme that, in order to be close to husband Cornel Wilde, she lets his crippled brother drown, sacks the handyman and throws herself down a staircase to abort their child.

In fact, under John M. Stahl's direction, with Alfred Newman's lush music underlining the quality of Tierney's madness, it was all pretty believable, even the ending that sees Ellen, her existence with her husband menaced by her adopted sister, poison herself in such a way that they are bound to take the blame.

Susan Anspach, in Dusan Makaveyev's very black comedy *Montenegro, Or: Pigs and Pearls* (1980), finds her mind disintegrating under the pressure of something very different: boredom. When her husband departs for Brazil on a business trip, she accidentally finds herself at a bawdy drinking-club, where she meets a handsome Yugoslavian labourer, Montenegro, with whom she has an affair.

Her husband, arriving back early, suspects she has been kidnapped – a supposition which his wife, in a phone call, seems happy to endorse. But her madness surfaces, she kills her lover with a huge knife and returns to the bosom of her family and friends, whom she then dispatches in their entirety by giving them poisoned grapes.

Hardly less chilling is the character played by Susannah York in one of Robert Altman's better films, *Images*, made in 1972. As Cathryn, she is besieged at her husband's holiday home in Ireland by hallucinations and confusions of identity. Does she really blast with a shotgun and stab with a chicken knife her two former lovers? Or are they figments of her demented imagination? Probably the former. At any rate, free of her besetting 'phantoms' she flees to her husband, Hugh. By the road, she sees an image of herself and runs it down. Later she realises it was Hugh . . . as she is greeted at her flat by another image of herself.

Nor would our list of psychopaths and mentally disturbed women be complete without the inevitable Janis Carter, most notably in a 66-minute 'B' feature from 1946 called *Night Editor* (in Britain: *The Trespasser*). Her character is frighteningly unpleasant for a minor film of the immediate post-war period.

We first meet Jill (Carter) necking in a

*Cathryn (Susannah York) blasts a former lover with a shotgun in* Images *(1972). Or is it all a figment of her demented imagination?*

secluded spot with Tony (William Gargan), a married police detective pushing 40, with whom she is having an affair. They witness a murder, which seems in some unpalatable way to turn Jill on.

Tony feels impelled to keep silent because of his wife, but Jill loses little time in tracking down the killer and blackmailing him, especially when another man is arrested for the murder. Tony finally confronts Jill and she stabs him in the stomach with an ice pick. She is taken by his colleagues, while Tony survives, although forced to resign from the force.

Just as dangerous was Nancy, the character played by Leigh Taylor-Young in *The Big Bounce* (1968). The film again seeks to make the dubious connection between compulsive love-making, thrill-seeking (especially in breaking the law) and an unbalanced mind. For Jack (Ryan O'Neal) an ex-GI with a criminal record, these elements lead to murder – and nearly his own.

Driving down the coast to pull off a $50,000 payroll robbery she has planned they will execute, Nancy enthusiastically forces another vehicle over a cliff and threatens to frame Jack for the crime if he talks. In reality, she plans to kill him too, and when Jack arrives for the robbery, shoots him in cold blood, only to find that in the darkness she has gunned down the wrong man. Nancy shrugs off the setback. 'It was more fun throwing rocks,' she remarks, before being arrested for – and acquitted of – the killing. Jack at least gets off with his life.

Like many films depicting women as figures to tangle with at a man's peril (it was also erratically paced), *The Big Bounce* was not popular at the box-office where audiences evidently liked bad girls larger than life and more identifiably evil. Thus an interesting film like *Guest in the House* (1944), which saw the first of Anne Baxter's sweet-faced destroyers (she plays a disturbed girl who is taken into a household whose members she turns against one another in an insidiously poisonous campaign, bringing chaos, tragedy and hatred), is almost forgotten today.

It is small wonder that such a long (two hours plus) and unrelievedly grim film was not to the liking of wartime audiences, but it is a film overdue for revival.

The quality of the films depicting psychotic women is often distressingly low, which accounts for some of them slipping from sight almost before they have surfaced. A pity, for the performances of, respectively, Carol Lynley, Robin Mattson and Elizabeth Ashley were the best things about *Once You Kiss a Stranger* (1968 – a sex-reversal remake of Hitchcock's *Strangers on a Train*), *Return to Macon County* (1975) and *Windows* (1980).

Likewise, Clint Eastwood's *Play 'Misty' For Me* (1971) brought the best performance of Jessica Walter's career. In her case, she was lucky that Eastwood's name (he also directed) brought her fine portrayal of a possessive, crumbling mind to a wider audience than might have otherwise have proved possible.

We first encounter Evelyn (Walter) as a disembodied voice on the phone, requesting 'Misty' of Eastwood's disc jockey Dave. Some time later, she propositions him in a bar and he is unwise enough, as it turns out, to spend the night with her on a 'no strings' basis.

When he tries to pick up his normal life, Evelyn pesters him constantly. Her neurosis begins to turn to violence when she breaks into his flat hoping to find him with his girlfriend Tobie (Donna Mills). Frustrated, Evelyn attempts suicide by slashing her wrists.

Returning the following day expecting to find Evelyn resting in bed after treatment, Dave discovers instead his apartment – and his cleaning woman – ripped to shreds with a razor. Evelyn is taken to a sanatorium, but six months later reappears in spectacular fashion, standing over Dave's bed at night with a carving knife, plunging it into the mattress as he rolls off.

From a reference to Poe's *Annabel Lee*, once quoted to him by Evelyn, Dave deduces with horror that Tobie's new flatmate Annabel may

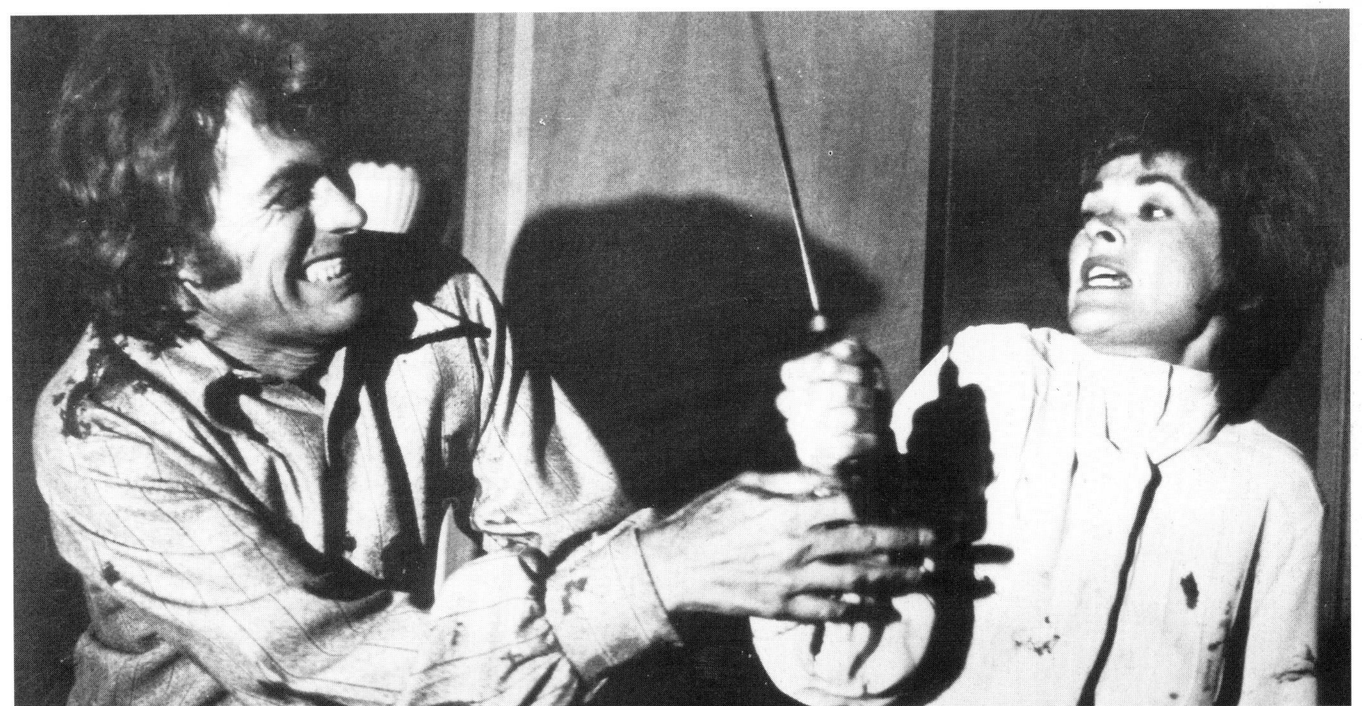

*Knives don't come much more fearsome than the one wielded by Jessica Walter in this final bloody confrontation with Clint Eastwood in* Play 'Misty' for Me *(1971)*

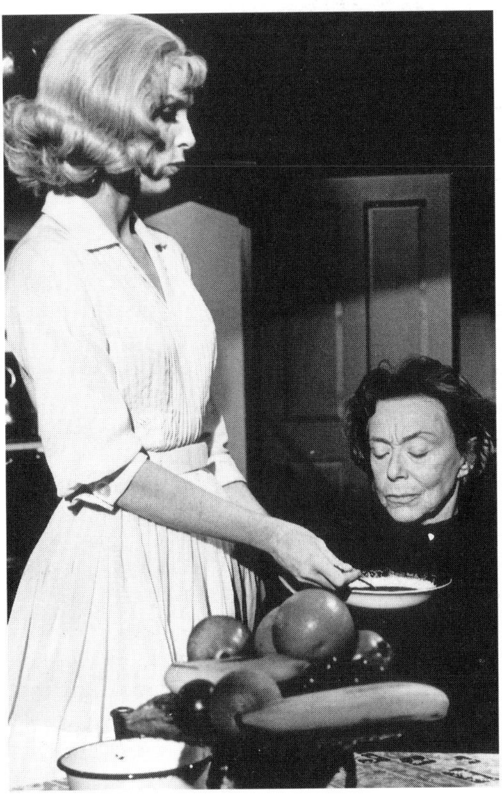

*Drink up . . . while you've still got a head on your shoulders. Jean Arless is, for the moment, kind to Eugenie Leontovitch in* Homicidal *(1961)*

be Evelyn, and dispatches a policeman friend to find out. He arrives at Tobie's coastal home to find the policeman well dispatched with scissors sticking out of his chest and a crazed Evelyn about to kill a trussed-up Tobie. Evelyn and Dave battle and she falls to her death on the rocks below the house.

Many of the screaming banshees of the screen with knives in their hands belong to another chapter, on fantasy and horror films, but before we leave them, perhaps we could bag two other borderline-category cases in Shelley Winters in *What's the Matter with Helen?* (1971) and Jean Arless in *Homicidal* (1961).

In the former, Helen is Shelley Winters and her problems stem from 1934 when her teenage son and that of a friend Adelle (Debbie Reynolds) are executed for murdering a young girl (shades of *Rope* and *Compulsion*). Together, the women set up a dance school for 'Hollywood kiddies' but anonymous phone calls undermine Helen's precarious sanity and she disrupts a dance show in hysterical breakdown.

Refused God's forgiveness by the church, Helen discovers and kills an intruder (he turns out to be an insurance man with an inheritance for her) whose body Adelle helps her dispose of. But Helen is tipped over into total insanity by a seemingly harmless incident in which she cuts her finger on the thorn of a white rose. It can be no coincidence that Adelle finds all her white rabbits slaughtered – not that she has much time to dwell on it, as Helen stabs her to death as well.

Shortly afterwards, a detective tells Helen that the dead man, of whom she denies all knowledge, was almost certainly her anonymous caller...

*Homicidal* was more blatantly pitched in *Psycho* territory, with frozen-faced Jean Arless clearly a bit odd from the start, with her household of wheelchaired mute (Eugenie Leontovitch) and Arless's effete brother.

Pretty soon a knife started flashing up and down, and it didn't surprise those who survived director William Castle's 'fright break' gimmick (which would only have got rid of those bored with the film) that Arless and brother were one and the same.

A rather more serious and frightening study of impending homicidal madness was offered by Roman Polanski's *Repulsion* (1964). Catherine Deneuve plays the Belgian girl who, repelled by the touch of men (the last shot of the film hints at sexual abuse by her father) begins to hallucinate when left alone in the flat she shares with her sister. In the film's most famous effect, she shrinks from disembodied hands that reach through corridor walls to clutch her.

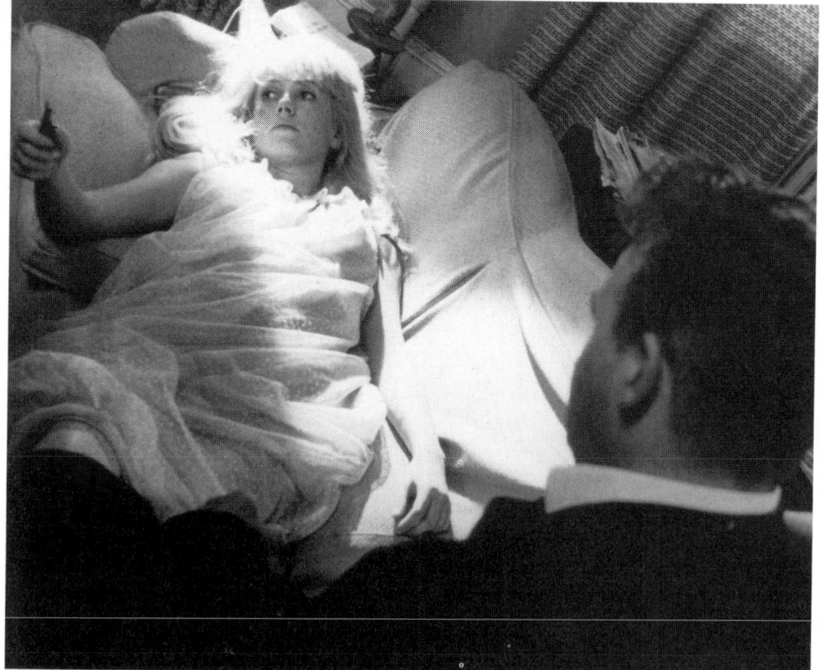

*Carol's (Catherine Deneuve) worst nightmares descend on her in the shape of her oafish landlord (Patrick Wymark) in* Repulsion *(1965). A razor is to hand . . .*

Visits from her boyfriend (John Fraser) and the landlord (Patrick Wymark) result in both men being hacked to pieces. The film is masterly (and chilling) in its demonstration of dangerous withdrawal and deep-seated fears turning to violence when left alone to fester.

A somewhat glossier tale of sexuality linked to murder was Jean Becker's *L'été meurtrier/One Deadly Summer* (1983). It was reminiscent of another French film, Truffaut's *La mariée était en noir/The Bride Wore Black* (1968), but whereas in the latter film Jeanne Moreau killed the men who were accidentally responsible for the death of her bridegroom, the resistible Isabelle Adjani in *Summer* had the wrong three men.

Her father's revelation, that he had hunted down and killed the three who raped Adjani's mother years before, sends the already disturbed girl into a catatonic trance. But a note in which she accused two of the innocent men of the rape passes into the hands of her recently-wedded husband, who guns them both down.

Even more lethal on the loose was the maniac played by Margot Kidder in one of Brian de Palma's earlier (and better) thrillers, *Sisters* (1972. In Britain: *Blood Sisters*), with the star as (separated) Siamese twins, one a homicidal psychopath who has committed murders, one of which (in true *Rear Window* fashion) *may* have been witnessed by reporter Jennifer Salt.

Things get quite complex from this point on, with a doctor falling in love with the 'good' twin, and trying to help by capturing the reporter and brainwashing her into forgetting the murder. Thankfully, good old movie shocker plots have not been forgotten, and there turns out to be only one twin after all (the other having died) who now has two personalities, one normal, one psychotic. She thanks the doctor for sorting it out by stabbing him to death with a scalpel. And, as the reporter now insists she didn't see the first murder, heaven only knows (in a fashionably open-ended finale) what will happen next.

More thoroughly unpleasant was an asylum-set thriller described by its star, Lauren Bacall, as 'truly tacky'. This was *Shock Treatment* (1964) and Bacall is a warped psychiatrist who enjoys inflicting pain and becomes interested in a garden-shears murderer (Roddy McDowall!) whom she feels may not only be less unbalanced than he seems, but may have a million dollars stashed away stolen from his last victim.

An unemployed actor (Stuart Whitman) is hired by the victim's lawyer to feign insanity to find out just what's going on in Bacall's institution. But she eventually rumbles him, and gives him injections which render him catatonic.

Days later, he recovers and, escaping, reaches the victim's home (the lawyer has died) in time to see Bacall and McDowall digging up the treasure which consists of bags of ashes of money, presumably burned by the really demented McDowall.

Bacall's mind completely snaps, McDowall almost kills her with a pitchfork, but Whitman intervenes and McDowall dies instead. Bacall becomes a patient in her own institution. Like the lady said, pretty tacky all round.

But if these were complex characters, then what was one to make of the girl played by Edana Romney in the British *Corridor of Mirrors* (1948)? Romney, whose co-scripting in this arty but intriguing piece was more interesting than her acting, is Mifanwy, believed by painter Paul (Eric Portman) to be the reincarnation of a girl in a picture who lived 400 years before.

When his mistress is found strangled, Paul hangs for the murder. Years later, his housekeeper realises that Mifanwy is the killer and that there's something frighteningly strange about her. Running away from Mifanwy, the housekeeper is killed by a car.

Split personalities and schizophrenics quite often received happy endings from Hollywood, but in Britain Phyllis Calvert came to a sticky end in *Madonna of the Seven Moons* (1944). One half of her life has her as the wife of an Italian wine merchant, the other as the mistress of a notorious jewel thief. Trying to find Calvert, her daughter is trapped by the thief's brother. Finding them together, Calvert confuses brothers, and she and the man knife each other to death.

Nymphomaniacs in films often seemed to be involved in mayhem of one kind or another. If not, like Sandra Julien in *I Was a Nymphomaniac* (1972), they tend to be plain boring. Dyan Cannon in *Doctors' Wives* (1971) got herself bumped off, while Suzanne Pleshette in the ludicrous *A Rage to Live* (1965) could ultimately hold herself responsible for both her mother's and her husband's deaths.

Joyce Redman's sexual gluttony was nearly the death (via a vengeful husband) of Albert Finney in 1963's *Tom Jones*. And both Marianne Faithfull and Janet Munro came to nasty ends in the final few frames of two more British films from the 1960s, *Girl on a Motorcycle* (1968) and *Bitter Harvest* (1963).

It's difficult to tell what sins another nymphomaniac, Carmen Sternwood, isn't up to in

*Is this a razor that she sees before her, the blade towards your neck? Carol Lynley is slashingly destructive in 1970's* Once You Kiss a Stranger

*Philip Marlowe (Humphrey Bogart) finds Carmen (Martha Vickers) spaced out on drugs in the 1946 version of Raymond Chandler's* The Big Sleep

Raymond Chandler's *The Big Sleep*. In the 1946 version, as played by Martha Vickers, she's probably a killer, certainly a junkie and a blackmail victim over nude photographs. At the film's ending (which even director Howard Hawks didn't claim to understand), it seems she's just a wilful teenager in need of the proper care.

As vividly played by Candy Clark in the much inferior 1978 version, the nymphomania and drug addiction of Carmen (renamed Camilla) are put into overdrive. The nude photographs are given more prominence and there is no reprieve from the script for the character this time. She is proved to be a murderess, even if insane – and committed to a sanatorium.

For some reason, the films in which nymphomaniacs were involved all too often turned out to be turkeys. They didn't come much worse than *Youngblood Hawke* (1963), in which Suzanne Pleshette (a good actress but a bad chooser of scripts) strikes up an introduction with the hero with 'Shall I call you Youngy or Bloody?' In the same film, a young boy commits suicide complaining that 'They said mummy was Youngblood Hawke's harlot!' Ouch.

And Nadja Tiller's spirited and enigmatic performance as the mysterious nymphomaniac who drives besotted William Bendix into shooting himself was all adrift in the folly of 1959's *The Rough and the Smooth* (in America: *Portrait of a Sinner*), one of the most inept major British films of its decade.

Mari Blanchard's performance in 1958's *Man Mad* (*aka No Place to Land*) left much less to the imagination, as she caused three deaths in her efforts to win back the man (John Ireland) who has dumped her for lustrous Gail Russell. Her last victim (Jackie Coogan, the former child star!), who is losing his sight because of her, takes her up in his plane and kills them both.

Diane McBain, though, was a better actress than you would ever guess from her performance as the passionate pouter in *Claudelle Inglish* (1961. In Britain: *Young and Eager*), a ludicrous

*Diane McBain doesn't seem too impressed with Claude Akins' offer in the 1961 film* Claudelle Inglish *(aka* Young and Eager*). She'll come around . . .*

Warner melodrama from Erskine Caldwell's pulp novel about a country girl going off the rails after being deserted by her first lover.

Dorothy Malone, on the other hand, an actress previously noted for quiet roles (apart from her seductive bookseller in the 1946 *The Big Sleep*), made a big career switch (and went to blonde from brunette) by playing the spoiled-bitch daughter of a Texas millionaire in *Written on the Wind* (1956). In between lurching from man to man and bar to bar, she inadvertently brings about the death of her weak brother (Robert Stack) and nearly ruins the life of the man (Rock Hudson) she lies, cheats and blackmails to try to get.

*Smashed again. Lauren Bacall is obviously not bowled over by Dorothy Malone's state of permanent inebriation in* Written on the Wind *(1956)*

For Malone, the gamble paid off, and she won an Oscar for her performance. At the end of the film, her character, Marylee, is left alone in the family mansion.

One of the more fascinating characters in this category is Kathleen Byron's demented nun in the richly-coloured 1946 British film, *Black Narcissus*. One of a group of five nuns who open a school and hospital in a deserted palace deep in the Himalayas, Sister Ruth (Byron) is unnerved by the stillness and torrid atmosphere of the place, once the home of the ruler's concubines, as the fading erotic murals demonstrate.

Finally, her mind snaps with her desire for the local English agent (sweatily played by David Farrar) and she dons a red dress and paints her face with vivid makeup. Like some scarlet angel of death, she swoops on the gentle Sister Clodagh (Deborah Kerr) in the bell-tower with intent to kill. But in the nightmare struggle, it's Sister Ruth who falls to her death in the lush jungle far below.

On the subject of minds snapping, one of the most memorable examples, in addition to Bette Davis in *What Ever Happened to Baby Jane?* (1962), comes from Gloria Swanson's fabulous comeback role as Norma Desmond in *Sunset Boulevard* (1950). She is discovered soon after the outset of the film, a now-forgotten silent superstar living in a fading mansion set in a half-ruined estate. Unemployed writer Joe Gillis

*Sister Ruth (Kathleen Byron) opens the door to madness in* Black Narcissus *(1947)*

(William Holden), wandering into this marble web, soon becomes her plaything.

Soon tiring of Norma's world of dreamed-of comebacks and past glories, Joe tries to escape to the love and friendship of a girl at the nearby film studio. But Norma's suicide bid sucks him back in and, when he later walks out for good, she kills him. As his body floats in the pool, Norma walks down her ornate staircase to greet her public (the police) preparing to make a grand comeback in the role of Salome.

That dominant Australian actress Judith Anderson was back in her native country when she gave an astounding performance at the age of 76 in Terry Bourke's *Inn of the Damned* (1974). She and Joseph Furst play a couple at whose inn travellers are wont to disappear – a situation that owed more than a little to the 1951 French film *L'auberge rouge* (*The Red Inn*). Here doyenne French actress Françoise Rosay was the murderous innkeeper, with Julien Carette as her husband and accomplice.

The delight of the psychotic pair is untold when an entire coachload of passengers descends upon them. A monk to whom Rosay has just confessed her sins is unable to break the vow of the Confessional and warn them. Nonetheless, Rosay and Carette are, through a monkey belonging to a previous victim, arrested – but their servant saws through the pillars of the bridge over which the ongoing coach must pass. As the passengers hurtle to their deaths, the monk, watching, loses his mind.

It was hard to know into which category to

*'All right, Mr DeMille. I'm ready for my close-up.' Gloria Swanson comes down the staircase and round the bend at the end of* Sunset Boulevard *(1950). At left: Erich von Stroheim*

*Love-making at the point of a knife is interrupted by a knock on the door. Kyle MacLachlan and Isabella Rossellini in the scabrous* Blue Velvet *(1986)*

pigeonhole Isabella Rossellini's Dorothy Vallens in the controversial *Blue Velvet* (1986). A torch singer at a nightspot in a middle-sized American town, she is also a nymphomaniac and a masochist. Psychotic, too, in so much as the kidnap of her child – over which she feels compelled to supply bizarre sexual favours to a sadistic drug-dealer (Dennis Hopper) – has accentuated these deviant qualities to such a degree as to partially unhinge her mind.

Teenager Jeffrey (Kyle MacLachlan) becomes involved in this bed of worms after accidentally finding a severed ear that turns out to belong to Dorothy's husband, also a hostage. Surprised searching Dorothy's apartment, her becomes her lover at knifepoint and finds himself being asked to beat her as well. Her later appearance, nude, bloodied but unbowed, on his front lawn, triggers off a final confrontation in which MacLachlan shoots Hopper from the same cupboard he hid in while acting as burglar, and Rossellini gets her child (but not her husband, who is killed by Hopper) back.

One doesn't for a moment discount the danger that will attach itself to all of Dorothy's future relationships. For her, and the audience, the asylum doors are still wide open.

# 5
# BADDIES OF FANTASY AND HORROR

'I'll get you, my pretty'
Margaret Hamilton of Judy Garland
in *The Wizard of Oz* (1939)

Like a cross between a pterodactyl and a banshee, filmland's female frighteners of fantasy and horror have shrieked and swooped upon their victims in more cold-blooded and fearsome fashion than their male counterparts for more than 50 years. Yet producers of these genres have not on the whole heeded the old maxim that the female of the species is deadlier than the male, even though this most ghoulish variety of the screen's wicked ladies proved more merciless in films than any other.

Women in horror films might often have been frightened by things that went bump in the night. But they were just as likely to turn into them. While male villains usually stayed in some kind of human form, female denizens of darkness were liable to transform themselves into everything from panthers to snakes, possibly to make their death-dealing exploits that much more believable – and gruesome.

Barbara Shelley, almost as perennial a 'heroine' of the horrors as dark-eyed Barbara Steele (whose cinematic misdeeds are recorded in a separate chapter), had her first taste of horror (and blood) by 'changing' into a panther in *Cat Girl* (1957). Well, actually, her spirit enters the panther's body at night, to be technically correct. But the net result is the same: her enemies are mauled to death.

*As if from behind a cloud of chiaroscuro, Simone Simon looms palely as one of the* Cat People *(1942)*

True transmogrification was achieved by the silky Simone Simon in *Cat People* (1942), a low-budget horror film that saved its studio, RKO, from bankruptcy by making a profit of several million dollars. It was remade in 1981, with the appropriately catlike Nastassja Kinski, and the predictably visceral (if excellent) special effects. But the original remains far superior, conveying many of its terrors by suggestion rather than actuality.

Both Simon and Kinski frighten the life out of their victims and the audience, before being cornered and killed at the end while trying to release a panther from captivity at the zoo.

Dusky Pam Grier was a 'panther-woman' in the awful *Twilight People* (1972), but this, in Dr Moreau fashion, was more as a result of overdoses of animal serum than any connection with the supernatural.

Although women did manage to turn themselves into various 'creatures of the night', there was many a catchpenny title that sent horror fans away disappointed. In *Cobra Woman* (1943), for example, Maria Montez does not change into a snake (the film might have been livelier if she had) and June Lockhart in *She-Wolf of London* (1946) wasn't really a lycanthrope killer, even though she had been conned into thinking she was.

But the suitably cold Faith Domergue did manage to assume the form of a snake in *Cult of the Cobra* (1955), a dose of horror so mild that the British censors gave it a 'U' certificate. So did Jacqueline Pearce in *The Reptile* (1966), one of the best of Hammer's later films, with Pearce's performance arousing pity as well as horror, as the girl afflicted with this ophidian curse.

One could hardly expect, however, that Coleen Gray would turn into a leech in *The Leech Woman* (1959) and indeed she didn't, even though Susan Cabot did assume a sort of insect-like appearance the same year in a Roger Corman low-budgeter, *Wasp Woman*, another result of a serum overdose. But Barbara Shelley was up to

*Paul (Richard Pasco) may be signing his own death warrant in falling for the enigmatic Carla (Barbara Shelley) in the 1964 Hammer shocker* The Gorgon

*'Well, my pretty, I can cause accidents too.' Margaret Hamilton, clearly peeved at the demise of a sister witch, threatens Judy Garland in* The Wizard of Oz *(1939)*

new tricks in *The Gorgon* (1964), changing into a snake-haired woman who turns all those who gaze upon her to stone. Eventually, this being a Hammer film, someone managed to chop off her head, snakes and all.

Two favourite film forms of female fiends are witches and vampires. Probably the most famous witch in the history of cinema isn't a particularly horrific one at all, but Margaret Hamilton's cone-hatted cackler in *The Wizard of Oz* (1939), plotting with her army of monkeys, and finally dispatched by Dorothy (Judy Garland) with a bucket of water that melts her away.

Others in more serious horror films might have wished the remedy were that simple. Although witches *were* occasionally figures of fun and even romance – as Kim Novak in *Bell, Book and Candle* (1958) and Teri Garr and Lana Turner in *Witches Brew* (1978) – they were mostly bent on dealing out death and destruction.

There was certainly no mistaking the malevolence of Patricia Jessel in *City of the Dead* (1961) or Yvette Rees in *Witchcraft* (1964). In the 1966 film *The Witches* (in America: *The Devil's Own*), another Hammer production, Hollywood's Joan Fontaine found herself confronted with a whole coven of them. Forcibly initiated into the cult, she breaks an occult spell by shedding her own blood and the head witch (Kay Walsh) dies.

Like Kay Walsh in this film, many other witches' invoked the power of evil to further their own ends. Fritz Leiber Jr's novel *Conjure Wife* proved a popular source for film-makers and Hollywood used it first, as the basis for 1945's *Weird Woman*, with Evelyn Ankers trying to get Anne Gwynne to murder husband Lon Chaney Jr. A more ambitious effort emerged from the British group Independent Artists in 1961, titled *Night of the Eagle* (in America: *Burn, Witch, Burn*), with Margaret Johnston as a professor's wife who uses black magic to get Janet Blair to dispatch husband Peter Wyngarde.

When that fails, she brings a stone eagle to life. It chases the terrified man through the

*Head witch Kay Walsh goes into a trance, while Ingrid Boulting prepares for the worst, in the 1966 horror film* The Witches

corridors of his school, but as Johnstone leaves the building, an effigy of an eagle that stands above the entrance crashes down and kills her, breaking the curse.

Witches rarely have time to be sexy as well, but a couple of exceptions are Linda Hayden, trying to seduce a priest in his church, before meeting a sticky end (as the leader of a group of teenagers conjuring up demons) in 1970's *Satan's Skin/Blood on Satan's Claw*, and Carroll Baker in *Baba Yaga – Devil Witch* (1973).

The latter character goes back further in time than the strip cartoon on which the film is based, being the inspiration for one of the pieces of music for Moussorgsky's *Pictures from an Exhibition*, where the witch is supposed to live in a house on stilts. Although Baker plays Yaga as a modern Lesbian witch, the space beneath her house still provides the place for a bottomless pit, into which she herself falls at the end of the film.

Billie Whitelaw's Mrs Baylock in *The Omen* (1976) was a witch in all but name. Certainly she possessed supernatural powers which enabled her to get rid of heroine Lee Remick before herself being overcome by Gregory Peck in his efforts to kill his own son, the reborn anti-Christ. He doesn't succeed, of course, or we wouldn't have had two (inferior) sequels.

Perhaps the most extraordinary shape of all (at least outside the cartoon witches recorded in another chapter) was achieved by Wanda Ventham in 1967's *The Blood Beast Terror* (in America: *The Vampire-Beast Craves Blood*). She managed to transform herself into a giant death's head moth that fed upon its prey in vampire fashion – although the film's budget was too low to allow the special effects its audience would doubtless have liked.

There are many examples of female vampires (apart from the kind created by Pola Negri) in filmic lore, dating back to Dracula's sinister 'wives' in the classic 1931 version of Bram Stoker's horror story. But they weren't to hold centre stage for another five years until the austere Gloria Holden appeared (in her screen debut) as *Dracula's Daughter*.

After burning her father's body, his daughter, Countess Marya, tries to lead a normal life. But love (and her natural vampiristic tendencies!) prove too much for her, and she dies protecting the man she loves (Otto Kruger) when her assistant fires an arrow which goes through her heart.

Generally speaking, vampires were not good to the ladies who played them. Despite her fine performance, Gloria Holden could rarely find better than character roles in films. Nor did her successors fare any better. The vampires played

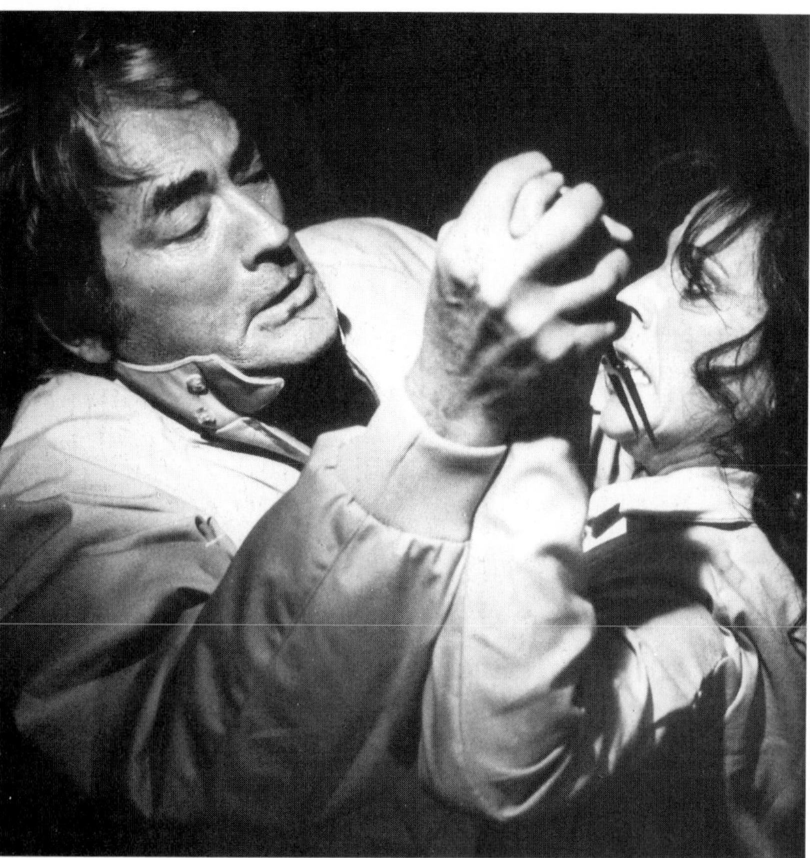

*To-the-death struggle between Robert Thorn (Gregory Peck) and his son's witchlike nanny, Mrs Baylock (Billie Whitelaw) in* The Omen *(1976)*

*Horror fans got a triple dose of Ingrid Pitt in* The Vampire Lovers *(1970). She played Mircalla, Marcilla and Carmilla, vampires all*

by Valerie Gaunt and Carol Marsh in the 1958 version of *Dracula* (in America: *The Horror of Dracula*) were pretty well relegated to the sidelines, and Jennifer Jayne had only the last of five segments to herself in the portmanteau horror film *Dr Terror's House of Horrors* (1964).

Fanged females, however, did receive a boost in the late 1960s, mainly from the works of J. Sheridan le Fanu, a distinguished and very scary writer of chillers who had invented the infamous Carmilla Karnstein and other vampire ladies. Carmilla was ferociously embodied by Ingrid Pitt in *The Vampire Lovers* (1970) and by Yutte Stensgaard in *Lust for a Vampire* the following year. Hammer Films mixed the traditional chills with lots of fashionable Lesbianism and excessive gore, and Miss Pitt carried on with the mixture in *Countess Dracula* (1970), as a noble-woman who must bathe in the blood of virgins to preserve her youth, and in *The House That Dripped Blood* (also 1970).

Wanda Ventham recovered sufficiently from her demise as the death's head moth in *The Blood Beast Terror* (*qv*) to rear her head briefly as a vampire in *Captain Kronos – Vampire Hunter* (1972), before being disintegrated again, while across the Atlantic, Celeste Yarnall was a sexy bloodsucker in Stephanie Rothman's *The Velvet Vampire* (1971).

Meanwhile, Hammer were plundering the stories of le Fanu yet again in *Twins of Evil* (1971). As the *Playboy* centrefold Collinson twins, Mary and Madeleine, were cast as the daughters of a Puritan witchhunter – one escapes the clutches of evil while the other becomes a vampire – the accent was once more on sex. And the settings seemed little changed from those employed in the same studio's *Vampire Circus* (1971), in which the stage musical star Elizabeth Seal was among the vampires able to change into animals to plague Serbian villages in the guise of a travelling circus.

Continental cinema also had a go at the theme with *Le rouge aux lèvres/Daughters of Darkness* (1971). A modern reworking of *Countess Dracula* – the character played by Delphine Seyrig even has the same name – its sole merit was its original method of dispatching the vampire. Involved in a car crash, Seyrig is flung through a window and impaled on a branch.

Inside a few years, however, this new vein was emptied of its box-office blood. One of the last to drink the red liquid was the distinguished stage actress Anna Massey in *Vault of Horror* (1973), another of the in-vogue multi-story horror films, playing a girl murdered by her brother. An incident in a restaurant reveals that he is the only non-vampire in town – and his sister gains her revenge...

In the same film, Glynis Johns made an uncharacteristic venture into villainy as a wife driven mad by her husband's passion for tidiness. She kills him and cuts him up into tiny pieces which she stores in neatly labelled jars.

These comic-book-style compendiums mostly emanated from Amicus Productions. Hammer remained aloof from such vulgarities (although it must have envied Amicus their 1972 near-classic of the genre *Asylum*), prefering to stick to its female fiends in sideshoots of established stories of the macabre.

Thus, Angharad Rees as Anna carries on the work of her father Jack the Ripper in *Hands of the Ripper* (1971). A kiss sets off the homicidal tendencies that stem from having watched her father murder her mother, but she is finally cornered in the Whispering Gallery of St Paul's Cathedral, and plummets to her death.

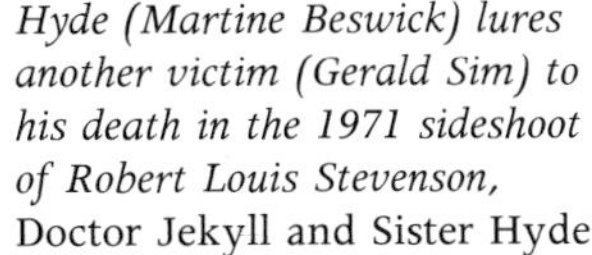

*Hyde (Martine Beswick) lures another victim (Gerald Sim) to his death in the 1971 sideshoot of Robert Louis Stevenson,* Doctor Jekyll and Sister Hyde

(ABOVE RIGHT) *A devotee of black magic, the evil Juliana (Hazel Court) brands herself with the sign of the inverted cross in* The Masque of the Red Death *(1964)*

Both this and the next Hammer film, *Doctor Jekyll and Sister Hyde* (1971), were only semi-successful, yet the latter is partially redeemed by Martine Beswick's performance of Barbara Steele-like intensity as Sister Hyde, a murderess who eventually loses her new-found identity when her alter ego, Dr Jekyll (Ralph Bates), is killed during pursuit by police.

Completing a trio of Hammer Films released at this time, *Blood from the Mummy's Tomb* (1971), another embellishment on a familiar literary theme, is regarded in some quarters as the best of the studio's later work. It certainly contains the best (indeed, only major) performance of its statuesque leading lady, Valerie Leon, storming through the night looking suitably possessed as the girl 'taken over' by the spirit of an Egyptian queen with great supernatural powers.

The last shot of the film leaves the viewer to decide which identity has survived the final holocaust – in similar fashion to the two girls, one dead, one alive, played by Elizabeth Shepherd in Roger Corman's best film, *The Tomb of Ligeia* (1964).

Another good villainess in the Corman films based on the works of Edgar Allan Poe was British-born Hazel Court, who showed in these films to much better advantage than she had in milk-and-water roles in her native country – both in *The Raven* (1963) in which she deserts sorcerer Vincent Price for a rival (Boris Karloff) and especially *The Masque of the Red Death* (1964), in which she makes a breast-branding pact with the Devil but is later ripped to death by the beak and talons of a falcon.

Servants of the Devil came in many and varied forms – but one of the most chilling was not in a horror film at all. In *The Devil and Daniel Webster/All That Money Can Buy* (1941), Simone Simon, the self-same 'heroine' from *Cat People* (*qv*) 'materialised' as Belle Dee, seductive assistant to the satanic Mr Scratch (Walter Huston).

She is seen off in the end by Edward Arnold's 'Everyman' character Daniel Webster, but not before seducing hero James Craig away from his wife and bringing a bizarre, other-wordly aura to her role that almost belongs in another film.

Back in Britain, one of the most striking villainesses of early creepies was Mary Clare, always a formidable actress, in *The Night Has Eyes* (1942. In America: *Terror House*). She plays a housekeeper who, with her husband (Wilfrid Lawson), is committing the Yorkshire moors murders of which her employer (James Mason) is suspected.

After a good many scares – the film is said to have frightened wartime audiences considerably – Clare and Lawson meet their own doom in the quicksands on the moors.

Two of the most extraordinary figures of more recent times have been created by the same woman – Tina Turner, basically a singer who occasionally takes acting roles. But her voracious acting style, part instinct, part showmanship, enlarges her bad girls beyond lifesize. In *Tommy* (1975), she plays The Acid Queen, a gorgon in steel and leather, who pumps the title character full of drugs, supposedly to cure him of his deafness, dumbness and blindness; it permits him only to see a transitory red image of himself in a mirror.

Although Turner tore the screen apart in this brief appearance, she did very little acting until permitted to hold rather more of centre stage in *Mad Max Beyond Thunderdome* (1985), as Aunty Entity, the chainmail-clad ruler of the futuristic

*Tina Turner as Aunty Entity, the duplicitous ruler of Bartertown, with her imperial guards, in the futuristic adventure* Mad Max Beyond Thunderdome *(1985)*

Bartertown. She consigns her enemies to duels to the death in the great vaulted netting of the Thunderdome, having no mercy on those who break its rules. She also leads her warriors into battle at the head of an army of jeeps and Heath Robinson contraptions across the desert, but fails to get the better of Mel Gibson's intrepid loner hero.

Few of these chapters would be complete without an appearance by the indomitable Shelley Winters. In *Whoever Slew Auntie Roo?* (1971. In America: *Who Slew Auntie Roo?*), she is not so much wicked as merely deranged, a sad, tormented woman who keeps her daughter's skeleton in a coffin, and now plans to replace the tragic child with a Christmas visitor from the local orphanage.

The child (Chloë Franks) is quite happy to be 'kept' by Auntie Roo. Not so her brother (Mark Lester), who believes Roo to be a witch, and roasts her alive in a cupboard even as she tries to break out with an axe.

The devilishly angelic Miss Franks, who, like so many talented child players, never quite matured into an adult leading lady, moved from protagonist to antagonist in *The House That Dripped Blood* (1970) as a little girl frightened of fire and forbidden to play with dolls. Unfortunately, her new governess cures her of the first and allows her the second – to her own cost, for the child, like her mother, is a witch...

Curtis Harrington, who had directed Shelley Winters in *Whoever Slew Auntie Roo?* (and *What's the Matter with Helen?*), went on to disappoint thereafter, one of his few remaining cimema films being *Ruby* (1977), which seemed to be inspired by the the renewed popularity of Piper Laurie, Oscar-nominated on her comeback to acting in *Carrie* (1976), in which she plays a religious fanatic eventually crucified by the telekinetic powers of her repressed daughter (Sissy Spacek).

In *Ruby* she plays a gangland moll whose lover is shot down by the hoodlum who 'owns' her. She bears her lover Nicky's mute daughter and gouges out the hoodlum's eyes in revenge, taking over his mob. Sixteen years later (in 1950), the daughter is possessed by Nicky's spirit and starts killing members of the gang.

While a parapsychologist frees the girl of Nicky's vengeful influence, Ruby is trying to persuade his spirit to release its grip by producing the eyes she plucked from the gangster's head! Those members of the cast still alive at the end arrive at the scene in time to see Ruby embracing Nicky by the lake where he was shot

*There's trouble in the kitchen and Shelley Winters' Auntie Roo has that stern Jewish mama look in* Who Ever Slew Auntie Roo? *(1971). Could mean trouble for Mark Lester . . .*

down, before both disappear beneath the water.

The same Curtis Harrington had previously directed Simone Signoret in *Games* (1967), the second of her two 'fiendish plot' films that hover between this chapter and the one on schemers. The more famous of the two, however, is Henri-Georges Clouzot's *Les diaboliques/The Fiends* (1954), in which Simone Signoret and Vera Clouzot (the director's real-life wife) play, respectively, mistress and wife of a master at a run-down boys' school.

As the wife is browbeaten and the mistress physically beaten, the two women band together to rid themselves of the brute. The murder is messy – they get him drunk and drown him in a bath – and doesn't do much for Clouzot's weak heart. They dump the body in the swimming pool, but, when the pool is drained – no body. A school group photograph shows a shadowy face at the window in the background that could be the 'murdered' man.

Hounded by a scruffy ex-policeman, Signoret flees the scene. Left alone, Clouzot has a nightmare in which disembodied sounds combine to drive her to the bathroom. There, in the full bath, she finds the body of her husband. As she succumbs to a heart attack, he rises, takes out his false eyes and goes to congratulate Signoret on the success of their plot together.

There is a sting in the tail. Another school photograph. Another shadowy figure at a window in the background. It looks like Clouzot...

There is no reprieve for the victim of *Games*. The puzzle the film sets is once again who are the tormentors and who the tormented. This time it's James Caan and Katherine Ross as wealthy eccentrics who indulge in bizarre games and welcome Signoret to their household when she faints while trying to sell them cosmetics.

She initiates them into more dangerous games, involving duelling pistols and Russian roulette, with the result that one of their macabre jokes ends with Caan shooting a delivery boy through the eye while Signoret is not there. They hide the body, but Ross's sanity begins to crack, and Signoret's Tarot cards and crystal ball say she is being haunted by an unquiet spirit.

While Ross is alone, the body of the delivery boy, which had been encased in plaster, comes to life. She shoots – he dies, for real, the unknowing patsy in a plot by Signoret and Caan to drive Ross insane, or to murder or both, and make off with her money. Signoret then poisons Caan and leaves, carefully watched by the little old lady (Estelle Winwood) next door.

It became fashionable for *grandes dames* of the cinema to indulge in such vivid shockers in the 1960s, and the crone-voiced Tallulah Bankhead seized her piece of the action in 1965's *Fanatic* (in America: *Die, Die, My Darling*).

As Mrs Trefoile, brooding in her dark country mansion, her welcome for her dead son's ex-

*Frozen-faced Simone Signoret (right), with Vera Clouzot, prepares a bottle of whisky that will give the man they hate more than a hangover, in* The Fiends *(1954)*

*Nursing the midget Hans (Harry Earles), who loves her, trapeze star Cleopatra (Olga Bacalnova) plans to poison him and make off with his fortune – and her lover, in* Freaks *(1932)*

fiancée (Stefanie Powers) soon turns into a reign of terror. A religious fanatic with a strange dislike of mirrors, she locks the girl in an attic and gives her readings from the Bible to rid her of her 'sinful desire' to marry another man.

The girl tempts the handyman (Donald Sutherland), who had foiled an escape bid, into helping her, but they are discovered. The handyman decides to get rid of Mrs T, from whose death he will benefit, but she outwits him and shoots him in the cellar. Ultimately, the girl's boyfriend arrives just in time to prevent her from becoming a human sacrifice to the portrait of Mrs Trefoile's son. Mrs T instead becomes the sacrifice when she is stabbed to death there by the handyman's vengeful wife.

Veteran villainesses continued apace even in Italy, where, in *The Evil Eye* (1962), the mild and ladylike Valentina Cortese proved to be the hatter-mad woman behind a nightmarish series of stabbings of girls whose names begin with A, B and C (shades of Agatha Christie).

Before she can dispatch girl D (Leticia Roman) Cortese is shot by her reluctant accomplice husband, whom she has also just stabbed – but not until a final five minutes of hand-rubbing histrionics in which Cortese proves herself more than a match for Davis, Bankhead and Crawford.

A rather more subtle shade of growing evil was assumed by Catherine Lacey (once the high-heeled nun in the 1938 version of *The Lady Vanishes*) in *the Sorcerers* (1967). In a performance described by one critic as 'superbly baleful', she plays the wife of a professor (Boris Karloff) who has perfected a system of telepathic control over the human mind.

Sharing the experiences of their 'subject' (Ian Ogilvy), the couple, with Karloff's will dominated by Lacey's, go on to vicariously experience robbery, violence and finally murder. After a second killing, Karloff makes Ogilvy's getaway car crash, the flames consuming all three protagonists.

Ruth Gordon, best-known in her later years for crusty but basically kind-hearted termagants, showed no such mercy in *Rosemary's Baby* (1968), in a role that won her an Oscar. She and her husband turn out to head a coven of Satanists, the demon they have called forth having apparently raped the girl in the next apartment and impregnated her.

It was rather more extraordinary to find that gentle actress Betsy Palmer, briefly a Columbia contract player of the 1950s, required to kindle her natural warmth into a maniacal flame in *Friday the 13th* (1980), a movie which spawned numerous gory sequels and consists almost entirely (as did all the sequels) of teenagers being slaughtered while on vacation at a lakeside summer camp.

Palmer's character turned out to be the killer, having been driven insane by the death of her son in a swimming accident some 20 years earlier, but, alas for filmgoers, her death did not bring about the end of the story.

From the other end of the acting scale, sex queen Marilyn Chambers emerged briefly from softporn films to become the 'heroine' of David Cronenberg's 1976 Canadian film *Rabid*. Involved in a road accident, her character, Rose, is subjected to experimental surgery which seemingly leaves her with an insatiable desire for blood, and a rather gruesome new organ for extracting it.

Seemingly unaware that she is decimating the countryside, Rose leaves a trail of devastation behind her. Her victims behave like rabid dogs, foaming at the mouth and going around biting other people willy-nilly. Finally confronted with evidence of her 'disease', the plague-carrier 'bleeds' another victim, then waits until he comes round. Her body is later cleared away by anti-contamination squads cleaning the city.

In another Cronenberg film, *The Brood* (1979), Samantha Eggar is the mental patient who goes around literally giving bloody birth to 'children of rage', malevolent midgets who kidnap and kill at her will. Finding her in the middle of giving birth to one, husband Oliver Reed wisely strangles her, and her 'brood' dies with her.

Rather more colourful portraits of villainy from the world of fantasy were painted by Helen Gahagan and Ursula Andress in the two versions (1935 and 1964) of H. Rider Haggard's *She*, chronicling the exploits of 'She who must be obeyed', the ageless ruler of a mysterious city who finally ages and crumbles to dust in her own flame of youth. And, from the realms of legend, several actresses have had a stab at the treacherous Morgan le Fay, the witch-warrior who assailed King Arthur, notably Anne Crawford in *Knights of the Round Table* (1954) and Helen Mirren in *Excalibur* (1981).

Perhaps the worst fate of all befell Olga Baclanova as the trapeze artist Cleopatra in *Freaks* (1932). She plans to marry the midget who is infatuated with her, then poison him for his money and end up with her lover, the circus strong man. However, at the wedding ceremony, she is reckless enough to reveal her true colours.

The rest of the freaks exact a terrible revenge one lightning-lit night, and Cleopatra ends as a freak herself – a limbless 'chicken woman' doomed to eternal agony.

# 6
# SCHEMERS AND DOUBLE-CROSSERS

You're an improbable person, Eve,
and so am I. We have that in common.
Also a contempt for humanity, an inability
to love or be loved, insatiable ambition – and
talent.
We deserve each other.'

George Sanders to Anne Baxter in *All About Eve* (1950)

She was the lady with the bedroom eyes and the enigmatic smile. The hero had usually fallen for her so heavily that he had to believe she was on the level, blinkering himself to the double-cross that a less infatuated man would have known was just around the next corner.

She was most likely to turn up in the *film noir* world of the 1940s, perhaps as Anne Baxter, Virginia Mayo or Ava Gardner, but a few classic examples of screen schemers stray in from later years, such as Kathleen Turner in 1981's *Body Heat*. One thing was certain: the schemer and double-crosser was after her own ends in life, and didn't have a sympathetic bone in her body for those whose emotions she deliberately used.

Most poker-faced of all this particularly deadly species (whose victims often ended up dead or, at best, demoralized) was Anne Baxter, whose surface sweetness always seemed suspicious after her appearances as chilling charmers.

Her evil exploits in *Guest in the House* (1944) are chronicled in another chapter but, despite an Oscar for her dipsomaniac widow in *The Razor's Edge* (1946), Baxter was cast in 'nice girl' roles until the emergence of her Eve Harrington in 1950's *All About Eve*.

The apparently guileless Eve ingratiates herself into the role of secretary-companion to doyenne actress Margot Channing (Bette Davis), while harbouring secret ambitions to replace Margo as the queen of the Broadway stage. Only Birdie the maid (Thelma Ritter) is on to her from the start, but Margo has a blazing row with Eve for being over-attentive to her director lover (Gary Merrill) and tries to get shot of her by arranging a job elsewhere.

But when Margo is late for an audition reading, she learns that Eve appeared and took her place, and has been appointed her understudy. A playwright's wife (Celeste Holm), also taken in by Eve, arranges for Margo to miss a performance and Eve takes her place for a personal triumph. Eve now feels free to fly her real colours by slanging Margo in a newspaper interview and blackmailing the playwright's wife into pressuring him to give Eve the leading role in his new play. But she loses Margo's lover, who rejects her.

Basking in the warmth of her latest theatrical triumph, Eve is herself taken in at the end of the film by a girl (Barbara Bates) just like her.

Both Davis and Baxter were nominated for Oscars for reaching such heights of screen bitchery, although in the event both were to lose out to Judy Holliday for *Born Yesterday*.

But Baxter's portrayal is the archetypal schemer, only her crocodile eyes betraying her mask of deception. She was to be notably devious only twice more in her long film career, firstly as an unscrupulous con-woman mixed up to her neck in murder in *The Come-On* (1956).

She seemed to be the victim of a diabolical plot in *Chase a Crooked Shadow* (1957), in which she plays Kim, an heiress who returns to her Costa Brava villa to find a stranger claiming to be her brother, who was killed in a car crash. She thinks she will unmask the imposter (Richard Todd) by calling in her uncle and the local police chief, but to her terror they both back his story. A few more twists in the tale and Kim herself is revealed as a devious schemer, a thief and a murderess, thanks to a complex plot against her by the authorities.

The grandmother of all *film noir* double-crossers, of course, is Mary Astor in *The Maltese Falcon* (1941), lying, cheating and killing to lay her hands on the black statuette of the title, and never telling private eye Humphrey Bogart the whole story as she sweet-talks him into helping her. In the end, though, she pays the penalty. Bogart deduces that she shot his partner (whom he despised) and he turns her over to the law because 'when a man's partner is killed, he's supposed to do something about it' and because he 'won't play the sap' for her even though he loves her.

Astor can't quite believe it, and even turns on the feigned tremulous lip once more, to no avail. Never mind, Bogart will be waiting for her if she ever gets out of jail.

Between 1945 and 1949, enough of these two-faced women followed the Astor trail to fill the cells in Death Row several times over. The escapism required by wartime audiences had reduced such roles to a few outstanding examples – such as Barbara Stanwyck's burnished

*Margo (Bette Davis) introduces Eve (Anne Baxter) to Addison (George Sanders) and his 'protegée' Miss Casswell (Marilyn Monroe) in* All About Eve *(1950). Addison recognizes a fellow-opportunist when he sees one . . .*

blonde in *Double Indemnity* (1944). The following year Warner Brothers made a film from Vicki Baum's novel *Hotel Berlin*, a sort of follow-up to the same author's *Grand Hotel*, filmed in 1932. The 1945 film is set in a once-grandiose, now crumbling edifice which, providing a haven for refugees from the Nazis, looms as a sort of *Casablanca* of the hotel world.

The appearance of Helmut Dantine and Peter Lorre heightens the comparison, but mainly the film provided an interesting role (the best of her film career) for Andrea King, a fairly bland actress whose Hollywood days came mainly between the ages of 29 and 38. Here, quite successfully cast against type, she is Lisa Dorn, actress and Nazi supporter who, setting her cap at a Prussian general, falls incongruously in love with an Austrian underground worker. She helps him evade his pursuers but, when her love is not returned, plans to betray him to save her own skin. But he knows she has tipped the Nazis off, kills her and escapes.

Another lesser-known actress, Mary Beth Hughes, often played unsympathetic parts, but a change from blonde to brunette brought her one of her best, opposite Erich von Stroheim in an early Anthony Mann thriller, *The Great Flamarion* (1945). They are partners in a circus sharpshooting act, and Hughes banks on Stroheim's infatuation with her when they plot her unwanted husband's death in an 'accident' during his performance. Naturally, she intends going away not with Von Stroheim, but a typically caddish Dan Duryea. But the plot's final twists provide one or two surprises.

The svelte Ava Gardner was often cast in equivocal roles in these post-war years, the outstanding example coming in Robert Siodmak's 1946 version of Ernest Hemingway's *The Killers*, in which she deprives Burt Lancaster's boxer-turned-robber of even his will to live, after inveigling him into a payroll heist, then absconding with her kingpin gangster lover (Albert Dekker) and the loot.

Later, Gardner and Dekker have Lancaster murdered by contract killers, a fate he resignedly accepts. But, thanks to Edmond O'Brien's insurance investigator, they fail to get away with it. Gardner's role was reprised (with less fire) by Angie Dickinson in the 1964 remake.

Normally cast as a girl next door, the sweetly pretty Ellen Drew must have been pleased to get her teeth into the role of Nelle Marchettis in *Johnny O'Clock* (1946). She has her eye on her husband's gambling casino partner Johnny (Dick Powell) and, when Marchettis finds out about a diamond watch she has given Johnny, he orders his hitmen to gun him down.

Johnny escapes and, although wounded, shoots Marchettis (Thomas Gomez) dead. When he rebuffs Nelle, she turns him in as a cold-blooded killer. After a brief attempt to escape using a policeman as hostage, Johnny decides to give himself up and hope the evidence will free him to marry the girl he really loves.

Virginia Mayo occasionally broke away from Goldwyn frolics with Danny Kaye to thread together a string of duplicitous dames from the 1940s. First she was the floozy wartime wife who claimed to have wasted the best years of her life waiting for fighter pilot husband Dana Andrews in *The Best Years of Our Lives* (1946). In fact, she has run up a succession of lovers (glowering Steve Cochran is her current beau) which is swiftly continued when Andrews returns to his old job of soda-jerking.

After assuming centre stage as the brassy broad who endeavours to frame her own lawyer on a murder charge as *Flaxy Martin* (1948), Mayo had just about her best role as the faithless wife of manic hoodlum James Cagney in *White Heat* (1949). Much slapped around, Verna (Mayo) would like nothing better than to slip between the sheets with Cagney's right-hand man Ed (again Steve Cochran) and gets the chance when Cagney is sent down for robbery. She and Cochran also conspire to have his super-protective mother bumped off. And, although Cagney kills Cochran on his escape, Mayo typically wriggles (and wiggles) her way off the hook.

Gene Tierney who, like Anne Baxter, had cold eyes set in a lovely face, weighed in with the self-seeking Isabel Bradley in the 1946 version of Somerset Maugham's *The Razor's Edge*. Spoiled and bitter at having married a rich man (John Payne) she doesn't love, she attempts to win back the man she really loves (Tyrone Power) by driving his fianceé (ironically, Baxter) back to the drink she had given up, and suicide. But Power turns his back on her, to cheers from the audience, who were probably as pleased to see the end of a vastly overlong film as to relish Tierney getting her just deserts.

By and large, though, the crime drama held sway in offering the best and juiciest roles for actresses seeking red meat at the time. *Criss Cross* (1948) is a well-documented but strangely seldom-seen thriller from the Universal stable that provided one of the studio's prize female possessions, Yvonne de Carlo, with a character that made her for the first time seem convincingly treacherous as well as desirable.

The theme of sexual enslavement runs strongly through this black drama, even at the

*The treacherous Anna (Yvonne de Carlo) and her ex-husband Steve (Burt Lancaster) are cornered by her crooked gambler boyfriend, in* Criss Cross *(1948)*

outset when Steve, an armoured car guard (again Burt Lancaster, as besotted by de Carlo here, as his ex-wife Anna, as by Ava Gardner in *The Killers*, also directed by Robert Siodmak) is discovered drinking heavily, unable to forget.

His obsession with her is a terminal condition. Planning to marry Slim, a gambler (Dan Duryea), she encourages Steve to renew their own relationship on a clandestine basis, then convinces him to go through with a robbery plan which he has suggested to cover their almost-discovered liaison, but which the film hints has rooted itself in Steve's mind some time before as a means to getting away with Anna and the money she desires.

Slim goes along with it, but plans to set up Steve as the fall guy. Gunning most of Dundee's men down, Steve becomes a hero. But then he is kidnapped from his hospital bed to a final rendezvous with Anna, who in the best tradition of the double-crosser, has taken off with the money. Anna prepares to leave the wounded

*A double date with destiny for Ann Savage and Tom Neal in Edgar G. Ulmer's triumph of minimalist cinema,* Detour *(1945)*

Steve to his fate, but Slim tracks them down and kills them both before himself being mown down in hail of police bullets.

Just as fatal to the man she manipulates is a gritty little actress called Ann Savage in that classic of minimal cinema *Detour* (1945). A twitchy tubercular, she joins a hitchhiker driving a car whose driver has died of an accidental overdose and subsequent fall, and turns the situation to her own advantage.

When the hitchhiker (Tom Neal) confides in her, unaware she is the same girl who viciously attacked the dead driver when he made a pass at her, she eagerly blackmails him. Her first idea is merely to sell the car, but a newspaper report tells her that the dead man was a dying millionaire's son, returning to the father who had not seen him since he was a child. The girl hatches a plot to pass the hitchhiker off as the heir. If he refuses, she will call the police.

The girl dreams of a health-giving life in the sun, but, like the equally tubercular Dustin Hoffman in *Midnight Cowboy*, she is never to get there. Drunkenly quarrelling with the hitcher at a motel, she pretends to make good her threat to phone the law by rushing into the adjoining room, but collapses on the bed. Pulling desperately on the phone cord from the other side of the locked door, the hitcher accidentally strangles her with the cord which is wound round her neck.

*Detour* was made in five days for $20,000. But it provided Ann Savage with easily the best role of an otherwise disappointing career. Neither did the cinema make the best use of strong-jawed Helen Walker, largely requiring her to play passive dramatic roles, whereas she excelled when asked to be warmly comic (as in 1945's *Murder He Says*) or coldly manipulative. In this vein, she played the unscrupulous psychologist who drops meal-ticket trickster Tyrone Power when he blows an important con-trick, and the frigid wife whose schemes to bring about the death of her trusting husband (Brian Donlevy) in *Impact* (1949) ironically rebound on her. By the time she died from cancer at 47, Walker's screen career was long over.

And the Swedish actress Signe Hasso, who lacked warmth as a leading lady, despite a long Hollywood attempt to make her a major star in appealing roles, was ideally cast as the glacial, manoeuvring woman who inspired robbery and murder in Ray McCarey's very minor but watchable 1946 thriller *Strange Triangle*.

Screen schemers became thinner on the ground with the turn of the decade, but Marilyn

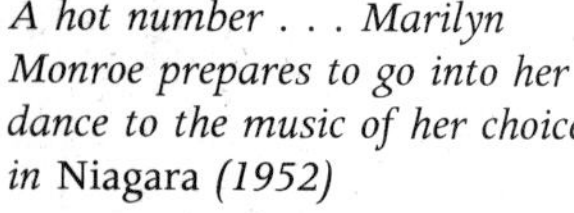

*A hot number . . . Marilyn Monroe prepares to go into her dance to the music of her choice in* Niagara *(1952)*

*Poisoner or saint? Richard Burton never really finds out the truth about Olivia de Havilland in* My Cousin Rachel *(1952)*

Monroe was certainly one, and a hot number too, seducing her boyfriend into a hoped-for murder of her husband (Joseph Cotten) in Monroe's breakthrough film, *Niagara* (1952). But it's the adulterous couple who die at the hands of the wised-up husband.

Over in Britain, Elizabeth Sellars helped send unwanted lover John Mills to jail for 12 years by perjuring herself. But on his release, and once the man Mills was supposed to have killed has been dispatched for real, she proves beneath his contempt.

Doubts about whether Olivia de Havilland was schemer, a poisoner, or neither, were never resolved in *My Cousin Rachel* (1952); but there was finally no doubting the duplicity of Mary Murphy in *Hell's Island* (1955), a grimly dark sideshoot from *The Maltese Falcon*, and made in Technicolor for some reason best known only to the producers.

She plays Janet, who, in order to marry a wealthy man, ran out on her fiancé, a district attorney (John Payne) who subsequently lost his job through drinking. Now her husband is suspected of sabotaging a plane to steal a priceless ruby aboard, and Payne is the man offered a princely sum to recover the gem.

He shouldn't be pleased to see her again, but he is, poor sap, only to find out at the end of the story, after nearly losing his own life, that Janet sabotaged the plane, stole the ruby and planned to bump off her husband for his insurance. Ruefully, he turns her over to the cops.

Nor had Fred MacMurray learned from his painful experience with Barbara Stanwyck in *Double Indemnity*. Here he was in 1954, ten years older and ten years wearier, but no wiser and the perfect patsy for another blonde, this time Kim Novak, in *Pushover* (1954).

Playing Leona, the mistress of a bank robber,

*No mercy in the eyes of Mieko Harada, seducing and killing her way to power in Akira Kurosawa's* Ran *(1985)*

she seduces MacMurray, as the cop on the case, and suggests that he kill her lover before making off with her and the money from a recent 'job' – more than $200,000. At first disgusted with the idea (just like MacMurray's insurance investigator in the earlier film), his sexual obsession with the girl leads him to carry it out...but the murder is witnessed by another policeman.

Killing his colleague, too, MacMurray also kidnaps a girl who had spotted him leaving Leona's apartment after the killing. But inevitably he is gunned down at the end and, lying in the street badly wounded, tells Leona bitterly that 'we didn't really need the money, did we?'

Another buxom blonde who played a bevy of bad-girl roles, albeit in much cheaper films than Novak, was round-faced Cleo Moore. In *The Other Woman* (1954), for example, one of several seedy low-budget pictures she made for Czech writer-director Hugo Haas, she plays Sherry, an aspiring actress bitterly resentful at being refused a role by Haas, actually playing a movie director in the film.

Persuading him to take her to his apartment to talk things over, she drugs him, pretends they have had sex and later announces herself pregnant, demanding $50,000 not to break the news to his wife. The director plans and executes an ingenious murder involving a sound loop on the moviola in his editing room. But, in best *Columbo* tradition, a cunning detective unpicks his alibi and the director confesses.

Shakesperian schemers have been largely male, but Judith Anderson made a formidable Lady Macbeth in the 1960 film. A pity she did not get to play the role until she was 62. An interesting variation on the role was played by Ruth Roman in *Joe Macbeth* (1955), a modern-day gangster variation on Shakespeare's play.

Roman, an actress well-suited to cold charmers, played Lily Macbeth opposite Paul Douglas' Joe. She steers him to the top in the underworld by egging him on to murder rivals, but a series of bungled killings leads to Joe shooting Lily by mistake. He himself is gunned down by the son of one of his victims.

More recent times have brought an extraordinary performance by the Japanese actress Mieko Harada in Akira Kurosawa's *Ran* (1985), an impressive and spectacular relocation of Shakespeare's *King Lear* to sixteenth-century Japan.

Harada's character is a Lady Macbeth-type schemer who marries first one brother, then another, to further her own ends, and the actress plays her with such ferocious single-mindedness that she dominates the whole film, a lot of life going out of it with her bloody demise towards the end.

Sometimes lady plotters in films were more concerned with driving a rival out of her mind than grasping the reins of power. Natasha Parry, once the prettiest of British screen ingénues in the early 1950s, combined with Rex Harrison to try to drive Harrison's wife (Doris Day) round the bend and, hopefully, to her death, in the shivery suspense film *Midnight Lace* (1960), while in *Night Watch* (1973) it was Billie Whitelaw and Laurence Harvey who were scheming (or were they?) to push Elizabeth Taylor to a second mental breakdown. After she goes off her rocker, she lures them both to the derelict house where she has 'seen' bodies ('visions' supplied by Harvey and Whitelaw) and slashes them to death with a knife.

More plotters routed were Samantha Eggar and Curt Jurgens in *Psyche 59* (1964), a turgid affair whose title I have never been able to figure out. They flaunt their affair in front of his wife (and her older sister), who is blind. Since the wife is played by Patricia Neal, at least the more melodramatic aspects of all this are never allowed to get out of hand, and you can bet that, when Neal gradually recovers partial sight without telling anyone, the adulterous duo are due for a nasty come-uppance.

Memories of *The Fiends* were revived by some of the developments in *Hush...Hush, Sweet Charlotte* (1964), director Robert Aldrich's follow-up to *What Ever Happened to Baby Jane?* two years earlier.

The gruesome plot, which might equally well fit into our chapter on fantasy and horror, deals with a complex scheme (it takes 134 minutes to unravel) woven by Miriam (Olivia de Havilland) and her lover Dr Bayliss (Joseph Cotten) to gain control of the fortune at present being sat upon by Charlotte (Bette Davis), Miriam's cousin – a half-dotty recluse beset by hallucinations about the beheading of her married lover (Bruce Dern) 37 years before.

Miriam's contributions to Charlotte's mental collapse include lullabies played late at night and the discovery of a disembodied head and hand in the music room. Velma (Agnes Moorehead), Charlotte's devoted housekeeper, is suspicious of Miriam, but the latter surprises and kills her, Bayliss contriving the death to seem like an accident.

Miriam then convinces Charlotte that she has killed Bayliss and they dispose of the 'body' together in a swamp. Returning to her mansion, Charlotte is confronted by the 'walking corpse' of Bayliss, and collapses. When she comes to, not quite in the condition of total dementia the conspirators had hoped for, she overhears them talking and everything falls into place – including the cement pot pushed over the balcony by Charlotte on top of Miriam and Bayliss.

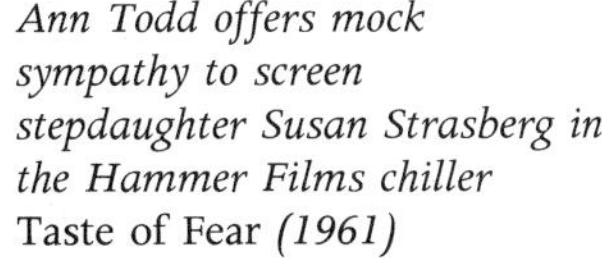

*Ann Todd offers mock sympathy to screen stepdaughter Susan Strasberg in the Hammer Films chiller* Taste of Fear *(1961)*

Taken away by police, Charlotte is handed a copy of a letter by an insurance investigator. It is, in an ironical twist ending, the deathbed confession of the woman (Mary Astor) who really beheaded Charlotte's lover decades before, and had paid Miriam to withhold the truth.

Over in Britain, it was Ann Todd's turn to assume the wicked stepmother role in 1961, in *Taste Of Fear* (in America: *Scream of Fear*) in one of Jimmy Sangster's typically convoluted plots, possibly all inspired by the success of *Chase a Crooked Shadow*. The recipe in this case is: Take one crippled heiress, Penny (Susan Strasberg), add a tight-lipped Todd, throw in Ronald Lewis as the chauffeur who rescues Penny from the pool into which she falls at the sight of her father's body in a wheelchair and, just for luck, stir in a red herring in the form of Christopher Lee as a sinister doctor.

Further appearances by daddy's corpse convince Penny that it's a plot by stepmum and the doctor to drive her insane. She's not got it quite right, though, and, despite the fact she isn't really a cripple, it almost costs her her life when the conspiratorial lovers turn out to be stepmum and the chauffeur. The climax, however, sees Todd falling from the top of a cliff to be smashed on the rocks below – the fate she intended for her stepdaughter.

Throwbacks to the snaky charmers of *noir* years have been rare in recent times, but the poker-faced Jacqueline Bisset played one in the 1976 Charles Bronson thriller *St Ives*. Sporting the Chandleresque name of Janet Whistler, she's the 'companion' to a wealthy recluse, Procane (John Houseman), and double-crosses everyone in sight in her attempts to lay hands on the ransom money demanded for the return of five ledgers which comprise Procane's criminal diary. This includes the safecracker who stole them, pushed to his death from a hotel window, the two crooked detectives in on the deal (both shot) and Procane himself, deceived by Janet and her lover (Maximilian Schell) his psychiatrist. In a final shootout, the latter fatally wounds Procane, but is in turn shot by Bronson as the hero, an ex-crime reporter who also had the wool pulled over his eyes by Janet.

There is a suggestion at the end that she may yet escape justice, by seducing the police captain on the case into absconding with her, and the money. One wonders how long he will last.

Rather more sympathy is attracted for the coolly calculating Geraldine Chaplin of *Remember My Name* (1978), especially since she has just served 12 years for a death for which her ex-husband (Anthony Perkins) may have been responsible. She harasses him and his new wife to an alarming degree, which culminates in the man being fired from his job. Finally getting her ex-husband to make love to her, Chaplin has him locked in his room while she buys herself a suitcase full of clothes on his credit cards and leaves town.

But the deadliest of all *noir*-type heroines has to be Kathleen Turner in her screen debut in *Body Heat* (1981). Echoes of *Double Indemnity* are wholly intentional as writer-director Lawrence Kasdan's fiendishly complicated plot unwinds.

Sexually obsessed with Matty Walker (Turner) to blood-heat level, Florida lawyer Ned Racine (William Hurt) is soon sucked into a plan to kill her shady businessman husband (Richard Crenna). The grisly business is not accomplished easily, but the couple burn the body with an explosive device Ned has obtained from a friend, Teddy Lewis (Mickey Rourke).

Things Ned later learns lead him to suspect the 'spontaneous' nature of the lovers' conspiracy. Matty has handed in a new will, which she claims Ned helped her draw up. A judge, remembering a similar case involving Ned, has declared the will invalid under a technicality, leaving Walker intestate and Matty with the money. Ned further discovers that Mary Ann Simpson, witness to the will, has disappeared and that Teddy Lewis has been taken by police and has told them that a woman asking about the explosive device gave him Ned's name.

Smelling a svelte blonde rat, Ned goes to see Matty at her boathouse and spots a suspicious wire attached to the door. Matty, claiming that she initially contrived their affair but subsequently fell for him, walks down to the boathouse, which blows up. Arrested for the Walker murder, Ned seems to have proved in prison that the body found in the boathouse was Mary Ann Simpson's and that Matty is still alive and enjoying her ill-gotten gains. He's right too. The film's last shot shows Matty sunning herself on a South American shore.

The French as usual played their own variation on the game. In 1957's *Retour de Manivelle* (in Britain and America: *There's Always a Price Tag*), that enigmatic green-eyed blonde Michèle Morgan plays the gold-digging wife of an alcoholic financier who commits suicide. To collect his money, she must make the death look like murder and, with the help of an infatuated drifter, it's achieved. But a plan to frame one of her husband's associates proves her downfall. Asked to hit her, the drifter misjudges the blow and kills her.

Meanwhile, Hollywood still hadn't finished with *The Maltese Falcon* and it turned up yet again revamped as *Target: Harry* (1969), with Vic Morrow as Sam Spade (thinly disguised as Harry Black), Suzanne Pleshette as the intelligent murderess Harry has eventually to hand to the police, and Victor Buono predictably given the Sydney Greenstreet role. This time they're all after a set of plates stolen from the Royal Mint in London. Inevitably, the magic of the original had all but evaporated.

Nowadays, scheming women too often play second-fiddle to other elements in the plot. In *They're Playing with Fire* (1984), a voluptuous Sybil Danning was intriguing casting as the teacher who lures a teenage pupil into helping her bump off her mother and claim an early inheritance she has no intention of sharing with him; unfortunately, there's a killer with a knife on the loose as well, and the film soon disintegrates into a routine 1980s bloodbath along *Friday the 13th* lines.

Finally a tribute to two little ladies who

*The tension shows on the faces of Matty (Kathleen Turner) and Ned (William Hurt) as they prepare to murder her husband in the latter-day* film noir, Body Heat *(1981)*

deceived practically a whole town and a whole army. In the delicately titled *A Big Hand for the Little Lady* (1966. Changed by Britain to *Big Deal at Dodge City*), Joanne Woodward is the wife of ex-gambler Henry Fonda riding into town and into an annual poker game played by five filthy-rich businessmen for enormous stakes.

Much to his wife's distress, Fonda joins in the game, but collapses after staking all his savings on one hand. Told by a doctor he has had a heart attack, Fonda asks his wife to take over. 'How do you play this game?' she asks, before going to the bank manager for a loan. His reaction to the hand she holds is to raise the stakes hugely, leaving the other players so awestruck that they all throw in and leave Woodward with the money.

Outside town, Fonda, Woodward, the doctor and the banker meet to split the thousands of dollars netted by their elaborate plot.

No such happy fate awaited Gia Scala in *The Guns of Navarone* (1961). As a girl supposedly struck dumb following brutal Nazi torture, she is later discovered to be a traitor trying to sabotage an entire Allied expedition against giant guns on an Aegean island. When the men hesitate at exterminating such pretty vermin, Greek partisan Irene Papas does the job for them. A good few movie heroes might have wished for the help of such a woman before being destroyed by one of the schemers of the screen.

# 7
# OUTSIDE THE LAW – CROOKS AND FEMALE MASTERMINDS

'When women go wrong, men go right after 'em'
Mae West in *She Done Him Wrong* (1933)

This is a chapter dedicated to those ladies who flaunted the law in ways that varied from amusing to vicious, yet don't fit quite snugly into any of the other categories in this book. Small-time lawbreakers trying to stay alive mingle with those with grandiose schemes to land them a lifetime of luxury – or just a soon-spent bankroll until the next crooked idea occurred to their devious minds.

Blackmailers were a nasty breed, who, since they were often part of a whodunnit or detective thriller, could easily end up dead before the end of the film. One who survived – only to keep an assignation with the hangman – was Jean Simmons, playing a steel-minded housemaid in gaslit London of the early 1900s in *Footsteps in the Fog* (1955).

Finding out that her employer, Lowry (Stewart Granger), whom she has ambitions to marry, poisoned his late wife, the maid quickly blackmails her way to a position of housekeeper. Following her in fog with intent to finish her off, Lowry gets the wrong girl and finds himself on trial for the murder of someone he never met.

Acquitted, he feeds himself slow doses of poison in the hope that the malevolent maid will be taken for attempted murder. But he dies, and the maid faces the gallows for a crime she didn't commit.

Diana Dors' blackmailing habits in 1952's *The Last Page* (in America: *Manbait*) got her bumped off in a struggle with her confederate over the money, but pinch-faced Elsa Lanchester just about survived *Mystery Street* (1950), which cast her unusually but successfully as a grasping landlady out to squeeze a killer whose victim was one of her tenants.

He intends to kill her for her pains, but is interrupted by the policeman hero, who discovers a key to a railway station locker, where it turns out the landlady has hidden her blackmail insurance – the murder gun.

Many of the women in this chapter were thieves in some way or another. In *The Killer That Stalked New York* (1950, in Britain: *The Frightened City*), Evelyn Keyes plays a nefarious lady who visits Cuba to collect stolen diamonds on her husband's behalf. While there, she contracts smallpox, becomes a carrier and, like Marilyn Chambers in the later *Rabid* (see *'Baddies of Fantasy and Horror'*), leaves a trail of death behind her when she returns to the United States.

She becomes progressively more ill and alienated from society, eventually reaching her husband only to find he is planning to run off with the loot and another woman. She tries to kill him but finds that, in more ways than one, she cannot summon up the strength. The husband dies falling from a building after police pursuit, while Keyes gives the authorities a full list of people she has contacted before succumbing to the disease herself.

Gangland molls were usually shunted to the sidelines, and were cheap rather than callous, but an early example played by Jean Harlow is integral to the plot of *The Beast of the City* (1932). She it is who lures the detective brother of the

*Dr Wood (William Bishop) at last corners the girl criminal (Evelyn Keyes) who is carrying a deadly disease, in* The Killer That Stalked New York *(1950)*

*About to stew in their own mess of poison, Lily (Jean Simmons) and Lowry (Stewart Granger) act out the last rites of a bizarre duel in* Footsteps in the Fog *(1955)*

crusading senior policeman hero into the gang, dying with both of them in an apocalyptic shootout at the end. Fortunately, the character is also endowed with a Mae West sense of humour. Asked by an aggressive cop if she likes to get hurt, Harlow is allowed to curl her lip and drawl: 'Oh I dunno. It can be fun if it's done in the right spirit.'

More of a would-be gangland moll than an underworld intimate: that was Peggie Castle playing one of her many women whose longing for luxury led them to step across the tracks, in Phil Karlson's *99 River Street* (1953). At the start of the film we find her morosely married to ex-boxer John Payne, who now has to earn a living as a cabbie. In between nagging Payne, Castle starts an affair with Brad Dexter, as a crook who has just pulled off a jewel heist.

After a fence objects to her involvement, however, Dexter kills her, a not unfamiliar fate for Castle, often seen as hard-bitten types in tough thrillers, including two from the works of Mickey Spillane, *I, The Jury* (1953) and *The Long Wait* (1954). In 1956, she was involved with a gang of forgers in Britain's *The Counterfeit Plan*.

It was art forgery that was Lucille Ball's interest in *Two Smart People* (1946), but 'art' of a different kind occupied the attention of the screen's occasional poison-pen writers, who always seemed to turn out to be women.

Flora Robson was first out of the starting stalls in 1939, as Britain used the obvious title of *Poison Pen*. Playing the repressed spinster sister of the village vicar, Robson includes among her victims Catherine Lacey, for once, not a wicked woman herself, but a dressmaker driven to suicide by one of Robson's letters. It's a way out that Robson herself eventually takes, throwing herself off a cliff when unmasked, but not before more letters have led to heartbreak and murder.

It's a film that the French director Henri-Georges Clouzot might have seen before co-writing and directing his famous film *Le corbeau* in 1943. Again, the theme is of a village torn apart by a series of anonymous letters, which begin when a psychiatrist's young wife (Ginette Leclerc) gets a letter accusing her of an affair with a reclusive doctor.

The doctor himself investigates and discovers, though not in time to prevent the suicide of a cancer victim, that there was not one writer, but three. The first letter had been written by the 'victim', Leclerc, out of unrequited passion for the doctor. The spate of letters had then been taken over by her seemingly gentle, but actually vicious and insane husband, to prove his theory of 'insanity of two', with a crippled girl proving the writer of another letter.

The wife is taken away, and the psychiatrist killed by the cancer victim's wife, with the same razor used by her husband to commit suicide.

Hollywood remade the film in a French-Canadian setting as *The Thirteenth Letter* (1950), with Constance Smith as the hapless originator,

*Denizens of the early Hollywood underworld. Pietro Cholo (J. Carrol Naish) and Daisy (Jean Harlow) in* Beast of the City *(1932)*

*Medium – and kidnapper. Kim Stanley goes into a candlelit trance in* Seance on a Wet Afternoon *(1964)*

Linda Darnell as the cripple and Charles Boyer as the demented psychiatrist, who is dispatched in this version in the act of writing a letter, by the *mother* of the suicide, here a war veteran.

Kidnappers were usually pretty vile characters, male or female, but often they remained shadows in the background, or mouths at a telephone, until near the end of a film. Ruth Roman and Paul Stewart had kidnapping forced upon them in the 1949 suspense classic *The Window*, in which a young boy (Bobby Driscoll) sees Roman abetting husband Stewart in his efforts to rob, and then kill a drunken sailor.

Known for telling lies, Tommy is unable to convince his parents of what he saw, and his eventual attempt to escape his apartment and tell the police only leads to his being taken by Roman and Stewart. Placed unconscious on a high ledge, the boy survives and it is Stewart who dies while pursuing him along a wooden beam. Roman is arrested by police.

A very different, but hardly less dangerous kidnapper was played by the great stage actress Kim Stanley in *Seance on a Wet Afternoon* (1964). She's a barely-sane medium who plans to boost her reputation by getting her downtrodden but devoted husband Billy (Richard Attenborough) to kidnap a little girl so she may reveal her whereabouts (and those of the ransom) by 'clairvoyance'.

But when the medium, whose 'contact' with the spirit world is through her stillborn son Arthur, moves from this chapter to the one on psychos, by deciding that Arthur has told her the kidnap victim will be happier with him forever, the plan is doomed. Refusing to 'send the girl to Arthur', Billy hides the child in a wood. The police duly ask the medium to help locate the girl but, in her crazed state, she reveals the entire substance of the plot.

The most recent lady kidnapper has been *Supergirl* herself, Helen Slater, in the hugely successful *Ruthless People* (1986). But her inept amateur hardly qualifies as a wicked woman!

Those without the brains to go for the big money sometimes tried their hands at a little shoplifting. Margaret Rutherford was a comic shoplifter in *Trouble in Store* (1953) and the British cinema showed the more serious side of the coin in the same year both with Olive Sloane as Nellie in *The Weak and the Wicked* and Kathleen Harrison's Mrs Quilliam in *Turn the Key Softly* – both jailed for their crimes. Nellie stayed behind bars, but Mrs Quilliam, an elderly, dog-loving kleptomaniac, celebrates her release by going on a shoplifting spree, which ends when she is run over searching for her lost dog.

In Hollywood, Lee Grant made an auspicious film debut as the shoplifter arrested in *Detective Story* (1951). Five years later, her powerful personality was well suited to the role of a bank robber in *Storm Fear*. In the end, though, she breaks her ankle in her flight from the law, and is callously abandoned by her fellow-robbers, who get their just deserts before the close.

Smuggling was an occupation that also concerned British films spasmodically over the years. Often, especially when appearing in Ealing Studios films, these lawbreakers were played for laughs. However in *Forbidden Cargo* (1954), Elizabeth Sellars and Terence Morgan were brother and sister currency smugglers. She baulks when he starts to deal in drugs, their split resulting in his eventual death in a car crash.

Rather more ruthless was the smooth Lena in the interestingly-plotted *Sail into Danger* (1957). Played by Kathleen Ryan, a gentle-seeming Irish actress who was surprisingly often found on the wrong side of the law, she blackmails ex-smuggling comrade Steve (Dennis O'Keefe) into sailing her and her Spanish confederates to Tangier.

*Della (Martha Vickers) keeps Nat (Dan Duryea) prisoner – but not for long, as* The Burglar *(1957) moves towards a violent finale*

Murder and the theft of a priceless madonna follow before the 'worm' turns and, between Steve and the police, Lena and her gang are brought to book.

'Playgirls' who flirted with the world of crime fascinated Hollywood through the decades from the coming of sound. Two films actually earned the title provided by these creatures who found dangerous men and dangerous living so irresistible. In *Play Girl* (1940), the ladylike Kay Francis, of all people, was a sort of glamorous Fagin: a bright golddigger who trains younger girls of similar inclination to use their shapely wiles to rook rich clients of money for a communal kitty.

Francis got her come-uppance in the end, but it was one way to earn a living, and certainly preferable to 1954's *Playgirl*, a turgid affair which introduced busty brunette newcomer Colleen Miller, tangling with Shelley Winters, both girls becoming involved with gangsters and murders. And, in another of Universal-International's street-level thrillers, *The Sleeping City* (1950), it was Coleen Gray as a nurse, a figure more tragic than wicked, who became trapped into participation in a racket involving the stealing of drugs from a city hospital.

Despite her 'cynical blonde' looks, MGM's Ann Sothern was rarely handed 'bad girl' parts, even though she had excelled as the spiteful murderess in *Shadow on the Wall* (1950). So it was quite a surprise when she turned up, plump and blowsy, as a prostitute who helped terrorise Olivia de Havilland, trapped in a lift, in 1964's *Lady in a Cage*, a film much criticized for its sado-masochistic content. In the end the tables are turned and Sothern's character, appropriately called Sade is, after looting the house, trapped (presumably forever) in a wine closet.

Another sleazy thriller, *The Burglar* (1955), also had two leading ladies in Jayne Mansfield and Martha Vickers – and both of them were crooks.

Mansfield helps Dan Duryea and his gang steal a fabulous diamond necklace, but Vickers and her partner, a crooked cop, kidnap Mans-

*The gargantuan Hope Emerson (centre) enjoyed her nastiest film hour as the sadistic prison matron of* Caged *(1950), who owes her position to crooked political influence. Star Eleanor Parker is second from right*

field to lay their hands on the gems. Predictably, Duryea is killed before the end, both girls are caught, and nobody gets the diamonds. Mansfield tried the wrong side of the law again four years later in the British-made *The Challenge*, but this time a happy ending is arranged for her character, a glamorous gang boss who has just pulled off a bullion robbery.

Robbery was also on the mind of *The Ragman's Daughter* (1972), played by a young Victoria Tennant long before her success in television's *The Winds of War*. The film is a sort of bucolic English *Bonnie and Clyde* set in the Midlands, with Tennant as a spoiled rich girl who falls in love with a petty thief (Simon Rouse) and joins him in his criminal escapades, dividing their time between robbing, loving and tearing around the countryside on his motorcycle.

Inevitably, he is caught, and later she, pregnant by him, marries another man. On Rouse's release, he learns she has been killed in a road accident.

Also sent down for complicity in a robbery was Eleanor Parker as Marie in *Caged* (1950). Prison films were, naturally, packed with wicked women characters, but this one has more than its fair share. Between the attentions of sadistic wardress Hope Emerson (see *Bitches and Dominatrixes*), Lee Patrick, as the head of a prostitution ring, and Betty Garde, who organizes a group of shoplifters, the once-naïve Parker has very little chance. As the Warden observes on her release to become a callgirl: 'she'll be back'.

Bucketsful of baddies were released by the 'female gang' cycle of exploitation movies in the 1970s. Many of these were prison films with heavy emphasis on sex and violence, but they also include *Switchblade Sisters* (1975), whose alternate title of *Playgirl Gang* is self-explanatory, and the most famous of this group, *Truck Stop Women* (1974).

A raucous black comedy, it deals with the girls of Anna's Truck Stop, a highway station that gives service a new meaning as it provides a front for prostitution run by Anna (Lieux Dressler) and her daughter Rose (Claudia Jennings). This in itself disguises an even more lucrative hijacking racket also masterminded by the women.

Anna is betrayed, both by her daughter, and by another associate, whom she has trampled to death in a cattle stampede. In the end Rose and her partners are gunned down and Anna wounded. Fortunately, no such fate awaited Julie Walters in *Personal Services* (1986), as a real-life brothel-keeper in modern London serving the famous and not-so-famous alike.

Another echo of *Bonnie and Clyde* was struck by *Wanda*, which was written, directed and starred by Barbara Loden in 1970, ten years before her early death from cancer. Few men would want anything to do with the drifter she portrays, alienated, confused and newly-divorced, who picks up men in bars before accidentally interrupting a holdup and taking up with the thief concerned.

They carry out a series of robberies culminating in an elaborate bank job. But Wanda gets lost on the way, arriving in time to see her confederate carried away after being shot by police. She flees and resumes her life cruising bars, although her hysterical rejection of a new man suggests that violence may soon end her story.

In *Gideon's Day* (1957. In America: *Gideon of Scotland Yard*), Dianne Foster, who three years earlier had lured Mickey Rooney off the hairpin bends of racing to become a getaway driver in *Drive a Crooked Road*, was again up to no good, this time as a crooked artist involved in fake paintings and shady financial dealings. She and her husband run down a bent copper in their car, but Superintendent Jack Hawkins of the Yard traps, disarms and captures her.

Female pickpockets are extremely rare, but Vivien Leigh, who was usually wilful and tempestuous rather than rotten through and through – as in *Gone With the Wind* (1939) and *That Hamilton Woman/Lady Hamilton* (1941) – did play one in 1938's *St Martin's Lane* (in America: *Sidewalks of London*). An unemployed actress driven to street crime for a living, she also leads busker Charles Laughton a merry dance, although she does disillusion him before the end of the movie.

Moving from the tiny crimes of little minds to blondes and big deals, Ursula Andress could be found in the unlikely role of Britt, Lady Dorset in *Perfect Friday* (1970). Going to see her bank manager (Stanley Baker) about an overdraft, she soon has him planning to rob his own bank to the tune of £300,000, with the connivance of herself and her work-shy husband.

The robbery comes off at the second time of trying, but two of the conspirators are left empty-handed when Britt makes off with the entire proceeds.

There weren't too many female masterminds around before World War II, although massive Alison Skipworth certainly filled the bill in *Satan Met a Lady*, the 1936 version of *The Maltese Falcon*, in which she played the role later inherited by Sydney Greenstreet!

In *The House on 92nd Street* (1945), Signe Hasso plays Elsa Gebhardt, whose fashion shop hides her real activity as leader of a Nazi espionage ring, which is subsequently infiltrated for the FBI by Dietrich (William Eythe). As the authorities close in, she tries to slip away disguised as a man, but is shot by one of her own men in mistake for Dietrich.

The usually timid Dame May Whitty, the original vanishing governess from Hitchcock's *The Lady Vanishes*, made an unexpected mistress of evil in a highly-praised low-budget film called *My Name is Julia Ross* (1945). She it is, as wealthy matron Mrs Hughes, who offers down-

*No, Ralph is not practising his needlepoint, as mother and son (Dame May Whitty and George Macready) discuss the necessary dispatch of their prisoner Julia, in* My Name is Julia Ross *(1945)*

*Max Thursday (Zachary Scott) finds that the disreputable Smitty (Mary Boland) is really a mysterious underworld figure, and forces her to lead him to his kidnapped son. From* Guilty Bystander *(1950)*

on-her-luck Julia Ross (Nina Foch) a job as secretary. Julia is drugged and wakes up to find herself on the Cornish coast, the victim of a complicated plot.

She is informed that she is Mrs Hughes' son's wife, Marian; in ıact the son has killed his wife, and Julia is being set up as a 'suicide' to cover up the murder. She pretends to have taken poison, but Mrs Hughes gets the butler to pose as the doctor and Julia tells him of an appeal for help she has smuggled out. It is only when the butler is caught trying to steal the letter that the truth comes out and Julia is saved, with Mrs Hughes arrested and her son (George Macready) killed trying to escape.

Jean Gillie was a vivacious British dancer, singer and actress, a bit like Jeannie Carson if a shade more acid. Her talents were never quite properly showcased in Britain (from 1935) or Hollywood (from 1945) and she was dead by 1949 at only 33. Her most exciting performance came in one of her first American films, *Decoy*, in 1946.

She plays Margot Shelby, the pretty but extremely dangerous brains behind a gang of thieves, one of whom, Frankie (Robert Armstrong), about to die for murdering a policeman, has nearly half a million stashed away in a place not even Margot knows about. But she plans to rescue his body from the gas chamber and, through a doctor she has taken great pleasure in seducing from the straight and narrow, to administer an antidote to the cyanide gas.

The plan works. Frankie draws a map and gives Margot half. Her other partner Vincent (Edward Norris) shoots Frankie and takes his half. On the way to the loot, Margot pretends she has a flat tyre and runs (back and forth, to make sure) over Vincent when he gets out to fix it, calmly taking the rest of the map from the body and getting the still-infatuated doctor to dig for the money.

As the money-chest appears, Margot opens it and, laughing ecstatically, shoots the doctor. But he crawls to her apartment for revenge and, although this time she plugs him for keeps, he wounds her badly enough to prevent her escaping the police. Still laughing, she tells them the money chest contained a single dollar bill and that Frankie's secret died with him.

Also involved with large sums of money was Andrea King as Nora Craig in 1950's *Southside 1–1000* (in Britain: *Forgery*). But she, like her father before her, is an ace counterfeiter. Ostensibly the manager of a hotel, she runs her father's racket *in absentia* while he works on counterfeit plates in his prison cell.

A treasury agent, John Riggs (Don DeFore) infiltrates the gang, but a sketch drawn by her father in prison alerts Nora to his identity. She traps him in the gang's house, which is set on fire. Police arrive in time to save him and round up the gang, except Nora, whom Riggs pursues to a downtown freight yard. Surprising him on a trestle bridge, she tries to push him off a narrow ledge – but falls to her own death instead.

For King, who only seemed to function on screen as characters rotten to the core, it completed a trio of such charmers, begun in *Hotel Berlin* (see *'Schemers and Double Crossers'*), that also included her unfeeling villainess Marjorie in *Ride the Pink Horse* (1948), succinctly described by hero Robert Montgomery as 'a dead fish with perfume on the outside'.

That delightful ditherer Mary Boland, best remembered for a series of man-and-wife comedies opposite Charlie Ruggles, assumed a very different character for the final role of her long career, in *Guilty Bystander* (1950). Zachary Scott plays an ex-cop discharged for alcoholism and now house detective for a large, if seedy, hotel run by Boland as a character called Smitty.

When Scott's son is kidnapped, the trail leads him through various underworld characters including a crooked doctor and a smuggler, before deducing that the mysterious 'St Paul' who is behind everything is none other than Smitty. Ignoring her offers to share the money from her various rackets, Scott recovers his son and turns Smitty over to the police.

This film, incidentally, contains a second wicked woman in a rare early film appearance by Broadway character star Kay Medford, who plays Angel, the sadistic girlfriend of the original kidnapper, Scott's brother-in-law.

Britain produced two female gang leaders in 1956, both in films made for American companies. In *No Road Back*, which also gave employment to a young Sean Connery, Margaret Rawlings plays blind and deaf Mrs Railton, who runs a club as a front for her activities as fence and boss of a gang of jewel thieves led by Clem (Paul Carpenter).

Eventually, she has a change of heart when her son (Skip Homeier) becomes accidentally involved in her criminal activities, and forces Clem to sign a confession. But he turns the tables and kills her, before being taken by police.

Grim-faced Faith Domergue headed a crooked London betting ring in *Soho Incident* (in America: *Spin a Dark Web*). A Canadian drifter (Lee Patterson) gets sucked into her gang, but, after the murder of a boxer who refused to throw a fight, he wants out. The gang threatens the life of the boxer's sister, of whom Patterson is fond, but the police are hard on their heels and, in a final shoot-out, Domergue's brother and partner (Martin Benson) is killed, and she is captured.

Gang-leader, Hollywood-style, was that forceful actress Mara Corday in *Girls on the Loose* (1958), who rarely got the calibre of roles she deserved. Here she's the vicious, quick-tempered brains of an all-girl gang that brings off a Brinks-type bank job.

The girls bury the loot in a remote spot. But, despite the fact that Corday is as handy with a knife as a slap in the face, thieves do fall out, murder rears its head and Corday and her lieutenant kill each other.

Ingrid Bergman appeared as a mastermind of a rather different sort in *The Visit* (1964). Returning to her native European village as 'the richest woman in the world', she is bent on revenge over the villagers and especially Miller (Anthony Quinn) whose seduction of her had resulted in her leaving the village in disgrace 20 years earlier.

She offers the run-down village a million dollars, plus another million to be divided equally among its inhabitants, if Miller is brought to trial and executed. At first they refuse, but by offering them luxuries on credit, the woman brings leading villagers so deeply into debt that they must betray Miller for the money. After they condemn Miller to death, the woman decrees that he shall live – in the village, as a reminder of its shame.

Larger-than-life lady masterminds, a throwback to silent days, became fashionable again after the impact of Lotte Lenya as Rosa Klebb, with her deadly steel-tipped shoes, in the James Bond film *From Russia With Love* (1963). This led inevitably to those who wanted to rule the world, led off in great slinky style by Shirley Eaton in 1967's *Sumuru* (in America: *The Million Eyes of Sumuru*) and a 1969 sequel *The Seven Men of Sumuru*. If the characters had a similar feel to those in the contemporaneous Fu Manchu films, that's because both of these megalomaniacs were created by the same novelist, Sax Rohmer.

Superintendent Stewart Granger had to track down two female felons when his murder and robbery investigation in *The Trygon Factor* (1967) led him to a gang led by Susan Hampshire and Cathleen Nesbitt. Even worse was Lex

*Jim (Lee Patterson) falls under the spell of Bella (Faith Domergue) and becomes enmeshed in her illegal London rackets in* Soho Incident *(1956)*

*She's got the whole town in her hands . . . Karla (Ingrid Bergman) is 'welcomed' back to her home town by the Mayor (Ernst Schroeder) and her former seducer (Anthony Quinn) in* The Visit *(1964)*

(OPPOSITE) *A toast to supercrime from a supercriminal. Bette Davis dressed to make a killing in her 1971 film* Madame Sin.

Barker's lot in 1958's *The Strange Awakening* (in America: *Female Fiends*). In a plot that bears a superficial resemblance to *My Name is Julia Ross*, he's drugged while on holiday in France and finds himself living in a villa, apparently married to Selena (Carole Mathews).

Trying to escape, he stumbles across the body of the real husband, and soon deduces that he's the fall guy in a plot by Selena, her sister (Lisa Gastoni) and her mother (Nora Swinburne) to inherit the man's fortune. A fire eventually puts paid to their diabolical scheme.

That most clinical of calculators, Nadja Tiller, rivetingly played a true-life mistress of blackmail in 1958's *The Girl Rosemarie* (in America: *Rosemary*). She's a street singer who becomes intimate with various members of a powerful business cartel, installing a tape recorder in her apartment so that she can record the 'careless talk' of its members.

Blackmail looks like making her a rich woman, but then she is strangled by a killer who has never been identified. Several relieved industrialists are able to pick up their lives where they left off.

It was left perhaps to Bette Davis to supply the last word on the genre with her *Madame Sin* (1971). An international criminal directing operations from her headquarters in an isolated Scottish castle, she is planning to steal a Polaris missile when confronted by the unwanted intrusion of ex-government agent Anthony Lawrence (Robert Wagner) hunting for vanished fellow agent Barbara (Catherine Schell).

Lawrence's meddling eventually pays dividends, it seems. Madame Sin is forced to flee her castle, and he finds Barbara alive. But she has been indoctrinated during her incarceration. She poisons Lawrence, and makes a getaway in the company of Madame Sin.

# 8
# SIRENS, VAMPS AND FEMMES FATALES

'She came at me in sections.
More curves than a scenic railway'
Fred Astaire on Cyd Charisse
in *The Band Wagon* (1953)

Ever since Theda Bara husked 'Kiss me, my fool!' (it had to be translated by title card in 1914), men have been getting themselves seduced away from respectability in the cinema, mere pawns in the hands of the sirens, vamps and femmes fatales of the screen.

Some met death, others were broken in spirit. About the best they could expect was disillusionment and a chance to do better next time – not that it was likely to do these no-hopers much good. A curve, a flash of stocking, an inviting glance and they would be off again down the pink brick road to destruction.

*Great Garbo strikes a vaguely vampiric pose as the woman who drives men to destruction in* The Temptress *(1926). The film was an unhappy one for the star: her favourite director Mauritz Stiller was replaced by Fred Niblo*

As we have seen from the careers of Theda Bara and Pola Negri, this kind of woman made a showcase for any actress, during the silent days when the vamp reigned supreme. Memorable silent seductresses were Nita Naldi in the 1922 *Blood and Sand* (the role later claimed by Rita Hayworth), Barbara LaMarr in *Trifling Women* (1922) and *The Heart of a Siren* (1925), Lya de Putti in *Variety* (1926), Greta Garbo in *The Temptress* (1926), Margaret Livingston in *Sunrise* (1927) and the purse-lipped Mae Murray in almost anything.

Classic temptresses were also popular and Bara's *Cleopatra* (1917), Gloria Swanson's *Sadie Thompson* (1928) and Garbo's *Mata Hari* (1932) were only early examples that would provide juicy meat for actresses from several different decades. On the other hand there was the odd role that never caught fire, such as Emile Zola's tempestuous prostitute *Nana*, the 1934 version of which pretty well torpedoed the Russian actress Anna Sten's Hollywood career.

The siren was, by and large, not a popular figure through the 1930s and Depression era cinema. When leading actresses did essay them, as with Barbara Stanwyck in *Baby Face* (1933), Kay Francis in *I Loved a Woman* (1933), Joan Crawford in *The Gorgeous Hussy* (1936) or Jean Harlow in *Reckless* (1936), the results were hardly among the most popular films of their careers. Vivien Leigh's Scarlett O'Hara in *Gone With the Wind* (1939) certainly fancied herself as a vamp and was bitch and schemer in turn. Finally, though, she falls into no category but her own.

In the same year, Betty Field grabbed attention as the sluttish wife of a barley rancher in John Steinbeck's *Of Mice and Men*. As Mae, she is a vixen permanently on heat, parading her half-available talents to her husband's ranch-hands. The situation turns to tragedy when she flirts with the hulking, simple-minded Lenny (Lon Chaney Jr) who cannot take the confusion of emotions that temptation and rejection brings and strangles her. His own life is ended by his partner (Burgess Meredith) who prefers not to hand the simple giant over to the law.

*With her father (Thomas Mitchell) demented by the ravages of war, Scarlett (Vivien Leigh) vows to rebuild Tara, her home, in* Gone With the Wind *(1939)*

Two classic femmes fatales of the 1940s were portrayed by Joan Bennett, who was graduating from delicate heroines to hardened women, in Fritz Lang's *noir* thrillers *The Woman in the Window* (1944) and *Scarlet Street* (1945).

In *The Woman in the Window*, Edward G. Robinson plays a mild professor fascinated by a painting of a beautiful woman in an art gallery window. One day while staring at the window, he meets the real-life original, Alice (Joan Bennett) and finds himself in her apartment drinking champagne. But her lover arrives unexpectedly and knocks Alice down before nearly throttling the professor, who stabs the man in the back with a pair of scissors handed to him by Alice.

They dispose of the body, only for Heidt (Dan Duryea), a blackmailer, to get on their trail and make demands that go up according to the police reward. Alice and the professor make plans to get rid of him with an overdose of tranquillizers which the professor knows will leave no trace. Heidt is too smart to drink the drugged glass Alice offers him but, as the professor himself takes an overdose, Heidt is shot down in a gun battle with police, who assume he is the murderer, through his possession of the dead man's watch. Alice calls to give the professor the good news, but he cannot hear the phone. A final scene reveals that the professor is asleep in his club and it was all a dream.

No last-minute reprieves exist for Robinson in *Scarlet Street*, which has the same leading trio of players and is based on a 1931 French film, *La chienne*, made by Jean Renoir.

This time Robinson is a downtrodden cashier, Chris Cross, whose interest in painting gives him his only respite from a dull job and a shrewish wife (Rosalind Ivan, an expert at such harridans). Kitty (Bennett), known as 'Lazy Legs' is a classy prostitute who, in her plastic see-through raincoat, is a sex object who ensnares Cross totally.

He is even willing to swallow her story that she is an actress who has been mugged by a purse thief when she has in fact been beaten up by the pimp Johnny (Duryea) she adores, for not earning enough money. Eagerly he embezzles company funds to provide her with lovely clothes for 'auditions'. Then a luxury apartment for her to live in, where Chris can come to paint and escape his wife.

He even agrees to Kitty signing his paintings and selling them. Thinking of murdering his wife, Chris is saved from this course when her 'dead' first husband turns up. Racing to tell Kitty they are free to marry, he sees her in Johnny's arms. When Johnny leaves, he confronts her, loses control and stabs her frenziedly to death with an ice-pick. Johnny is arrested and executed for the murder. Chris tries to hang himself but fails and is last seen as a down-and-out, haunted by voices from the past, and shuffling into oblivion.

*While the passion lasts, Joe (Harry Belafonte) is glad he deserted the Army to be with Carmen (Dorothy Dandridge) in* Carmen Jones *(1954). But the moment is fleeting . . .*

Dorothy Dandridge enjoyed a similar stoat and rabbit relationship a decade later with Harry Belafonte in *Carmen Jones* (1954). In the all-black revamp of Bizet's opera, which had originally appeared on the Broadway stage in 1943, she plays a parachute packer who makes a play for a military policeman, Joe, trying to seduce him away from his sweetheart.

The moment Joe starts to respond, he is doomed. As Carmen's song puts it: 'You go for me, and I'm taboo. But if you're hard to get, I go for you. An' if I do, then you are through . . . boy . . . Baby that's the end of you.'

It certainly is. He becomes a deserter to stay with Carmen, but it's she who deserts him – for a boxing champion. Finally rejected by Carmen, Joe strangles her and is taken away by the military.

Dandridge never quite repeated her success as Carmen Jones, even when she played a not dissimilar role five years later in *Porgy and Bess*. The slit-skirted mistress of a gambler, Bess moves in with the cripple Porgy (Sidney Poitier), but is eventually retaken by the gambler, whom Porgy kills.

Cleared of murder, Porgy returns to the slums of Catfish Row to find that gambler Sportin' Life (Sammy Davis Jr) has persuaded another Bess to go off the New York City with him. Porgy decides to make the journey from South Carolina to New York in search of her.

Another American actress who never *quite* found a regular niche at the top was the tall, sophisticated Alexis Smith. In 1954, she came to Britain to play one of her best roles, as the slinky Glenda Esmond, very willing to launch into the excitement of a full-blooded affair with one of her psychiatrist husband's criminal patients, Frank (Dirk Bogarde).

Frank has a change of heart about the affair when the psychiatrist (Alexander Knox) provides him with an alibi for a robbery. But the voracious Glenda refuses to let go, and spitefully pretends that Frank has attacked and raped her.

Seeing through her story, Esmond pretends to shoot Frank to enable him to get away. But Glenda is not finished – even until death do her and Frank part. She picks him up in her car and crashes it through a hoarding and over a cliff. Smith, a former Warner Brothers' contractee in the heady days of the 1940s, must have revelled in a role of the kind usually commandeered at that studio by Bette Davis.

The mid 1950s saw the emergence of what might be called the baby vamp or, perhaps, according to her victims' wives, the baby tramp. Brigitte Bardot's many pouting sexpots are dealt with in a separate chapter, but she had no lack of rivals on the Continent. Tawny bombshell Marina Vlady, for example, certainly steamed up a few pairs of spectacles, with her deadly teenage temptresses in *Les salauds vont en enfer/The Wicked Go to Hell* (1955) and, in the same year, *La sorcière/The Sorceress*.

In the first of these, she is the young mistress of an artist, who is killed at their isolated cabin by two convicts. The girl encourages each of the men in turn until there is a violent quarrel and one shoots the other. Watching them stagger off across the beach, the girl knows that she has won: they are heading for the quicksands.

*La sorcière* finds Vlady as a nymphet witch of bleak Scandinavian forests, seemingly the possessor of mysterious powers. A French engineer falls under her spell, but the girl foresees that the affair will end in her own death. When she dares to defile a church by entering it during a service, the women worshippers abuse and beat her. She is later found dead in the forest.

American nymphets were triggered off in 1956 by Carroll Baker as *Baby Doll*. The thumb-sucking, cot-sleeping child wife of a blustery Southern States cotton miller she is eventually seduced by an oily business rival (Eli Wallach) bent on a particular kind of revenge. By 1963, though (and after all Baker was then 32) she was a much more mature charmer, both as the girl generating smouldering sexual tension (and violence) among the pipeline workers of *Station Six Sahara* and as the superstar nymphomaniac of *The Carpetbaggers*.

Still later, Baker was turning to Continental sexploitation films to keep working in star roles, invading the territory of the queen of such roles, Algerian-born Edwige Fenech, who had provided an unusually erotic *Madame Bovary* in 1969. Ironically, Baker and Fenech eventually co-starred in a typically overheated offering called *La moglie vergine/The Virgin Wife* (1975), in which Baker plays Fenech's mother, and seduces her own son-in-law.

Even as recently as 1979, a still-game Baker could be found rushing out to vamp her lover, clad in a fur coat and nothing else, in such

*Screen nymphets went on the rampage after the advent of Carroll Baker's thumb-sucking, lip-pouting, cot-sleeping* Baby Doll *in 1956*

*The title of Pia Zadora's 1981 film,* Butterfly, *proved all too prophetic. Her life as a nymphet of the cinema was over after two major films*

bottom-of-the-barrel British sexploitation as *The World is Full of Married Men.*

The baby vamps finally reached the height of absurdity with the appearance of Pia Zadora in the 1981 pot-boiler *Butterfly.* A former child actress, her career as a teenage sex-kitten was disastrously launched (and sunk) by this adaptation of a James M. Cain novel.

Arriving at an Arizona tin mine in the late 1930s, Kady (Zadora) has come to avenge herself on the mine owner, who had refused to let her marry his son, although she had borne him a child. Much of the film is devoted to her gradual seduction of her own father, played with much sweating and staring by Stacy Keach, who turns out in the end not to have been her father anyway. Few people cared, and after one more (even worse) film, *The Lonely Lady* (1982), Zadora seems to have called it a day. These days, it appears, the public likes a good script as well as a femme fatale, as proved by the success of the 1981 Jessica Lange remake of *The Postman Always Rings Twice.*

In the 1960s, however, such disillusion had still to set in. While Sophia Loren had gone in for comedy, romance and adventure Hollywood-style, her long-time rival Gina Lollobrigida, in between making less successful Hollywood films, was still playing vamps, notably in *Go Naked in the World* (1961), in which she was cast as Giulietta, an expensive call-girl for whom hero Anthony Franciosa falls without knowing her profession. Ultimately, she kills herself rather than let him go.

A couple of years later, in *Imperial Venus* (1963), La Lollo regaled us with the little-known saga of Paolina Bonaparte, Napoleon's (very) hot-blooded sister who, as power-hungry as her brother, distributed her charms around what seemed like half his army officers in her bid to climb to the top.

In Britain, green-eyed Swedish import Mai Zetterling was the slinky wife of a town councillor in a Welsh town, who ensnares oversexed librarian Peter Sellers into an abortive affair in *Only Two Can Play* (1961). The film achieved some notoriety when Zetterling protested about the use of a stand-in for her nude bottom in a scene she had refused to do.

Home-grown actresses relished the chance to kick over the traces after years of hiding curvy figures and untapped aspects of their range in milk-and-water roles. None more so than Janet Munro, who followed her Welsh trollop in *Bitter Harvest* (1963) with a sexy opportunist in 1964's *A Jolly Bad Fellow* (in America: *They All Died Laughing*).

She ends up dead in both films, the second of which presents her as Delia, the curvy laboratory assistant, and later mistress, of university chemist Leo McKern, who plans to murder his way to a previously out-of-reach professorship by using a non-detectable poison he has concocted himself. After luring the podgy professor into her bed, Delia, seeing McKern is on course for success, progresses to blackmail by threatening to squeal to the police unless he marries her. The result, not unnaturally, is her own mysterious death.

Some newer British actresses made a name for themselves by following Hollywood in taking up the baby vamp theme. One of the first was

*Delia (Janet Munro) leads Professor Bowles-Ottery (Leo McKern) on to his downfall – and hers, in* A Jolly Bad Fellow *(1963)*

(predictably blonde) Gillian Hills, who played a precocious teenage tease, making trouble for a whole lot of people in 1959's *'Beat' Girl* (In America: *Wild for Kicks*). She becomes involved with a Soho strip club, does a strip herself at a party, runs away from home and is almost seduced by the club owner (Christopher Lee), who is stabbed to death by a vengeful stripper for his trouble.

Another to show the serious side of the gymslip sexpot played for laughs in St Trinian's films was the early Sarah Miles. She made her screen debut as the sensual schoolgirl in *Term of Trial* (1962) who falls in love with her teacher (Laurence Olivier) – seeking solace in the bottle from his unsympathetic wife (Simone Signoret) – and tries to get him to sleep with her.

When he refuses, she accuses him of assault and he stands convicted until the girl breaks down at the end of the trial and admits lying. To save his marriage, however, the teacher feels compelled to tell his wife a lie himself – that the girl's accusation was true.

There was more of the serpent than Eve in Miles' next portrayal, in *The Servant* (1963). A the freely-available 'cousin' (mistress) of the butler Dirk Bogarde, she helps him take over the grandiose home of his weak upper-crust master (James Fox) in a campaign of creeping decadence.

The archetypal nymphet of modern literature was brought to the screen in Stanley Kubrick's film of *Lolita* (1961). A 12-year-old half-knowing predator (Sue Lyon), she captivates middle-aged lecturer Humbert Humbert (James Mason) who marries her mother (Shelley Winters) to be near her. Learning from Humbert's diary of his feverish attraction for the child, Winters obligingly rushes out under the wheels of a car.

*(*RIGHT*) The character of* Lolita *was 12 in the Nabokov novel. Since Sue Lyon was 15 when she played the role, the 1961 film was rather more cagey about the nymphet's age*

Humbert promptly whisks Lolita away from her summer camp, and they embark on a doomed cross-country idyll which lasts as long as Lolita is flattered by his passion for her and fascinated by her hold on him.

Humbert becomes her slave and Lolita treats him cruelly, boredly sipping her coke while he paints her toenails and dances to her every whim. They quarrel and make up, but eventually Lolita runs off with Quilty (Peter Sellers), a degenerate playwright. Years later Humbert finds Lolita again, long since detached from Quilty, hard-up, married and pregnant. Learning Quilty's identity, Humbert tracks him down and shoots him, completing his own moral disintegration.

*When it takes one rotten apple to . . . destroy an entire family. Linda Hayden sizes up the situation in 1968's* Baby Love

With the advent of the British pop musical, under-age vamps went to ground for much of the decade. It was 1968 before anything substantial in the field emerged and again it was based on a best-selling novel, though hardly one of similar stature.

In *Baby Love*, Luci (Linda Hayden) is the illegitimate teenage daughter of a woman who commits suicide, entrusting Luci, in a dying note, to the care of her ex-lover Robert, a doctor. Luci's seemingly contradictory needs to be loved and at the same time be independent of those she makes dependent on her, soon make her an insidious home-wrecker.

She leads on Robert's teenage son Nicholas, then rejects him and turns to Robert's wife Amy, embroiling her in a Lesbian affair. Only Robert refuses her proffered body: she slashes his face with a fork. When Nicholas slips in the shower and is knocked out during another of Luci's attempted seductions (she momentarily beats his fallen body, begging for the love her mother denied her) the family decides to be rid of her.

However, Luci uses her sexuality to secure her position, forcing both adults to admit their attraction for her – to their mutual horror – and beginning a flirtation with Robert's colleague when he calls round.

If all this seemed overheated, then the goings-on of *Three Into Two Won't Go* (1968) rang even less true. Here, it's Judy Geeson as Ella, a blonde hitchhiker who seduces the salesman (Rod Steiger) who gives her a lift and proceeds to completely tear apart his marriage, home and life, contemptuously playing him and his wife (Claire Bloom) off against each other, until they finally leave their house in separate directions. After watching television for a while there, Ella packs up and wanders off into the night.

One best-seller that fell well and truly from grace was Terry Southern and Mason Hoffenberg's mostly delightful pornographic pilgrim's progress, *Candy*. All trace of subtlety and charm had disappeared from the 1968 film version, with creme-puff blonde Ewa Aulin undergoing various forms of initiation at the hands of the generals, doctors, gurus, poets and movie-makers she innocently ensnares.

Another Candy appeared in the form of Patricia Wymer in *The Babysitter* (1968), a teenager whose affair with an assistant district attorney leaves him open to blackmail when a gangster's mistress takes compromising photographs of them together. But a group of Candy's tough ex-lovers soon strongarm the mistress into destroying the negatives, though not before a copy has been delivered to the attorney's (amazingly understanding) wife.

Aulin and Wymer were little seen after these farragos. Hardly more successful was the brief career of Austrian scorcher Susan Denberg, who came on like a more worldly-wise Brigitte Bardot while seducing hero Stuart Whitman in the 1966 film *An American Dream* (In Britain: *See You in Hell, Darling*). Denberg certainly gave off a unique erotic smoulder in that film, but, after one more role, as the creature stitched together by Peter Cushing in *Frankenstein Created Woman* (1967), she disappeared from sight.

As the 1960s drew to a close, the works of Vladimir Nabokov (author of *Lolita*) were again raided to provide source material for a thoroughly unpleasant number called *Laughter in the Dark* (1969), which provided anything but as far as cinema audiences were concerned.

In a story that reverberates with echoes of *The Servant*. Anna Karina is cast as Margot, a minxish usherette who quickly makes use of her position as mistress to art dealer Sir Edward More (Nicol Williamson) to drive his wife out of the ancestral home through a strategically-compromising telegram. When the enamoured noble gives a party in her honour, she throws in her lot with an ex-lover who's a guest there; together they scheme to relieve Sir Edward of his family fortune.

She keeps him sweet for a while but, when he finds out about their liaison, Sir Edward crashes his car and is blinded. Pretending that her lover, Hervé, has left the country, Margot takes Sir Edward to convalesce at a remote villa, where Hervé awaits them, torturing Sir Edward in ways that never quite reveal his presence.

Finally catching on, Sir Edward tries to kill the guilty pair with a gun. Hervé takes flight, but Margot whirls round the blind nobleman until he accidentally shoots himself.

Tuesday Weld offered another of her extremely potent doses of pretty poison in *I Walk the Line* (1970). As moonshiner's daughter Alma McClain, she's the bait that ensures the silence of the infatuated local sheriff (Gregory Peck), who is so obsessed with her that he even helps dispose of the body of his own deputy after the moonshining McClains murder him.

Believing that the girl will come away with

*Kim Novak seduces Laurence Harvey back into her life in the third screen version of Somerset Maugham's* Of Human Bondage *(1964)*

him to California, the sheriff allows his wife to walk out and advises the McClains to make their escape. But they take Alma with them and, when he attempts to retrieve her, she helps her family drive him off.

This familiar theme, of the girl who draws an older man like a magnet, only for him to find she wasn't worth it in the end, was finally given a comic twist by director Blake Edwards in *10* (1979). Dudley Moore is the man who sees his perfect *10* in bride Bo Derek and follows her half-way across the country before saving her from drowning and finding out that the alabaster exterior and classic curves conceal a coarse interior he can't even begin to come to terms with.

Perhaps the final fling of the half-innocent nymphet also came late in 1979 with Louis Malle's *Pretty Baby,* which had actually been made two years earlier. Like so many child stars, Brooke Shields gave a memorable early performance she was never to equal as the child of the whorehouse who sets her cap at the photographer (Keith Carradine) who frequents her mother's brothel – but only to take pictures of the girls.

He eventually succumbs to her childlike advances, becomes devoted to her and ultimately marries her, although he is unresisting when her family, driven out of business by the US navy, returns to reclaim her.

Cleopatras, of course, have continued to flourish through virtually the entire history of the cinema – surely the most-played femme fatale of them all. Claudette Colbert was uncharacteristically underdressed for the De Mille version in 1934; Vivien Leigh, having had something of a dry run with Scarlett O'Hara in *Gone With the Wind* (1939), was a vixenish ruler in *Caesar and Cleopatra* (1945); Rhonda Fleming was an all-American Cleo in *Serpent of the Nile*; and Elizabeth Taylor proved surprisingly miscast as an inanimate Egyptian in the much-troubled 1963 *Cleopatra*.

Cleo clones were played by Joan Collins in *Land of the Pharaohs* (1955) and Debra Paget in *Princess of the Nile* (1954). Paget must have liked the locale, for she also played *Cleopatra's Daughter* in 1960. Finally, the subject was inevitably lampooned (by Amanda Barrie) in *Carry On Cleo* (1965).

It's surprising that Jennifer Jones never had a go at the role, in view of her obvious liking for lip-curling femmes fatales, as evidenced by her performances in *Duel in the Sun* (1946), *Carrie* (1952) and *Ruby Gentry* (1952).

*White Cargo* also provided a memorable screen siren in a half-caste temptress called Tondelayo. She was played in an early British (silent and sound) version by Gypsy Rhouma, and provided a notable career highlight for Hedy Lamarr in the 1942 Hollywood version. It's for love of her that the prosperous manager of a West African rubber plantation – played in the two versions by Leslie Faber and Walter Pidgeon – goes down and down until he has become a derelict. In the end, the girl is caught trying to poison him, and compelled to take the poison herself. Her broken lover is shipped back home as 'white cargo'.

In *Lassiter* (1983), Lauren Hutton was the prewar melodramatic figure of the German Mata Hari-type spy to the life, flourishing scarlet fingernails and moistening crimson lips in unsubtle indication of all sorts of inviting perversions.

*Moonshine whiskey girl Tuesday Weld, looking all of 14, though 27 when she made the film, comprehensively entrances local lawman Gregory Peck in* I Walk the Line *(1970)*

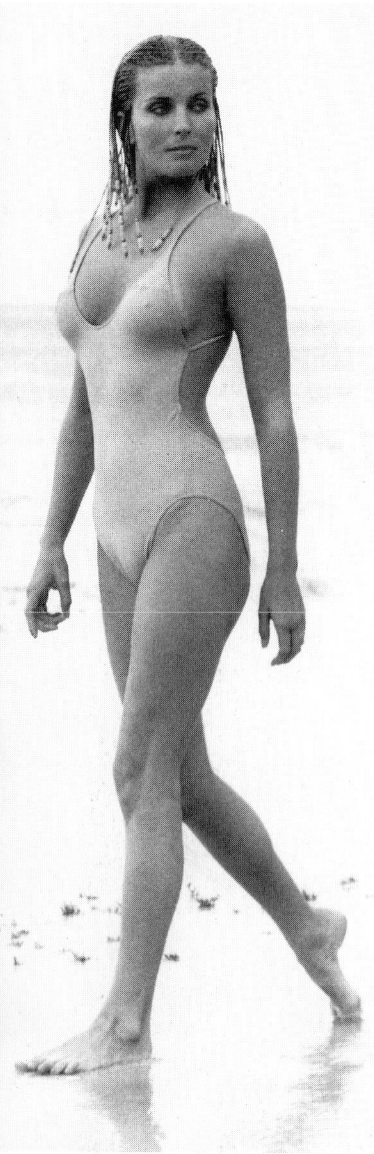

*So near and yet so far . . . as the subject of Dudley Moore's desire, Bo Derek created a sensation by wearing a swimsuit a couple of sizes too small in '10' (1979)*

*Is there life after sex? Anne Bancroft is the rapacious Mrs Robinson, with Dustin Hoffman as Benjamin Braddock, in* The Graduate *(1967)*

*It's 1942, and Hedy Lamarr was never lovelier as Tondelayo, the bewitching but poisonous native girl of* White Cargo. *The poor unfortunate man is Walter Pidgeon*

*A very fishy femme fatale – but pure gold at the box-office. That was Glynis Johns as the amorous mermaid of the title, in* Miranda *(1948)*

In 1987, France's Isabelle Huppert was the femme fatale in *The Bedroom Window*, whose refusal to testify in a murder case because of compromising her marriage ultimately led to her own death at the hands of the killer.

Perhaps the cinema's most unusual siren was Miranda the Mermaid as incarnated by the husky-voiced, green-eyed Glynis Johns in *Miranda* (1948) and a sequel, *Mad About Men* (1954). But Miranda must have limited her capers to flirting as she was unable to grow human legs like that other mermaid, Madison (Daryl Hannah) in *Splash* (1984).

And the screen's fiercest man-eater of all? Possibly Anne Bancroft as the slavering Mrs Robinson, surveying Dustin Hoffman like a tasty sheep a wolf must steer into her lair, in the 1967 classic *The Graduate*.

# 9
# BITCHES AND DOMINATRIXES

'Why don't you go . . .
He doesn't love you . . . You've nothing
to live for really, have you? I've opened a window
for you. Look down there. It's easy, isn't it?
Why don't you? Go on . . . Don't be afraid . . .'

Judith Anderson to Joan Fontaine in *Rebecca* (1940)

Flint-hearted females, from hussies to housekeepers, all determined to dominate their fellow-beings and have their own way. Goodie-goodies rarely stood a chance against these wicked women; that is until fate sometimes lent them a hand. These were the women we didn't even love to hate – they were cruel, calculating and in deadly earnest. And they often dominated their scenes in a film as much as they did a hapless heroine.

Perhaps one of the finest examples of the breed was played in *The Manchurian Candidate* (1962) by Angela Lansbury, nowadays more associated with cosy spinster detectives. Lansbury had proved before in such films as 1944's *Gaslight* (In Britain: *The Murder in Thornton Square*) and 1949's *Samson and Delilah* that she could be convincingly spiteful, vindictive and treacherous, and she brought all these talents to bear on Mrs Shaw in *The Manchurian Candidate*, a role that brought her a third Oscar nomination in the best supporting actress category.

*Hail the conquering hero comes . . . to kill. Angela Lansbury as the venal, power-seeking wife of a radical politician in* The Manchurian Candidate *(1962); here with Laurence Harvey, as the son she drives to murder, and James Gregory*

This power-hungry woman helps manipulate, and intends to profit by the zombie-like condition of her war veteran son (Laurence Harvey) who was brainwashed in Korea, and is now a tool of the Communists, a human time bomb who can be programmed to murder at his masters' behest.

Shaw hates his mother, but is powerless to resist when, as a test for a bigger assignment to come, he is programmed to kill, in turn, his employer, his father-in-law and his own bride. But the events trigger off suspicion in his previously zomboid mind.

So it is that he tries to battle hypnosis when instructed to gun down a presidential candidate and leave the way to power clear for his mother and his equally corrupt senator stepfather. He goes to carry out the assassination, but turns the gun on his stepfather, his mother and finally himself.

'Bitch' roles in early sound cinema are fairly rare for major actresses who, conscious of their images, may have had no great relish in playing them. When one did come along, like Ruth Chatterton's Fran Dodsworth in *Dodsworth* (1936), the odds seemed to be that the audience would be paying more attention to the nice girl (in this case Mary Astor) they hoped the hero (in this case Walter Huston) would end up with.

Fran is a woman in her late thirties, with a just-married daughter and a much-older husband. Seeing her youth slipping away, she determines to turn their trip to Europe into one last romantic fling. After a couple of flirtations, she embarks on affairs with Austrian aristocrats, tormenting her husband with letters.

When one of the Austrians asks her to marry him, Fran begs her husband Sam for a divorce and he drifts around Europe, re-meeting an American divorcee of whom he becomes fond. Fran's romance is soon over and she tells her husband she needs him. He comes running, but on board ship for home, the full realization hits him as to what a selfish, shallow, grasping person his wife is, and always will be. He disembarks and returns for good to the divorcee, leaving Fran to voyage back to America alone.

*Dodsworth* is one of the few occasions in pre-war cinema in which the 'other woman' figure became basically the heroine. Another was *In Name Only* (1939), hardly surprisingly since Kay

*Delia (Miriam Hopkins, right) breaks the news to Charlotte (Bette Davis) that the man she loves has been killed in the American Civil War, in* The Old Maid *(1939)*

Francis positively dripped malice as the wife from whom Cary Grant wants a divorce so that he can marry Carole Lombard.

One of the finest exponents of screen bitchery was the minx-like Miriam Hopkins. Especially when she got the chance of a sparring match with her Warners rival Bette Davis.

In *The Old Maid* (1939), a period melodrama, every fake smile from Hopkins is a prelude to an unleashing of claws. As Delia, cousin to Bette Davis' Charlotte, she throws over her handsome suitor Clem (George Brent) for someone more reliable. Charlotte subsequently has Clem's child after an affair but Clem is killed in the Civil War.

When Delia discovers that one of the children at Charlotte's nursery school for war orphans is Charlotte's (and Clem's) own daughter, she persuades Charlotte's new suitor not to marry her because of her bad health (an excuse cooked up by a doctor for Charlotte to have her child in privacy). Charlotte becomes an old maid, while the ruthless Delia, now a widow, takes over the child to such an extent that it calls her Mother. When the girl reaches marriage, Charlotte threatens to tell her the truth, but cannot go through with it. As a small gesture of reconciliation, Delia tells the girl to save her last pre-honeymoon departure kiss for her 'Aunt Charlotte'. And so the two women face bitterness and loneliness together.

In *Old Acquaintance* (1943), the two actresses are not cousins, but childhood friends, and rivals, the married Millie (Hopkins) being tensely jealous of bachelor girl Kit (Bette Davis) and the 'serious' book she has written.

Millie, full of her own self-importance and plans for the future, fancies herself as another Margeret Mitchell, her secret envy of her friend urging her on to write an immensely trashy but popular epic novel in soap-opera style. It's the first of many fatuous, flowery, sexy best-sellers typical of Millie, and success completely turns her head.

Her husband walks out, admitting that he has always loved Kit. In a showdown between the two, Millie accuses Kit (who has actually rejected her husband) of man-stealing and the two virtually come to blows. After several more plot developments, including Kit's loss of her new lover to Millie's daughter, the two 'old acquaint-

*Alicia (Ingrid Bergman) numbly realises she is being poisoned by her husband (Claude Rains) and his dominating mother (Leopoldine Konstanin) in Alfred Hitchcock's* Notorious *(1946)*

ances', more or less reconciled, drink a toast to approaching middle-age.

A 1981 remake, *Rich and Famous*, with Candice Bergen and Jacqueline Bisset in the Hopkins and Davis roles, proved, surprisingly from director George Cukor, to be a crude and vulgar travesty of the original.

Meanwhile, Hopkins herself had one more fling at bitchery with her memorable portrait of the vicious, venomous, bad-tempered wife of Laurence Olivier in *Carrie* (1952), who would rather destroy him and his hopes for a happy future with Jennifer Jones than part with a penny of his money. One reviewer thought Hopkins' performance 'almost too convincing'!

Another outstanding dominatrix from the 1940s, if only for one film, was Leopoldine Konstantin as Madame Sebastian in Hitchcock's *Notorious* (1946). Ingrid Bergman is the reluctant undercover agent infiltrating a Nazi ring in Rio de Janeiro by ensnaring its leader, Sebastian (Claude Rains) into marriage. Sebastian himself is completely under the thumb of his domineering mother and it is she who never loses her suspicion of the girl.

When the agent's duplicity seems certain, it is the forbidding figure of the mother who is the driving force behind a plan to slowly poison her to make her eventual death appear a developing illness. But she is rescued by the hero (Cary Grant) and Sebastian, a strangely sympathetic figure for a villain, must face some unpleasant music from fellow Nazis – especially his own mother.

Irish-born Geraldine Fitzgerald was a gentle-seeming actress who had an unhappy time in Hollywood, where she would liked to have played far more unsympathetic roles. Her role in *The Gay Sisters* (1942), as the wilful Evelyn, almost fitted the bill. 'I wore a monocle and stamped all over the place in high heels,' she recalled. 'If I had my way I'd be playing an absolute monster in every other film.'

Actually, she had to wait until 1945 and the role of Lettie in *Uncle Harry*. The possessive sister of John (George Sanders), Lettie is furious when he evades her dominance sufficiently to propose to a fashion expert (Ella Raines). So furious, in fact, that she feigns a heart attack on first learning of the engagement. Unable to rid himself of the termagant, John plans to murder her, but his other sister drinks the poison instead.

Convicted of her sister's murder, Lettie is willing to die rather than tell the truth, knowing that her death will forever stop John marrying the girl involved. A weak ending, which caused the film's producer to resign from the studio (Universal), reveals the whole thing to have been a dream.

Strangely Fitzgerald turned down the role in the British-made *So Well Remembered* (1947) that would have suited her powerful style, and was in the event played by another 'gentle' actress, Martha Scott. The part was that of Olivia, a ruthlessly ambitious woman whose father is in jail for the exploitation of grim housing conditions to his own advantage.

Tarred with the same brush, Olivia is only too ready to turn things to *her* own advantage, especially when she meets George (John Mills), councillor and newspaper editor, who con-

demns colleagues for pre-judging her and helps her get a job as librarian. Later they marry, and Olivia persuades George to run for Parliament. But, when their baby son dies in a diphtheria epidemic, George withdraws his candidacy and Olivia leaves him.

Years later, with George mayor, Olivia returns, still scheming for political power, planning to open her father's old mill, and squeeze the poor. She also plans to prevent the marriage of her son (by a second husband) to the orphan adopted by George's doctor friend. But George outmanoeuvres his ex-wife and she storms out of town for good.

More of a slut than anything else was Linda Darnell as Stella in another film from the 1940s, *Fallen Angel* (1945), made by director Otto Preminger as a follow-up to his previous success with *Laura*.

A waitress in a small Californian town, Stella has a string of men hanging on to her skirts, all of whom she treats with more or less equal contempt. She receives dog-like devotion from Pop (Percy Kilbride), for whom she works. Former detective Judd (Charles Bickford) comes to her café to be near her, smoothie Dave Atkins (Bruce

*Jealousy rears its head when John (George Sanders) introduces his fiancée Deborah (Ella Raines, left) to his domineering sisters, Hester (Moyna MacGill, standing) and the dangerous Lettie (Geraldine Fitzgerald) in* Uncle Harry *(1945)*

*The unscrupulous woos the promiscuous. Eric (Dana Andrews) plans to go off with Stella (Linda Darnell) with the help of another girl's money, in* Fallen Angel *(1945). But things don't work out that way . . .*

*His jealous, unsuccessful actress-wife (June Allyson) is tearing stage director José Ferrer apart piece by piece in* The Shrike *(1955)*

Cabot) would love to make it with her, and impoverished conman Eric (Dana Andrews) is also interested.

Stella tells Eric she might go off with him if he can arrange to get rich quick. Eric's plans to lay hands on wealthy June's (Alice Faye) money by a con-scheme or, if necessary, short-lived marriage, so that he can take off with Stella, are thwarted when Stella is murdered. No lack of suspects, that's for sure, but the killer turns out in the end to be the desperate Judd.

A cut above Darnell in society strata was Joan Fontaine in *Born To Be Bad* (1950). It could have been called *Ruthless* had that title not already been used two years previously, ironically in a film which featured one of Fontaine's co-stars, Zachary Scott. Here he's one of the men tugging at the apron strings of the scheming, selfish Christabel (others are played by Robert Ryan and Mel Ferrer) whose 'sweet' exterior is finally peeled away to reveal her true colours.

The role was, along with Fontaine's her poisoness in *Ivy* (1947), another attempt by the star to escape her demure image, although she wasn't a forceful enough actress to suggest anything more than skin-deep evil, and her best film performances remained as women under threat or domination.

Far more suitable to these roles was Audrey Totter, a beguiling blonde from American radio who never quite got the key role in a major film that might have given her top stardom. But her been-around-and-bitter-about-it prettiness enhanced most of her assignments, notably as the wife in *Tension* (1950) who takes sadistic pleasure in taking men's lives apart, the grasping, untrustworthy Althea in *The Unsuspected* (1947), a gun moll in *Man in the Dark* (1953) and Alexis Smith's bloodsucking sister in *Any Number Can Play* (1949), just dying to torpedo her romance with Clark Gable.

In contrast to the petite Totter, it was difficult for Hope Emerson, with her barn-door build, eagle features and 6ft 2in in height, to be seen in anything but dominant roles. Certainly, she loomed very large as the cruel and vicious prison matron, Harper, in *Caged* (1950).

Although Agnes Moorehead, cast for once against type as the progressive, well-meaning but blinkered warden, is in charge of the prison, it is Harper who runs it. Installed in her job thanks to crooked political chicanery, the sadistic Harper corrupts everything and everyone she touches, presiding over shoplifting rings and prostitution rackets virtually run from inside the prison. Ultimately, the heroine (Eleanor Parker) is broken in spirit, and released from prison only to become a prostitute. For her grim and frightening portrayal, Emerson was nominated for an Academy Award, although she found a wider range of roles in films hard to come by.

Five years later, it was Parker herself, the corrupted innocent in *Caged*, who played the lovely but hateful wheelchaired wife of drug addict Frank Sinatra in *The Man with the Golden Arm* (1955). Only her condition keeps him with her and, as we but not Sinatra can see, the possessive Parker is not really an invalid at all, but perfectly able to walk.

Under pressure from her, the addict, once cured, goes back to his drug dealer (Darren McGavin) who is later found murdered. The killer is Parker – because the dealer had found out she was not a cripple – and, when unmasked, she hurls herself spectacularly down a flight of

*A change of scenery does little for the relationship between Helen (Dora Bryan, right) and her daughter Jo (Rita Tushingham) in* A Taste of Honey *(1961)*

stairs to her death. Her husband undergoes a horrendous, but successful second cure.

A similarly destructive wife was played, unexpectedly, by Hollywood's perennial 'girl-next-door', June Allyson, in *The Shrike* (1955). José Ferrer is the Broadway producer married to Ann (Allyson), who proves not only to be a supernag, but fancies herself a better actress than she is. As the marriage falls apart, her possessive love turns to jealousy and hatred, and she drives him to a mental breakdown and the brink of suicide, committing him to the mental ward of a city hospital.

Unfortunately the film, apparently afraid of such unrelenting grimness, changed the down-beat ending of the original play to a happy one, with the hero freed and turning to a sympathetic 'other woman'. But the movie lacks the warmth to bring this twist off.

Ferrer himself had been through it all before in *Moulin Rouge* (1952), when harangued by the prostitute (Colette Marchand) who toys with the affections of Ferrer's dwarf painter Toulouse-Lautrec before deserting him.

Another husband driven firmly into the arms of another woman was Gary Cooper in *Ten North Frederick* (1958). The driver was none other than a tight-lipped Geraldine Fitzgerald, making one of her by-now-rare screen appearances as Cooper's prim and icily waspish wife, pushing him unwillingly into big-time politics with disastrous results.

She also forces her son to give up a musical career and go to Yale, and hushes up her daughter's affair with a musician, whom she pays to leave. The daughter has a miscarriage and Cooper, forced by his wife into shady political dealing, is abandoned by his backers.

Taunted by his wife with admissions of infidelity, Cooper, after giving up an affair with a much younger woman, takes solace from the virago in alcohol, which eventually kills him. The son, who has hated Yale, drunkenly turns on his mother at the funeral but, true to form, she rounds on him venomously and slaps him down.

Bitchy roles seemed to attract 'nice' actresses like moths to a flame and, although they were often very good in them, few could claim that they furthered their careers. In recent times, the Oscar-winning Sissy Spacek has fallen into the same trap with *Violets Are Blue* (1985) and in 1961 Dora Bryan's British Academy Award for *A Taste of Honey* seemed to put a complete stop to her cinema career.

Previously best known for comic cameos, Bryan's performance as Helen in *A Taste of Honey* (1961) was a brilliantly successful portrayal of a totally self-absorbed person. With one eye on 'a good time' and the other on the landlord coming for the rent, Helen and her schoolgirl daughter Jo (Rita Tushingham's screen debut) skip from lodging to lodging until one of Helen's frequent men friends decides to marry her.

Jo, finding herself pregnant (by a black sailor now departed) and alone, is helped by a kindly young homosexual, who eventually makes the mistake of going to tell Helen about Jo's situation. Helen, having been abandoned by her husband, turfs the youth out of the home he has made for himself and Jo, and the two women are once again left with each other.

Tushingham, who spent a lifetime as ugly ducklings and terrorised girls, herself tackled a bitch role in Sidney Furie's 1963 film *The Leather Boys*. A 16-year-old member of a motorcycle gang, she marries a boy from the gang but, lazy, empty-headed and a spendthrift, has no taste for routine married life. After she has mercilessly taunted his loveable grandmother, her husband leaves her. When he changes his mind and returns, he finds she has lost no time in bedding down with another man.

Tushingham grappled gamely with this totally unsympathetic character, but spent the rest of her career in a more delicate shade of role – until her illiterate mass murderess in *A Judgement in Stone* (1986), which she must have been pleased to hear one critic describe as 'a very nasty piece of work'.

The British cinema continued to toy with the bitch figure through the 1960s. Kim Novak was uneasily cast as the sluttish Mildred in the third film version of *Of Human Bondage* (1964), following Bette Davis in 1934 and Eleanor Parker in 1946. And Julie Christie played a very fashionable bitch in the now very dated *Darling* (1965), in which she breaks the hearts of several men in the furtherance of her seemingly not very successful career.

Modishly directed by John Schlesinger, this story of a heartless little social butterfly moved one critic to exclaim that 'people who were mean and nasty and corrupt and promiscuous were once thought to be answerable for their actions, Now it's more fashionable to blame society as a whole.' Well that was the (mostly fictitious) swinging sixties for you.

In Hollywood things were less complicated and Martha Hyer, an actress who didn't get to play as many bad-girl roles as she might have, had a chance to be thoroughly unpleasant in *Desire in the Dust* (1960), a sort of medium-budget Tennessee Williams/William Faulkner-style opus with Hyer as the spoilt and manipulative daughter of a powerful and rich Southern aristocrat (Raymond Burr).

After being responsible for the death of her own brother in a car crash, Melinda (Hyer) gets her father to talk her boyfriend Lonnie (Ken Scott) into going to prison for the crime, promising that he will be taken care of later. Six years on the chain gang later, Lonnie emerges to find that Melinda has married a wealthy doctor. He threatens to expose the truth, but Melinda sends him on the run from the law by accusing him of raping her.

It's only after a re-enactment of the original crash that Lonnie is cleared, Mrs Marquand (Joan Bennett) recovers from the mental breakdown she suffered at the time, and Melinda gets her just deserts. A heady brew, this, saved from disaster by the straight-faced performances of its stars.

Despite the comment by one critic that she 'screams non-stop and batters her daughter with Dickensian enthusiasm', Shelley Winters took her second Academy Award for her performance as the ranting, raddled mother of a blind girl in *A Patch of Blue* (1965).

Responsible for her own daughter's blindness (and rape, from one of her own clients when she was a prostitute), Rose-Ann (Winters) repeatedly beats the girl, who is now 18, and tries, but fails to stop her going to the park where she has struck up a friendship with Gordon (Sidney Poitier). The spiteful woman is quick to tell the girl Gordon is black, and furious when it makes no difference to her attitude.

Too old to attract men themselves, Rose-Ann and her blowsy friend plan to set up a brothel with the girl as one of the main attractions. Appalled, Gordon gets the girl away from her mother after a terrific battle and sends her to college where he has found a place for her.

Elizabeth Taylor's two 1960s attempts at fierce females also garnered her two Oscars, for her high-class call girl – 'Mama. Face it. I was the slut of all time' – eventually killed in a car smash in *Butterfield 8* (1960) and her all-stops-out harridan of a wife opposite then-husband Richard Burton in *Who's Afraid of Virginia Woolf?* (1966). In truth, neither of the performances was a match for sheer malice with the angel of death played by Barbara Hershey in *Last Summer* (1969).

A tease with a voluptuous figure, Hershey's Sandy is outwardly a fun-loving teenager enjoying a summer by the sea. She restores a wounded seagull to health, but the darker side of her nature emerges when, on recovering, it bites her finger. She crushes its skull with a stone. Sandy and her two boy hangers-on later leave a Puerto Rican friend to the mercy of a gang of toughs, to the horror of the fourth member of the teenage quartet, the freckled, teeth-braced Rhoda (Cathy Burns).

Later Sandy taunts Rhoda and stimulates one of the boys into raping the serious-minded girl, before wandering back to the beach, completely unperturbed, with the boys tagging behind. They are patently her slaves, but one doesn't give a penny for the chances of either of them finding happiness with her.

Around this time, Diane McBain, herself the portrayer of several teases, including the title character in *Claudelle Inglish* (1961. In Britain: *Young and Eager*) Warners' classic of kitsch, appeared in *The Mini-Skirt Mob* (1968) as Shayne, the prototype of numerous queens of sadism to appear in American-International/New World exploitation films over the next 15 years.

Leader of a motorcycle gang, she lays siege to the trailer of her ex-lover and his wife, and uses petrol bombs to kill what turns out to be her own sister who, disgusted at Shayne's viciousness and jealousy, has acted as a decoy to help the couple escape. Eventually the tables are turned and Shayne falls to her death down a cliff. Later examples of Shayne's breed include Lisa Todd's lesbian sadist in black leather in *Woman Hunt* (1972), an extraordinary rip-off of *The Hounds of Zaroff/The Most Dangerous Game* (1932), Pam Grier's prison torturess in *Women in Cages* (1972) and Barbara Steele's wheel-chaired warden in *Chained Heat* (1974), the latter performances being two of the *more* convincing portrayals of sadistic woman prison officers in the overcooked offerings of the 1970s and 1980s.

Some of the roles accepted by Britain's Charlotte Rampling certainly came in the overheated category, especially those in *'Tis Pity She's a Whore* (1971) and *The Night Porter* (1973). But she was never more bitchy than in one of her early successes, *Georgy Girl* (1966), as the heartless flatmate of Lynn Redgrave's Georgy who embarrasses Georgy with her casual affairs, generally lords it over her and even dumps her baby on Georgy when she goes.

With her slightly contemptuous attractiveness, Rampling found it difficult to escape such roles, and as recently as 1982 could be found selling Paul Newman up the river in *The Verdict*.

One of the worst monsters in this category also stepped on to our screens in 1982, as personified by Kim Stanley in *Frances*. Playing the publicity-hungry mother of tragic film star Frances Farmer (Jessica Lange), she has an all-devouring relationship with her daughter and when Frances, whose outspokenness has resulted in a sagging film career, is placed in her care after a drunk driving offence, Mrs Farmer commits her to a sanitorium.

Frances 'escapes' from the sanitorium, trustingly returning to her mother to recuperate. But, when she declares she will never go back to Hollywood after the way it has treated her, Mrs Farmer re-commits her. This time, Frances is straitjacketed and thrown in an insane ward.

*Alcoholic lawyer Galvin (Paul Newman) is assisted by Laura (Charlotte Rampling), only to discover that she is the daughter of the man opposing him in court, in* The Verdict *(1982)*

A brief family reunion following Frances's 'recovery' soon crumbles, and the vindictive Mrs Farmer incredibly manages to have her daughter put away for a third time, this time in an asylum from which she is only released after a experimental lobotomy which leaves her capable of only limited reactions.

Housekeepers, governesses and other senior figures of authority could be just as destructive – although it was usually weaklings or children who were their victims. Tight-lipped, sharp-faced, diminutive Mary Nash was absolutely beastly to Shirley Temple in *The Little Princess* (1939), which cast Shirley as a kind of Cinderella-figure in a period riches-to-rags-and-back-again story. It came as no surprise to some cinemagoers when Nash turned out to be the villainess mastermind masquerading as a garrulous schoolma'am in the following year's *Charlie Chan in Panama*.

That was the year in which, with all due deference to Gale Sondergaard (*qv*), the definitive wicked housekeeper appeared in the shape of Judith Anderson as Mrs Danvers in *Rebecca*. Devoted to the memory of her master's spoiled and amoral first wife Rebecca, who died under mysterious circumstances, Mrs Danvers soon launches an insidious campaign to destroy the fragile self-confidence of his new bride, played by Joan Fontaine.

Quickly establishing her mental superiority, the housekeeper has soon reduces the second Mrs de Winter (her Christian name is never mentioned) to a nervous wreck, gliding through the house and appearing as if from nowhere. But the girl gradually learns the truth about her predecessor, and it is Mrs Danvers who meets her doom in the flames at the ancestral home which she herself has set ablaze.

Fontaine was (indirectly) involved in a faintly similar situation in *Jane Eyre* (1943), in which her character when young (played by Peggy Ann Garner) suffers under all kinds of female oppressors, including such experts at the role as Agnes Moorehead (as Mrs Read) and Eily Malyon (as Mrs Sketcher). Jane Eyre herself becomes a governess in the course of the story, though her rule over her small charge (Margaret O'Brien) is hardly with a rod of iron.

Occasionally an actress who normally played benign, even motherly, characters would button up to the neck and become a menace. Hollywood's Fay Bainter did it as one of the conspiratorial quartet who threaten Merle Oberon's sanity – and her fortune – on a remote bayou plantation in *Dark Waters* (1944).

For British actress Freda Jackson, of shadow face and jagged smile, there was very little respite from villainy. In *No Room at the Inn* (1948), as the appropriately-named Mrs Voray(cious), she is the sluttish, sadistic and alcoholic landlady who makes life hell for the young wartime evacuees in her 'care'.

Appeals from the battered youngsters to authorities prove fruitless but, when two of them try to rescue a third imprisoned by Mrs Voray in a coalhole, the fiend plunges to her death down a rickety staircase while trying to catch them.

Jackson, whose ferocious acting style made her difficult to cast away from villainy, played a similar part in Britain's first 'X' certificate film in

*The vicious Mrs Voray (Freda Jackson) enjoys an alcoholic courtship with a sailor (Niall MacGinnis) in between ill-treating child evacuees in* No Room at the Inn *(1948)*

1952, *Women of Twilight* (in America: *Twilight Women*).

Again she is a landlady, Mrs Allister, a blackmailer and baby-farmer who takes in unmarried mothers-to-be. Her tenants are forced into prostitution, milked of what money they have and relieved of their babies, one of which dies when Mrs Allister refuses to call a doctor. Confronted by Vivianne (René Ray), the mistress of a condemned killer, Mrs Allister thrusts her down a flight of stairs and leaves her to die. She is only brought to justice when her fellow worker Jess (Vida Hope), sickened by her brutal reign of terror, turns against her.

*Mrs Danvers (Judith Anderson, right) tries to persuade the second Mrs de Winter (Joan Fontaine) to put an end to her troubles by leaping from a high window, in* Rebecca *(1940)*

In *The Last Man to Hang?* (1956), Jackson plays the housekeeper who frames the master (Tom Conway) she hates for the murder of his wife. After a long trial, the jury returns a not guilty verdict, and it transpires that the 'victim' is alive, the housekeeper having seized on the chance to pin her name to an unidentifiable corpse as part of a quickly-devised plan.

A little-known actress, Fay Baker, gave a glacially magnetic performance as the governess who seems to have had some kind of *Nightcomers* relationship with the trustee, Spender (Richard Basehart), of the estate to which her young charge becomes heir, following the suspicious death of his wealthy great-aunt, in *The House on Telegraph Hill* (1951).

Into this environment comes a wartime refugee, Victoria (Valentina Cortese), masquerading as the (dead) mother the boy has never seen. She inherits the estate and marries Spender, but a series of 'accidents' soon convinces her that the governess and Spender are planning to bump her, and probably Chris, off, and collect the inheritance themselves, having already murdered the aunt. In a showdown, Victoria outwits Spender and he drinks the poison he intended for her. The governess is arrested for murder.

Twenty-one years after unforgettably personifying the Wicked Witch of the West in *The Wizard of Oz*, bony-faced supporting treasure Margaret Hamilton finally got to play a sinister housekeeper (named Mrs Zacharides!) in William Castle's gimmicky *13 Ghosts* (1960). But her forbidding form proved not to be responsible for the mayhem in the end, rosy-cheeked Martin Milner unexpectedly emerging as the killer.

Characters such as these were not generally allowed too much glamour. An exception was Martha Hyer, whose alabaster beauty, unsympathetic screen character and screaming eyes were put to good use in the sometimes hysterical *Picture Mommy Dead* (1966). Hyer manages to play both a cruel governess and a wicked stepmother, as Francene, an icy schemer of the first order.

Thanks to Francene, her young charge Susan (Susan Gordon) had been committed to a sanatorium for three years following the death of her mother Jessica (Zsa Zsa Gabor) in a fire. Susan returns to find Francene not only married to her father Edward (Don Ameche), but determined to have her put away again to ensure her inheritance passing to Edward.

Francene also enlists the aid of her lover Anthony (Maxwell Reed) to terrify Susan into revealing the whereabouts of a fabulous necklace vanished in the fire. Finding the necklace, Susan is pursued by Francene. When Anthony intervenes, Francene stabs him with a grappling-hook. Her rampage is only stopped when she is strangled by Edward, who reveals that he did the same to Jessica for her infidelity with – Anthony.

Susan, driven completely insane, sets fire to the house and wanders out into the arms of the police with her equally traumatized father, leaving Hyer, like so many villainess matrons, consumed by flames at the end of the film.

# 10
# THE CARTOON VILLAINESSES

'Even as a kid I always went for
the wrong women...When my mother took
me to see *Snow White*...
I immediately fell for the wicked queen'

Woody Allen in *Annie Hall* (1977)

Many of the finest villains in the animated features produced over the past 50 years at the Walt Disney studio have been women. Almost always, they have provided the only 'frightening' element in the story – the one that has sent many a toddler wailing and turning to its accompanying parent for comfort.

The most terrifying of them all, the wicked witch in *Snow White and the Seven Dwarfs* (1937) set the pattern, and standard, for all Disney villains to come. Rather bizarrely described by Disney himself as 'a cross between Lady Macbeth and the Big Bad Wolf', she begins the picture as Snow White's vain and wicked stepmother, the queen, forever asking her magic 'Mirror, mirror on the wall – who is the fairest of them all?' Despite the queen's rather forbidding visage and Bette Davis lips, the mirror obviously knew what was good for it, as it always told her that she was.

Alas, one day a slip of the tongue occurs and the mirror reveals the truth, telling the malevolent matron that the Princess Snow White is now the fairest. This places the princess in a perilous predicament, especially when the queen orders her huntsman to take the girl into the deepest part of the woods, there to deprive her of her head with his axe.

Fortunately, the huntsman's nerve fails him, and he tells Snow White, in the nicest possible way, to skedaddle far away into the woods and never come back. Here she meets seven dwarf miners and becomes their housekeeper, a blissful state of affairs soon interrupted by the evil

*The Wicked Stepmother and her two spoiled and ugly daughters are horrified to find that Cinderella has managed to finish all her tasks and get ready for the royal ball, in* Cinderella *(1949). © Copyright Walt Disney Productions*

queen, who sees the truth in her magic mirror.

Delving deep into her book of evil spells, the witch turns herself into a cackling old crone in black cloak and hood, with a nasty wart on the biggest nose this side of Cyrano de Bergerac. She sets out to finish Snow White off with a poisoned apple.

Well, despite the fact that you wouldn't buy a second-hand car from an old hag like this, the princess-in-exile goes for it and biting into the tempting but tainted apple, doesn't die (or we wouldn't have a story) but falls into a sort of catatonic trance.

Finding her thus, the dwarfs, warned by their forest friends, pursue the queen in a storm up to the top of a cliff where, trapped, she plunges to her death. Snow White is restored to life by the kiss of a prince.

Originally Disney had asked the scriptwriters to make the queen's dialogue 'over-melodramatic, verging on the ridiculous'. In the context of a cartoon world, however, the character is all too convincing and gave many a whimpering child nightmares for weeks afterwards.

The facial characteristics that had made the queen so frightening – staring eyes, snarling mouth and eyebrows like a downward escalator – were cunningly integrated by Disney animators into subsequent villainesses from the studio. In *Cinderella* (1949), the wicked stepmother, with her light-streaked hair, spade-shaped chin, harsh elegance and dominating height, is clearly a figure to fear in the classic Disney tradition.

She treats poor Cinders like a skivvy and naturally ensures she cannot go to the ball after Cinderella does the impossible and gets her work and her dress (subsequently ripped to shreds by the ugly sisters) finished on time (with a little help from her friends the mice).

As we know, Cinderella eventually does go the the royal ball, there to dance with the prince and flee at midnight ere her coach turns back into a pumpkin. When the time comes to fit on the glass slipper, as the prince searches for his lost love, the stepmother tries one last throw, by smashing the slipper before Cinderella can try it on. However, the resourceful girl produces the slipper's mate from her pocket.

In contrast, the Queen of Hearts in Disney's underrated version of *Alice in Wonderland* (1951), voiced by Verna Felton (who had contributed to *Cinderella* as the voice of the Fairy Godmother!) is large, ill-tempered, fat and lazy and very fond of shouting 'Off with her head!' Equipped with arms like belaying pins, as well as a mouth like the Grand Canyon and the familiar Disney eyebrows, the Queen brooks no intervention from her tiny king, and soon has Alice condemned to death before the girl's flight from Wonderland and back to reality.

The studio produced perhaps its most bestial villainess in its 1958 film of *Sleeping Beauty*. The evil fairy Maleficent (lovely name) has inherited the mouth from *Snow White*'s witch and the alabaster-beard chin from the stepmother in *Cinderella*. The eyebrows are *de rigueur*. She also has a headdress like a pair of black horns, but undoubtedly her most endearing facet is the ability to turn herself into a fire-breathing dragon.

Angered at not being invited to the celebrations for the birth of Princess Aurora, Maleficent appears as the spectre at the feast in a flash of lightning, casting an evil spell on the baby which means that the prick of a needle from a spinning-wheel, any time up to the girl's sixteenth birthday, will have roughly the equivalent effect to Snow White sinking her teeth into the dreaded apple.

At her parents' behest, three good fairies keep the girl safe until then, but on her 16th birthday the glow from their magic while making a dress is spotted by Maleficent's raven with predictably disastrous effects. The girl is lured to a castle and obligingly places her finger on a spindle, while her princely boyfriend, with whom she has fallen in love incognito, is captured by Maleficent's minions and thrown into a deep and dingy dungeon.

Sprung by the fairies and armed by them with the sword of truth, the prince plunges its blade, after a ferocious battle, into the heart of the dragon into which Maleficent has transformed herself. With a shriek, she expires in charred embers. The rest is (fairytale) history.

One critic thought that 'the more terrifying aspects of the witch and her entourage make the film less suitable for unaccompanied children than the censor's certificate might indicate'.

*The evil Maleficent gasps with satisfaction as the Princess Aurora obligingly pricks her finger on the spindle of a spinning-wheel in 1958's* Sleeping Beauty. *© Copyright Walt Disney Productions*

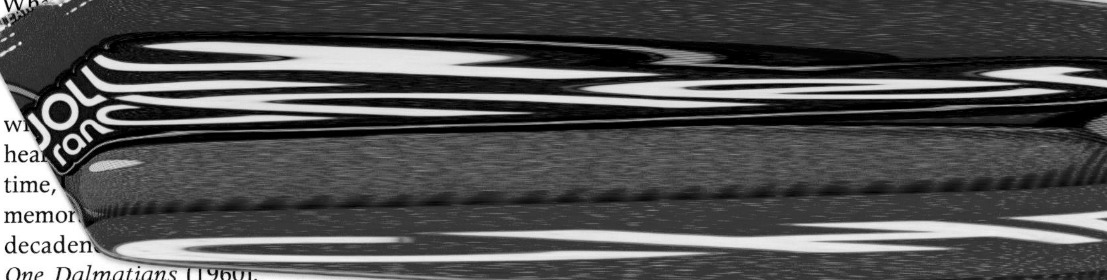

Wh…

wi…
hea…
time,…
memor…
decaden…
*One Dalmatians* (1960).

Cruella, the 'friend' of the heroine (well, they were at school together) looks as though she has been through death by fright and survived. She has two-colour hair that looks like a dead cockatoo and its shadow, cheekbones that make her seem as if she has a knitting needle jammed widthwise in her mouth, the obligatory purple lids and rollercoaster eyebrows and (unusually for a Disney villainess) a turned-up nose.

Her entrances, notably the first, are always spectacular occasions. Cigarette clutched in long holder away from her white fur coat contributed by some unfortunate animal, she surveys the hero and heroine's 15 Dalmatian puppies with evil delight flashing from her eyes, and greed dripping from her scarlet gash of a mouth – since she already has 84 puppies captive, planning to make a unique coat with their skins.

In no time at all, Cruella's ruthless if barely efficient thugs, Jasper and Horace, have dognapped the puppies and whisked them off to Cruella's remote country manor.

…get…

as 'an evil, crazy witch', … confirms that the accent is on craziness.

To begin with she is short and stumpy and has a gleeful grin which emphasises her double chin. The traditional Disney eyebrows are missing. But, although her sense of fun extends to riding her broomstick like a surfboard, it must be admitted that she is also a bit of a tartar, and will eat innocents for breakfast if she can.

One such innocent flies into her lair in the shape of the hero, Wart, one day to be king of England, but now transformed into a bird by his mentor Merlin the wizard, in the furtherance of his education. This is nearly ended abruptly by Madame Mim, who turns herself into a cat and tries to catch and eat him.

Merlin fortunately storms to the rescue, and a titanic duel of magic takes place between the two sorcerers. Battle rages bewilderingly back and forth as each tries to transform themselves into something that will defeat (or simply eat) the other. Finally Mim breaks the rules of the game

*Cruella de Vil congratulates her henchmen, Jasper and Horace, on an outstanding piece of bungling in letting their doggy prisoners go, in* One Hundred and One Dalmatians. *© Copyright Walt Disney Productions*

*Watched by the hero, Wart (who has been changed into a bird), mad witch Madam Mim shrinks herself to the size of a bird and flies over the table top, in* The Sword in the Stone *(1963). © Copyright Walt Disney Productions*

*Madame Medusa gives orders to her two crocodile minions as to where to take their girl captive in Devil's Bayou. But two mice have overheard her, in* The Rescuers *(1977).* *© Copyright Walt Disney Productions*

by turning herself into a great, fat, roaring dragon. 'We said No Dragons,' protests Merlin. Madame Mim, however, retorts that no-one said anything about purple dragons, and prepares to get on with the business of devouring him. But it's Merlin who has the last word. He disappears, turning himself into a tiny germ – and giving Mim's dragon the measles.

Disney's most recent villainess has been that flame-haired slouch Madame Medusa from *The Rescuers* (1977), voiced by the Academy Award winner Geraldine Page. With slumped shoulders, black-ringed eyes, shrill voice, pointy nose, plain looks, long nails, a nasty disposition and a figure that looks as though it's in dire need of a good girdle, Medusa hasn't much to recommend her.

She is, however, extremely fond of her two pet crocodiles, Brutus and Nero, and likes to cuddle them while dreaming of the fabled 'Devil's Eye' diamond. The Eye is located in a particularly inaccessible part of a pirates' cave near Medusa's headquarters in Devil's Bayou. To get it, Medusa kidnaps an orphan called Penny because she is thin enough to get through the narrow opening to the cave.

That's where the 'rescuers' come in – two intrepid mice who journey to the swamp and, after many adventures, prove to be Medusa's downfall, escaping with Penny in Medusa's swampmobile and leaving her to the mercy of Brutus and Nero, who have turned against her.

Recent Disney villains have been all male. But there must be some wicked women of children's literature left still, cowering away in some dark corner of the cellar – just waiting to jump out and scare the daylights from us. Let's hope they're soon brought to (animated) life.

# 11
# GUN GIRLS

'All you can buy up here is
a bullet in the head'

Joan Crawford in
*Johnny Guitar* (1954)

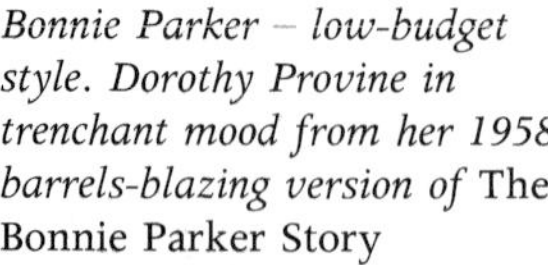

*Bonnie Parker – low-budget style. Dorothy Provine in trenchant mood from her 1958 barrels-blazing version of* The Bonnie Parker Story

Girls with guns in their hands in the movies are generally ruthless and snarling – especially when that gun is part of their way of life. Bank robbers, lady outlaws western and modern, hit-ladies and professional assassins, all were equally cool – even if they usually collected a bullet in the last reel.

Sometimes they were reckless, sometimes calculating, and many of them were based on real-life figures from America's violent past, such as Bonnie Parker, Belle Starr and Ma Barker. Male public enemies might be forgotten, but girls stayed in the memory.

Most of them were pretty uncomplicated, ugly (by nature) characters. Not so one of Hollywood's strangest fictional creations, Annie Laurie Starr (Peggy Cummins), the bug-eyed blonde beauty of a great unsung crime thriller called *Gun Crazy* (1949), originally just as appropriately released as *Deadly is the Female*.

Cummins, a diminutive but shapely British actress, was at the end of a brief stay in Hollywood, during which she had also played a blackmailing cockney actress in *Moss Rose* (1947). But she never had a role like Annie Laurie Starr, and turned in the best performance of her 20-year career, a memorable portrait of someone completely carried away by the heady success of criminal exploits.

*Gun Crazy* is set in contemporary times, but its two main protagonists seem somehow to belong to a more distant, primitive, lawless part of America's history. Annie is a sharpshooter with a carnival, while Bart (John Dall), just released from a corrective institution and the army in turn, has had an hysterical fascination with guns since childhood.

At first sight, the carnival owner recalls, the couple look at each other 'like wild animals', Bart challenging Annie to a duel, which he wins by a whisker, establishing (he thinks) his equality with her.

He joins the show, and marries Annie after only a few weeks, whereupon they are fired by the carnival owner, now denied Annie's sexual favours. As their money runs out, she sexually blackmails Bart not to pawn his collection of arms, then threatens to leave him unless he helps her rob a bank.

Acting as getaway driver, Annie distracts the attention of a policeman, whom she clubs down viciously when Bart emerges from the bank. Her lascivious smile at the moment of escape is really

*Until death . . . Annie Laurie (Peggy Cummins) and Bart (John Dall) acknowledge themselves bound to one another, and a life of violence, in* Gun Crazy *(1949)*

quite frightening, and the bank job proves to be just the opening shot in a career that ranges across the southwest from banks to gas stations and stores, and back to banks.

Violence and danger keep them on a high until, after several months of robberies, the pursuit becomes too hot. Annie decides on one last job before they hightail it to Mexico. Their immaculately-planned action to lift the payroll at a meat-packing plant goes like clockwork until Annie's itchy trigger finger guns down two employees and makes them the subjects of a nationwide manhunt.

Beaten back from the border by rallying police, Annie and Bart cannot bring themselves to separate because 'we go together...like guns and ammunition'. Cornered in a reedy swamp, Annie prepares to gun down as many policemen as she can, but Bart kills her with a single bullet before police bullets riddle his own body and their corpses fall together in the misty marshland in a lifeless embrace.

The climax of *Gun Crazy* is a direct ancestor of the balletic violence at the end of *Bonnie and Clyde*, although, whereas Faye Dunaway's Bonnie is intermittently terrified by violence, Annie Laurie Starr thrives on it – without it she would have no driving force to sustain her hyper-bright mental energies.

Before Dunaway made the role her own, Bonnie Parker had been previously portrayed on the screen by Dorothy Provine in a low-budget 1958 film called *The Bonnie Parker Story*. It caught quite well a feeling of backwoods austerity which the characters fought to escape, although it was an atmosphere that at least one sniffy critic found 'distinctly unhealthy'.

The name of Bonnie's partner in crime was even changed in this film to Guy Darrow, although Clyde Barrow was allowed to keep his own name in a much earlier version, *Persons in Hiding* (1939), made only four years after the couple were mown down by the law.

This was considerably sanitized, as one might expect, although the performances of Patricia Morison and J. Carrol Naish suggested that, with a bigger budget, the film's portrait of Bonnie and Clyde as romantic petty criminals could have been given considerably more depth.

Belle Starr, the fiery bandit queen of the west, was glamorized to a degree that would even have been disowned by Doris Day (whose Calamity Jane at least started off looking a bit like a hardened westerner) in three successive tellings of her story. It was to be expected that Gene Tierney (in 1941's *Belle Starr*) and Jane Russell (in 1952's *Montana Belle*, the gutsiest of the three) would hardly eschew powder and paint,

*Gene Tierney, with a gunbelt tailored to fit the dress, and perennial westerner Randolph Scott, as husband-and-wife outlaws in* Belle Starr *(1941)*

but when Elizabeth Montgomery weighed in with the beauty treatment in her 1980 version for television (also called *Belle Starr*), poor Belle must have been spinning in her grave. She was also played by Isabel Jewell as a minor character in the Randolph Scott western, *Badman's Territory* in 1946.

In the Russell version, actually completed as early as 1948, Belle is presented as a crack shot whose outlaw husband is killed, impelling her to ride the outlaw trail with the Dalton brothers, led by Scott Brady as Bob. Later, she goes on a holdup spree with two more outlaws, before the law finally catches up with her.

Poor Scott Brady seemed doomed to tangle with (and get billed below) some strong women of the filmic west. After co-starring with Yvonne de Carlo in *The Gal Who Took the West* (1949), the glutton came back for more punishment at the hands of Shelley Winters in *Untamed Frontier* (1951), Barbara Stanwyck in *The Maverick Queen* (1956) and Joan Crawford *and* Mercedes McCambridge in *Johnny Guitar* (1954), which gave us two gun girls for the price of one.

*Johnny Guitar*, which, despite its slower patches, is extraordinarily stylised and unusual for a western, is filled with characters whose hang-ups threaten to destroy their lives. Joan Crawford is Vienna, saloon queen and, according to bigoted townsfolk led by the dangerously unbalanced banker Emma Small (McCambridge), involved in a string of stagecoach robberies.

Vienna's hang-up is Johnny Guitar (Sterling Hayden), the ex-lover she hires to play in her saloon. Johnny's hang-up is guns; trying to give them up, he goes berserk when holding one in his hand. Emma's hang-up (besides herself) is Brady as the Dancin' Kid (though she won't admit it), while Brady's own hang-up is Vienna, whom he can see would go back to Johnny at the drop of a guitar.

There comes a posse of townspeople for the first time to give Vienna 24 hours to 'git'. But, as Vienna appears at the top of the staircase, Emma wants more. 'Go get her,' she grates. 'Drag her down.'

Crawford has her own riposte for that. 'Down there,' she flashes, 'I sell whisky and cards. All you can buy up here is a bullet in the head.'

But when the Dancin' Kid is falsely accused of the hold-ups, he and his men decide they might as well rob the bank before leaving town. Vienna, accidentally at the bank to collect money, is figuratively caught in the crossfire and this time the posse rides in earnest, barely able to keep up with the gun-toting Emma. 'Get 'em ready or I will,' she cries to the local bigwig (Ward Bond) adding, rather illogically, 'I wanted her out before she got in.'

Thanks to Emma, Vienna is dragged off for a hanging and the local marshal killed. Emma's parting shot is to gun down Vienna's huge chandelier and set fire to her saloon. When some reluctance is shown in kicking the horse from under Vienna at the lynching, Emma offers $100 to any man who will do it. No good. She has to do it herself – and does, only to see Vienna rescued in the nick of time by Johnny Guitar. They join the Dancin' Kid and his men holed up in their lair.

Comes the showdown and everyone concerned decides to let Vienna and Emma get on with it. 'It's what it was all about in the first place,' grumbles Bond, seeing the light. Almost bursting with nervous excitement and tension, Emma fires first, but Vienna is only winged which, considering Emma's aim for the rest of the film, is somewhat unlikely, especially as she swivels round and shoots the Dancin' Kid right

between the eyes. The diversion, however, gives Vienna a chance to recover. Result: Vienna gets Johnny, Johnny gets Vienna, and Emma gets hers.

There was another all-girl gun duel at the end of *The Woman They Almost Lynched* (1952). Sulky Audrey Totter fancies herself as the gunslinging bad girl, but is outgunned at the finish by heroine Joan Leslie who buckles on a gun over her skirts and gives Totter a lesson in accuracy.

There aren't many westerns about all-girl gangs, but the Dalton brothers, who turned up in the Belle Starr stories and many other westerns, begat one when their sisters took to the outlaw trail in *The Dalton Girls* (1957). One might have expected to find Marie Windsor, Carole Mathews and Beverly Garland as three of the strong-willed bandits in this film, but they were all away on duty making *Swamp Women*, and instead we got Merry Anders, Penny Edwards, Lisa Davis and Sue George, as Holly, Columbine, Rose and Marigold.

The girls bring off a number of hold-ups, but Pinkerton detectives are soon on their trail and a gambler (John Russell) in love with Columbine tries to prise her away from the rest before it's too late. She refuses and all four are then trapped an a hectic battle with the law. One lawman is gunned down by Holly, but Rose and Marigold

*Over the top for Forrest Tucker, as Mac, and Jane Russell, as Belle Starr in the seldom-seen RKO version of the Starr legend,* Montana Belle *(1952)*

*Rushing in where her posse fears to tread, Emma (Mercedes McCambridge) opens fire on a gunman whose own shot accidentally kills the town marshal, in* Johnny Guitar *(1954). Ward Bond is the horrified onlooker beside her*

*Unlikely-looking outlaws are Merry Anders and Lisa Davis as Holly and Rose Dalton in* The Dalton Girls *(1957)*

are shot dead and Columbine is wounded.

Holly goes out of her mind with grief and anger, but Columbine escapes and is helped to safety by the gambler. Despite an interesting performance by Anders as Holly, the film was too weakly scripted to make it a full-blooded addition to the genre.

The last of the great western outlaws were being cleaned out by the beginning of the twentieth century, and banditry went underground until the Depression hit America in the Twenties.

New lawlessness arose in the chain of states that formed America's midwest. From the Ozark backwoods of Arkansas and Missouri, came the flamboyant Kate 'Ma' Barker, a cigar-chewing hellion with four deadly sons who very quickly climbed America's 'Top 20' of public enemies.

Quickly off the mark to play her (she had been killed in January 1935) was that stern actress Blanche Yurka, who gave a powerful and passionate performance in *Queen of the Mob* (1940), even being allowed to survive at the end as the last of her sons lies dead at her feet.

The tale was then left alone until a furious flurry of atmospheric, low-budget gangster films of the late 1950s, fuelled by the success of television's *The Untouchables*. These included *Baby Face Nelson* (1957), *The Bonnie Parker Story* (1958), *Machine Gun Kelly* (1958), *Al Capone* (1959), *The Scarface Mob* (1959), *I, Mobster* (1959) – covering the career of 'Dutch' Schultz – *The Rise and Fall of Legs Diamond* (1959), *Pretty Boy Floyd* (1960) and, tagging on at the end, *Ma Barker's Killer Brood* (1960).

Lurene Tuttle's vigorous performance as Ma – who had been called Ma Webster in the Yurka version but now was allowed her real name – enlivened the penny-dreadful proceedings. However the role was to be definitively annexed nine years later by Shelley Winters in *Bloody Mama*.

Hardened and embittered by being raped by her father and brothers when a girl, Kate has brought her own four sons up as a violent but tight-knit family unit. As soon as they are old enough, she, like many another gangster of the era, 'rushes towards death' by taking them on a rampage of robberies which decimate the local population.

'Unless you're rich, you ain't free,' says Ma. 'I aim to be free.' But, with her spectacular headgear and noisy weaponry, Ma and her boys are soon hitting the headlines which threaten that freedom. A further note of warning is struck when one of the Barker boys, Lloyd (Robert de Niro), high on drugs, attempts to rape a local girl and Ma orders the 'witness' exterminated and helps to drown her in a bathtub.

The boys, despite their ruthlessness, are not happy about the incident, and, when Ma orders the killing of an affable kidnap victim they have grown to like, the boys rebel, Herman (Don Stroud) knocking Ma down and taking over leadership of the gang.

The change brings bad luck. Lloyd dies from a drug overdose and the gang is besieged in Florida, where Herman has taken them to a new headquarters. Their cohort Kevin (Bruce Dern) tries to run out on them, but Ma blasts him with her machine-gun.

After two of his brothers fall, Herman proves himself ultimately a coward by turning his gun on himself and leaving Ma to face the music alone. This she does, defiantly and ecstatically blazing away with her machine-gun even after being hit several times, until she is finally cut down.

It took another five years for a Ma Barker clone to appear, in the energetic shape of Angie Dickinson as Wilma McClatchie in *Big Bad*

*Ma Barker (Shelley Winters) and her son Fred (Robert Walden) flank a bandaged hostage (Pat Hingle) in* Bloody Mama *(1969)*

*Mama* (1974). Wilma is fiction rather than fact, and has two daughters rather than four sons. Her story starts a little later, in Texas in 1932, but runs along fairly similar lines.

When her bootlegger lover is shot down by federal agents, Wilma takes her girls and heads west. After getting the better of a striptease promoter and a crooked preacher, they become involved with a bank robbery headed by Diller (Tom Skerritt) and help him bring it off. A gambler (William Shatner) Wilma meets at the racetrack she is robbing is invited into her bed and becomes part of the gang.

Diller quits when Wilma launches a dicey scheme to rob a heavily-guarded oil refinery, but reappears to aid the getaway when the girls successfully carry out the raid.

As in *Bloody Mama*, it's a kidnap that precipitates the downfall of the gang. Inspired by their successful haul at a society ball, they kidnap a young heiress and her presence proves highly destructive. While Wilma is collecting the ransom, the heiress escapes, Wilma recapturing her just as police arrive for a showdown.

In a terrific gun battle, Diller and the gambler are shot down, but in the confusion Wilma and the girls manage to escape in their car and make off with the ransom money. Wilma, however, has stopped a bullet on the way and dies on the road.

The third film from the same New World stable, *Crazy Mama* (1975), is considerably lighter in style, more of a parody than anything else. It too starts in 1932, when an Arkansas farmer resisting eviction is shot dead before his wife Sheba and daughter Melba, but the body of its action takes place in the late 1950s, when Sheba (Ann Sothern) and Melba (Cloris Leachman) embark on a cross-country crime spree that involves robbing stores, garages, churches, box-offices and finally a bank.

For the third time, it is a kidnap (although a fake one of one of its own members) that provides a downswing in the gang's fortunes. Two of its ill-assorted members are killed at a gunfight at the rendezvous, a deserted zoo, and Melba resolves to make a final assault on reclaiming the family farm.

Triumphantly, with Sheba, she holds up the wedding reception there of the son of the man who had shot her father. In a subsequent gunfight with the police, Sheba is at last shot down. Melba and the last surviving members of the Crazy Mama Gang escape to Miami, Florida, where they start a fast-food restaurant. However, they are threatened with eviction by a debt collector...

The subject of women gang leaders can't be closed without reference to Judith Anderson, who followed her fearful Mrs Danvers in *Rebecca* with as desperate and dangerous a gunwoman as ever stalked the screen in *Lady Scarface*. You didn't argue when this Mama gave orders, although, like all the rest, she and her

*Two-gun Wilma McClatchie (Angie Dickinson) bears a charmed life . . . for a time, in the brassy 1974 melodrama* Big Bad Mama

gang are eventually hounded down and exterminated by the law.

In *Loophole* (1954), perennial bad girl Mary Beth Hughes was merely a gangster's girl, but colder and more ruthless than those with whom she associates. She's Vera, the blonde mistress of Tate (played by chubby Don Beddoe in a rare bad-guy role) who, pretending to be a bank examiner, lifts $50,000 from the till of cashier Donovan (Barry Sullivan) who, though proved innocent, subsequently loses his job.

Coming across Tate in later days, Donovan, now a cabby, forces the man to take him back to his apartment on a pretence of sharing the loot. Tate is willing, but Vera forbids it. As she is about to shoot Donovan, they are interruppted by an investigator (Charles McGraw) who has never believed Donovan's story.

The trio escapes and Donovan, calling the police, trails Tate and Vera to a beachhouse, where they trap him. Vera instructs Tate to kill Donovan and, when he refuses, guns down both men. Police arrive and, with the help of the injured Donovan, capture her before she can escape. Donovan uneasily returns to his bank job, the investigator still watching.

Even cooler than Vera were the screen's hit-ladies, female assassins for hire. Yvette Mimieux, usually seen as fragile flowers, played one in a television movie she wrote herself, *Hit Lady* (1974). In the same year, the exploitation movie *Girls for Rent* offered two of these dispatchers, one played by the fearsome Georgina Spelvin, whose character is eventually blasted out of existence in a speeding car by the boyfriend of one of her victims.

In *The Next Man* (1976), Cornelia Sharpe plays Nicole, a very high-class assassin who has just eliminated an Arab trying to patch up the fragile situation in the Middle East. Next assigned to bump off Khalil (Sean Connery), the Saudi Arabian Minister of State, she makes his acquaintance and they become lovers.

Together, they escape various terrorist bomb plots before Khalil's aide Hamid (Albert Paulsen), who turns out to be Nicole's employer, orders her to finish Khalil off. Nicole fulfils her mission – but not before turning her gun on Hamid as well. We last see her being trailed by the man who has already shot down her 'expendable' predecessor.

The cinema's most personable hit-lady of recent times has unquestionably been Kathleen Turner in *Prizzi's Honor* (1985). This highly-praised film from John Huston features the electric Turner as Irene, a very successful hit-lady whose work for the Mafia brings her into contact with Mafioso enforcer Charley Partanna (Jack Nicholson). It's love at first sight: they marry and even team up on a rather messy kidnap in which the victim is supposed to catch the 'baby' Turner throws at him, but goes for his gun instead.

Subsequently she is forced to kill a witness who turns out to be a police chief's wife. This gives Anjelica Huston, winning an Oscar for her portrayal of Maerose, Charley's seethingly rejected lover, a lever to push her successor out of the picture, especially as the Mafia suspect, correctly, that Irene still has $360,000 of their money from a previous double-cross. Charley is ordered to make a hit on his own wife. Irene, suspicious, arranges passage to Hong Kong, but Charley catches up with her.

Soon, they are warily circling each other in a hotel room like gunfighters at a showdown.

*Judith Anderson adopts the guise of a nurse to bump off a wounded witness in* Lady Scarface *(1941). That hand on her wrist suggests she's in trouble . . .*

Irene has a gun behind her back as she prepares to slip into bed, but from under the sheets, Charley flicks a knife with deadly aim and pins Irene by the neck to the wall.

A whole organisation full of female assassins was the subject of *Andy Warhol's Bad* (1976), with Carroll Baker fierce as Hazel, the female fiend who runs a home electrolysis parlour as a front for a dial-a-murder organization. Employing her first-ever male assassin proves a big mistake as he is unable to kill a child victim and begins a chain of events which end in Hazel being drowned by a once-friendly policeman in her own sink.

The perils of letting a female assassin off the hook were amply demonstrated in *Black Sunday* (1976), in which Israeli major Kabakov (Robert Shaw) corners Black September terrorist Dahlia (Marthe Keller) when he surprises her in her shower. He is unable to kill her and she gets away.

The result is that Dahlia reaches her American contact Lander (Bruce Dern), an embittered Vietnam veteran, now the pilot of an airship used for sports coverage, and a party to a horrendous plan to explode thousands of steel darts over the crowd at the Miami Super Bowl during the national championship final.

Unloading plastic explosives from a freighter, Dahlia is spotted but escapes again. Subsequently, she silences the ship's captain with a bomb, injuring Kabakov into the bargain. Trying to finish him off, she kills his assistant instead. Just before the game, Lander is replaced as the airship pilot, but he and Dahlia kill the new man and trick their way on to the 'blimp'.

Alerted to the danger when the body is found, Kabakov takes up a helicopter, and this time makes no mistake in cutting down Dahlia in a mid-air duel. Lander is killed just as he struggles to light the vital fuse that will explode the airship's lethal cargo.

The screen's latest gun girl takes the wheel full circle to the beginning of this chapter. John

*Mafia eliminators Kathleen Turner and Jack Nicholson dispose of a rather unexpected victim in John Huston's 1985 success,* Prizzi's Honor

Wisdom (Emilio Estevez) and Karen Simmons (Demi Moore) in *Wisdom* (1987) are in direct line of descent from Bonnie and Clyde, or Annie Laurie Starr and Bart Tare.

Shunned by society because of a minor conviction for car theft, Wisdom decides, after watching a TV programme about banks foreclosing on the mortgages of farmers and small businessmen, to become a modern Robin Hood.

Buying a powerful automatic rifle with the money he has saved for a car, Wisdom starts to raid banks – not for the money, but to 'torch' all the bank's mortgage records with home-made bombs.

His girl-friend Karen (Moore), at first the unsuspecting getaway driver, soon becomes converted to his cause. Fired by the thrill of a cross-country bank-burning spree, she joyously joins him in holding up customers who begin to treat the pair as folk heroes as they blaze across the midwest.

Wisdom's fatal slip comes when he disarms a bank guard and gives Karen the guard's gun. Confronted by a sheriff in a superstore, Karen 'freezes' and eventually panics herself into shooting him dead. Now on the run for murder, they head for Canada but only escape police after a running gun battle with numerous police vehicles. Foolishly abandoning their van (a gift to them earlier by an admiring fan), Karen and John try to go to ground in a town, but are separately raked with bullets from police weapons.

The cinema's gun girls almost always bit the dust in the end. For, unlike their male counterparts, they rarely laid down their arms.

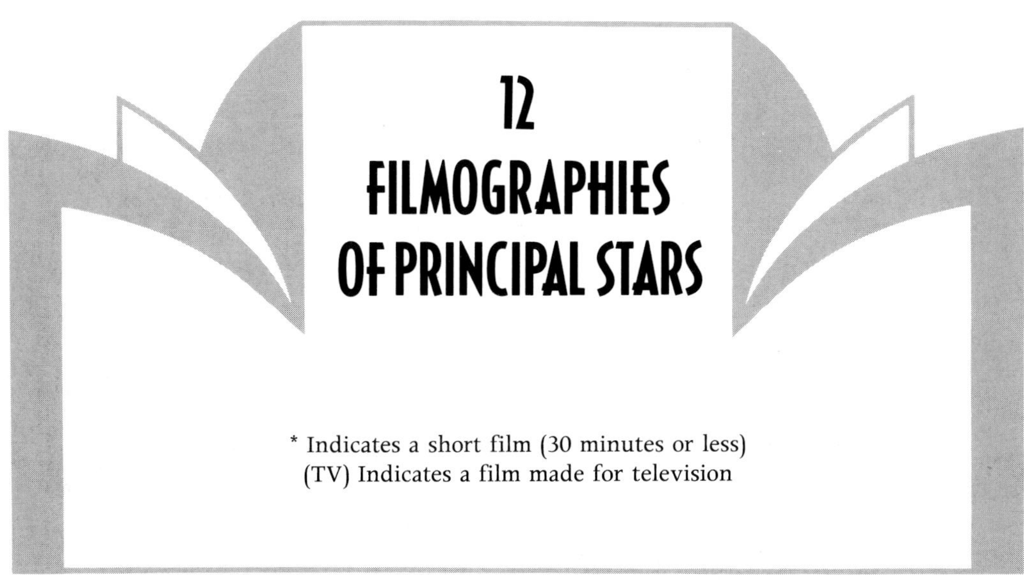


* Indicates a short film (30 minutes or less)
(TV) Indicates a film made for television

**Theda Bara**
*1914: A Fool There Was. 1915: The Clemenceau Case. The Devil's Daughter. The Kreutzer Sonata (GB: Sonata). Lord Audley's Secret. The Two Orphans. Sin. The Galley Slave. Destruction. Carmen. The Stain. 1916: The Serpent. Gold and the Woman. The Eternal Sappho. East Lynne. Her Double Life. Romeo and Juliet. Under Two Flags. Fires of Hate. The Vixen. The Tiger Woman. Darling of Paris. The Light. 1917: Cleopatra. Camille. Madame Dubarry. Her Greatest Love. Heart and Soul. The Rose of Blood. The Soul of Buddha. 1918: Salome. Under the Yoke. The Forbidden Path. When a Woman Sins. The She Devil. The Message of the Lilies. La Belle Russe. 1919: Siren's Song. When Men Desire. A Woman There Was. Lure of Ambition. Kathleen Mavourneen. 1921: The Price of Silence. Her Greatest Love. 1923: The Hunchback of Notre Dame. 1925: The Unchastened Woman. *Madame Mystery. 1926: The Dancer of Paris. *45 Minutes from Hollywood.*

**Brigitte Bardot**
*1952: Le trou normand (US: Crazy for Love). Manina (GB: The Lighthouse Keeper's Daughter. US: The Girl in the Bikini). Les dents longues. 1953: Le portrait de son père. Act of Love. Si Versailles m'était conté (GB: Versailles. US: Royal Affairs at Versailles). 1954: Tradita (US: Night of Love). Helen of Troy. Le fils de Caroline Chérie. 1955: Futures vedettes (GB: Sweet Sixteen). Doctor at Sea. Les grandes manoeuvres (GB and US: Summer Manoeuvres). La lumière d'en face (GB and US: The Light Across the Street). Cette sacrée gamine (GB and US: Mam'zelle Pigalle). 1956: Mio figlio Nerone (GB: Nero's Weekend). En effeuillant la Marguerite (GB: Mam'selle Striptease. US: Please, Mr Balzac). Et Dieu créa la femme (GB: And Woman . . . Was Created. US: And God Created Woman). La mariée est trop belle (GB and US: The Bride is Too Beautiful). 1957: Une Parisienne (GB and US: Parisienne). Les bijoutiers du clair de lune (GB: Heaven Fell That Night. US: The Night Heaven Fell). 1958: En cas de malheur (GB and US: Love Is My Profession). La femme et le pantin (GB: A Woman Like Satan). 1959: Babette Goes to War. Le testament d'Orphée. Voulez-vous danser avec moi? (GB and US: Come Dance With Me). 1960: L'affaire d'une nuit (GB: It Happened at Night). La vérité (GB and US: The Truth). 1961: La bride sur le cou (GB: Please, Not Now!). Les amours célèbres. Vie privée (GB and US: A Very Private Affair). 1962: Le repos du guerrier (GB: Warrior's Rest. US: Love on a Pillow). 1963: Le mépris (GB and US: Contempt). Paparazzi. Tentazione proibite. Une ravissante idiote (GB: A Ravishing Idiot. US: Adorable Idiot). 1964: Marie Soleil. 1965: Dear Brigitte . . . Viva Maria. 1966: Masculin-Féminin. Two Weeks in September. 1967: Histoires extraordinaires (GB: Tales of Mystery. US: Spirits of the Dead). 1968: Shalako. 1969: Les femmes. 1970: L'ours et la poupée. Les novices. Boulevard du rhum (GB: Rum Runner). 1971: Les pétroleuses (GB: The Legend of Frenchie King). 1973: Don Juan 1973 ou Et si Don Juan était une femme (GB: Don Juan, or If Don Juan Were a Woman). Colinot Trousse-Chemise.*

**Joan Collins**
*1951: Lady Godiva Rides Again. The Woman's Angle. Judgment Deferred. 1952: I Believe in You. Decameron Nights. Cosh Boy (US: The Slasher). 1953: Turn the Key Softly. The Square Ring. Our Girl Friday (US: The Adventures of Sadie). 1954: The Good Die Young. 1955: Land of the Pharaohs. The Virgin Queen. The Girl in the Red Velvet Swing. 1956: The Opposite Sex. 1957: Sea Wife. Island in the Sun. The Wayward Bus. Stopover Tokyo. 1958: The Bravados. Rally 'round the Flag, Boys! 1959: Seven Thieves. 1960: Esther and the King. 1962: The Road to Hong Kong. 1964: La congiuntura. 1967: Warning Shot. 1968: Subterfuge. Can Hieronymous Merkin Ever Forget Mercy Humpe and Find True Happiness? 1969: Drive Hard, Drive Fast (TV). If It's Tuesday, This Must Be Belgium. Breve amore. 1970: Up in the Cellar (GB: Three in the Cellar). The Executioner. 1971: Quest for Love. Revenge (US: Inn of the Frightened People). 1972: The Aquarian. Fear in the Night. Tales from the Crypt. 1973: Tales that Witness Madness. Dark Places. 1974: Call of the Wolf. The Referee (later Football Crazy). 1975: Alfie Darling. The Bawdy Adventures of Tom Jones. I Don't Want to Be Born. 1976: The Great Adventure. 1977: Empire of the Ants. 1978: The Stud. The Big Sleep. The Day of the Fox. Zero to Sixty. 1979: The Bitch. Sunburn. Game for Vultures. 1980: Growing Pains. Homework. 1982: Paper Dolls (TV). Nutcracker. The Wild Women of Chastity Gulch (TV). 1983: The Making of a Male Model (TV). 1984: The Cartier Affair (TV). Her Life as a Man (TV). 1986: Monte Carlo (TV).*

**Arlene Dahl**
*1947: Life with Father. My Wild Irish Rose. 1948: The Bride Goes Wild. A Southern Yankee (GB: My Hero). 1949: The Black Book (GB: Reign of Terror). Scene of the Crime. Ambush. 1950: The Outriders. Three Little Words. Watch the Birdie. 1951: Inside Straight. No Questions Asked. 1952: Caribbean (GB: Caribbean Gold). 1953: Desert Legion. Jamaica Run. Sangaree. The Diamond Queen. Here Come the Girls. 1954: Bengal Brigade (GB: Bengal Rifles). Woman's World. 1956: Slightly Scarlet. Wicked As They Come. 1957: Fortune is a Woman (US: She Played with Fire). 1959: Journey to the Center of the Earth. 1964: Kisses for My President. 1968: Les Poneyettes. 1969: Land Raiders. The Road to Katmandu. 1970: Du blé en liasses.*

**Bette Davis**
*1931: The Bad Sister. Seed. Waterloo Bridge. Way Back Home (GB: Old Greatheart). 1932: Hell's House. So Big. The Dark Horse. The Menace. The Man Who Played God (GB: The Silent Voice). The Rich are Always with Us. Cabin in the Cotton. Three on a Match. 20,000 Years in Sing Sing. 1933: Parachute Jumper. Ex-Lady. The Working Man. Bureau of Missing Persons. Fashions/Fashions of 1934 (GB: Fashion Follies of 1934). 1934: The Big Shakedown. Jimmy the Gent. Fog over Frisco. Housewife. Of Human Bondage. Bordertown. 1935: Front Page Woman. Special Agent. Dangerous. The Girl from 10th Avenue (GB: Men on her Mind). 1936: The Golden Arrow. The Petrified Forest. Satan Met a Lady. *A Day at Santa Anita. 1937: Kid Galahad. Marked Woman. That Certain Woman. It's Love I'm After. 1938: Jezebel. The Sisters. 1939: The Private Lives of Elizabeth and Essex. Dark Victory. Juarez. The Old Maid. 1940: All This and Heaven Too. The Letter. 1941: The Little Foxes. The Great Lie. Shining Victory. The Bride Came COD. The Man Who Came to Dinner. 1942: In This Our Life. Now, Voyager. 1943: Watch on the Rhine. Thank Your Lucky Stars. *Show Business at War. *A Present with a Future. *Stars on Horseback. Old Acquaintance. 1944: Mr Skeffington. Hollywood Canteen. 1945: The Corn is Green. 1946: Deception. A Stolen Life. 1948: Winter Meeting. June Bride. 1949: Beyond the Forest. 1950: All About Eve. 1951: Another Man's Poison. Payment on Demand. 1952: Phone Call from a Stranger. The Star. 1955: The Virgin Queen. 1956: The Catered Affair (GB: Wedding Breakfast). Storm Center. 1959: The Scapegoat. John Paul Jones. 1961: Pocketful of Miracles. 1962: What Ever Happened to Baby Jane? 1963: La noia (GB and US: The Empty Canvas). 1964: Dead Ringer (GB: Dead Image). Hush . . . Hush, Sweet Charlotte. Where Love Has Gone. 1965: The Nanny. 1967: The Anniversary. 1969: Connecting Rooms. 1971: Bunny O'Hare. Madame Sin (TV. GB: cinemas). 1972: The Judge and Jake Wyler (TV). The Scientific Card-Player. 1973: Scream Pretty Peggy (TV). 1976: Burnt Offerings. The Disappearance of Aimee (TV). 1977: Return to Witch Mountain. 1978: Death on the Nile. The Children of Sanchez. 1979: Strangers (TV). 1980: White Mama (TV). 1981: The Watcher in the Woods. Skyward (TV). Family Reunion (TV). A Piano for Mrs Cimino (TV). 1982: Little Gloria – Happy at Last (TV). 1983: Right of Way (TV). 1985: Murder with Mirrors (TV). As Summers Die (TV). 1986: Directed by William Wyler. 1987: The Whales of August.*

**Faye Dunaway**
*1966: The Happening. Hurry Sundown. 1967: Bonnie and Clyde. 1968: The Extraordinary Seaman. The Thomas Crown Affair. Amanti (GB and US: A Place for Lovers). 1969: The Arrangement. 1970: Little Big Man. Puzzle of a Downfall Child. 1971: Doc. The Deadly Trap. 1972: The Woman I Love (TV). 1973: Oklahoma Crude. The Three Musketeers. 1974: The Towering Inferno. The Four Musketeers. Chinatown.*

*1975: Three Days of the Condor. 1976: The Disappearance of Aimée (TV). Voyage of the Damned. Network. 1978: Eyes of Laura Mars. The Champ. 1979: Arthur Miller – on Home Ground. 1980: The First Deadly Sin. 1981: Mommie Dearest. Evita Peron (TV). 1983: The Wicked Lady. Supergirl. 1984: Ordeal by Innocence. 1985: Thirteen at Dinner (TV). 1986: Beverly Hills Madam (TV). 1987: Barfly. Casanova (TV). Midnight Crossing.*

### Gloria Grahame

*1943: Cry Havoc. 1944: Blonde Fever. 1945: Without Love. 1946: It's a Wonderful Life. 1947: It Happened in Brooklyn. Merton of the Movies. Song of the Thin Man. Crossfire. 1948: A Woman's Secret. 1949: Roughshod. 1950: In a Lonely Place. Macao (released 1952). 1952: Sudden Fear. The Greatest Show on Earth. The Bad and the Beautiful. 1953: Man on a Tightrope. The Glass Wall. The Big Heat. Prisoners of the Casbah. 1954: The Good Die Young. Human Desire. Naked Alibi. 1955: Oklahoma! The Cobweb. Not As a Stranger. 1956: The Man Who Never Was. 1957: Ride Out for Revenge. 1959: Odds Against Tomorrow. 1966: Ride Beyond Vengeance. 1971: Blood and Lace. Chandler. The Todd Killings. Black Noon. Escape (TV). 1972: The Loners. Julio and Stein. 1973: Tarot. 1974: Mama's Dirty Girls. The Girl on the Late, Late Show (TV). 1975: Mansion of the Doomed (GB: The Terror of Dr Chaney). 1979: Chilly Scenes of Winter/Head Over Heels. The Nesting. 1980: Melvin and Howard. The Biggest Bank Robbery (TV).*

### Rita Hayworth

*1926: †*:La Fiesta. 1934: †Cruz Diablo. 1935: †*Rose de Francia. †Under the Pampas Moon. †Dante's Inferno. †Charlie Chan in Egypt. †In Caliente. †Silk Legs. †Paddy O'Day. 1936: †Human Cargo. †A Message to Garcia. †Rebellion. †Meet Nero Wolfe. 1937: †Hit the Saddle. †Trouble in Texas. †Old Louisiana (GB: Treason). Criminals of the Air. The Game That Kills. Paid to Dance. Girls Can Play. The Shadow (GB: The Circus Shadow). 1938: There's Always a Woman. Who Killed Gail Preston? Juvenile Court. Convicted. Homicide Bureau. 1939: The Lone Wolf Spy Hunt (GB: The Lone Wolf's Daughter). Renegade Ranger. Only Angels Have Wings. Special Inspector (GB: Across the Border). 1940: Music in My Heart. Susan and God (GB: The Gay Mrs Trexel). Blondie on a Budget. The Lady in Question. Angels over Broadway. 1941: The Strawberry Blonde. Affectionately Yours. Blood and Sand. You'll Never Get Rich. 1942: My Gal Sal. Tales of Manhattan. You Were Never Lovelier. 1943: *Show Business at War. 1944: Cover Girl. Tonight and Every Night. 1946: Gilda. 1947: Down to Earth. 1948: The Lady from Shanghai. The Loves of Carmen. 1952: Affair in Trinidad. 1953: Salome. Miss Sadie Thompson. 1954: Champagne Safari. *Screen Snapshots No. 225. 1957: Fire Down Below. Pal Joey. 1958: Separate Tables. 1959: They Came to Cordura. The Story on Page One. 1962: The Happy Thieves. 1964: Circus World (GB: The Magnificent Showman). 1965: The Money Trap. 1966: The Poppy is Also a Flower (GB: Danger Grows Wild). L'avventuriero/The Rover. 1968: I bastardi/Sons of Satan. 1970: The Road to Salina. 1971: The Naked Zoo. 1972: The Wrath of God. 1976: Circle.*

†As Rita Cansino (when billed)

### Jean Kent

*1934: †The Rocks of Valpré (US: High Treason). 1935: †How's Your Father? 1939: ‡Frozen Limits. 1940: ‡Hullo Fame! 1942: It's That Man Again. 1943: Miss London Ltd. Warn That Man. 1944: Bees in Paradise. Fanny by Gaslight (US: Man of Evil). Waterloo Road. Champagne Charlie. Soldier, Sailor. 2,000 Women. Madonna of the Seven Moons. 1945: The Wicked Lady. The Rake's Progress (US: Notorious Gentleman). 1946: Carnival. Caravan. The Magic Bow. 1947: The Man Within (US: The Smugglers). The Loves of Joanna Godden. Good Time Girl. 1948: Bond Street. Sleeping Car to Trieste. 1949: Trottie True (US: Gay Lady). 1950: The Woman in Question (US: Five Angles on Murder). Her Favourite Husband (US: The Taming of Dorothy). The Reluctant Widow. 1951: The Browning Version. 1952: The Lost Hours (US: The Big Frame). 1955: Before I Wake (US: Shadow of Fear). 1957: The Prince and the Showgirl. 1958: Bonjour Tristesse. Grip of the Strangler (US: The Haunted Strangler). 1959: Beyond This Place (US: Web of Evidence). Please Turn Over. 1960: Bluebeard's Ten Honeymoons. 1976: Shout at the Devil.*

†As Joan Summerfield
‡As Jean Carr

### Margaret Lockwood

*1934: Lorna Doone. 1935: The Case of Gabriel Perry. Wild Justice. Some Day. Honours Easy. Man of the Moment. Midshipman Easy (US: Men of the Sea). Jury's Evidence. The Amateur Gentleman. 1936: The Beloved Vagabond. Irish for Luck. 1937: The Street Singer. Who's Your Lady Friend? Dr Syn. Melody and Romance. Owd Bob (US: To the Victor). Bank Holiday (US: Three on a Weekend). 1938: The Lady Vanishes. 1939: Rulers of the Sea. Susannah of the Mounties. A Girl Must Live. The Stars Look Down. 1940: Night Train to Munich (US: Night Train). The Girl in the News. 1941: Quiet Wedding. 1942: Alibi. 1943: Dear Octopus (US: The Randolph Family). The Man in Grey. 1944: Give Us the Moon. Love Story (US: A Lady Surrenders). 1945: A Place of One's Own. I'll Be Your Sweetheart. The Wicked Lady. 1946: Bedelia. Hungry Hill. 1947: Jassy. The White Unicorn (US: Bad Sister). 1948: Look Before You Love. 1949: Cardboard Cavalier. Madness of the Heart. 1950: Highly Dangerous. 1952: Trent's Last Case. 1953: Laughing Anne. 1954: Trouble in the Glen. 1955: Cast a Dark Shadow. 1976: The Slipper and the Rose.*

### Ida Lupino

*1931: The Love Race. 1932: Her First Affaire. 1933: Money for Speed. High Finance. I Lived with You. Prince of Arcadia. The Ghost Camera. 1934: Search for Beauty. Ready for Love. Come on Marines. 1935: Paris in Spring (GB: Paris Love Song). Peter Ibbetson. *La Fiesta de Santa Barbara. Smart Girl. 1936: Anything Goes. The Gay Desperado. One Rainy Afternoon. Yours for the Asking. 1937: Sea Devils. Artists and Models. Let's Get Married. Fight for Your Lady. 1939: The Lone Wolf Spy Hunt (GB: The Lone Wolf's Daughter). The Adventures of Sherlock Holmes (GB: Sherlock Holmes). The Lady and the Mob. 1940: The Light That Failed. They Drive by Night (GB: The Road to Frisco). 1941: The Sea Wolf. High Sierra. Out of the Fog. Ladies in Retirement. 1942: Moontide. Life Begins at 8.30 (GB: The Light of Heart). The Hard Way. 1943: Forever and a Day. Thank Your Lucky Stars. Devotion (released 1946). 1944: Hollywood Canteen. In Our Time. 1945: Pillow to Post. 1946: The Man I Love. 1947: Deep Valley. Escape Me Never. 1948: Road House. 1949: Lust for Gold. 1950: Woman in Hiding. 1951: On Dangerous Ground. 1952: Beware My Lovely. 1953: Jennifer. The Bigamist. 1954: Private Hell 36. 1955: The Big Knife. Women's Prison. 1956: While the City Sleeps. Strange Intruder. 1967: I Love a Mystery (TV). 1968: Backtrack (TV). 1971: Women in Chains (TV). 1972: Female Artillery (TV). Deadhead Miles. Junior Bonner. My Boys Are Good Boys. The Letters (TV). The Strangers in 7A (TV). 1975: The Devil's Rain. 1976: The Food of the Gods.*

As director: *1949: Not Wanted (uncredited co-director). 1950: Outrage. Never Fear. 1951: Hard, Fast and Beautiful. 1953: The Bigamist. The Hitch-Hiker. 1966: The Trouble With Angels.*

### Pola Negri

*1914: Niewolnicá Zomyslow. 1915: Czarná Ksiazeczka. Pokoj 13. 1916: Jego Ostátú Czyn. Zona. Studenci. Arabella. Die Bestie. 1917: Die toten Augen. Küsse, die man stiehlt im Dunketh. Nicht lange tauschte mich das Glück. Rosen, die der Sturm entblättert. Zügelloses Blut (GB and US: Hot Blood). 1918: Carmen (US: Gypsy Blood). Der gelbe Schein (GB and US: The Yellow Ticket). Die Augen der Mumie Mâ (GB and US: The Eyes of the Mummy). Camille (US: The Red Peacock). Mania (GB and US: Mad Love). Wenn das Herz in Hass erglüht. 1919: Comptesse Daddy. Karussel des Lebens. Kreuziget sie! Madame Dubarry (US: Passion). 1920: Vendetta. Arme Violetta. Das Martyrium. Die geschlossene Kette. Die Marchesa d'Arminiani. Sumurun (GB and US: One Arabian Night). Medea. 1921: Die Bergkatze. Sappho. Die Dame im Glashave. 1922: Die Flamme (GB and US: Montmartre). 1923: Bella Donna. The Cheat. The Spanish Dancer. 1924: Shadows of Paris. Men. Lily of the Dust. Forbidden Paradise. 1925: East of Suez. The Charmer. Flower of the Night. A Woman of the World. 1926: The Crown of Lies. Good and Naughty. Hotel Imperial. 1927: Barbed Wire. The Woman on Trial. 1928: The Secret Hour. Three Sinners. Loves of an Actress. The Woman from Moscow. Are Women to Blame? 1929: The Woman He Scorned. Forbidden Paradise. 1932: A Woman Commands. 1934: Fanatisme. 1935: Mazurka. 1936: Moskau – Shanghai. 1937: Madame Bovary. Tango notturno. 1938: Die fromme Lüge. Die Nacht der Entscheidung. *Rudolph Valentino. 1943: Hi Diddle Diddle. 1964: The Moon-Spinners.*

### Lizabeth Scott

*1945: You Came Along. 1946: The Strange Love of Martha Ivers. Dead Reckoning. 1947: Desert Fury. I Walk Alone. Variety Girl. 1948: Pitfall. 1949: Too Late for Tears. Easy Living. 1950: Dark City. Paid in Full. 1951: Two of a Kind. The Company She Keeps. The Racket. Red Mountain. 1952: Stolen Face. 1953: Scared Stiff. Bad for Each Other. 1954: Silver Lode. 1956: Overnight Haul (TV. GB: cinemas). The Weapon. 1957: Loving You. 1972: Pulp.*

### Gale Sondergaard

*1936: Anthony Adverse. 1937: The Life of Emile Zola. Maid of Salem. Seventh Heaven. 1938: Lord Jeff (GB: The Boy from Barnardo's). Dramatic School. 1939: Juarez. Never Say Die. The Cat and the Canary. *Sons of Liberty. 1940: The Llano Kid. The Mark of Zorro. The Blue Bird. The Letter. 1941: The Black Cat. Paris Calling. 1942: Enemy Agents Meet Ellery Queen (GB: The Lido Mystery). My Favorite Blonde. A Night to Remember. 1943: Isle of Forgotten Sins. Appointment in Berlin. The Strange Death of Adolf Hitler. Sherlock Holmes and Spider Woman (GB: Spider Woman). 1944: Follow the Boys. Christmas Holiday. The Invisible Man's Revenge. Enter Arsène Lupin. The Climax. Gypsy Wildcat. 1946: Anna and the King of Siam. Spider Woman Strikes Back. The Time of Their Lives. A Night in Paradise. 1947: Road to Rio. Pirates of Monterey. 1949: East Side, West Side. 1969: Slaves. 1970: Comeback (later copyrighted 1973 as Savage Intruder). 1973: The Cat Creature. 1976: The Return of a Man Called Horse. Pleasantville. 1977: Hollywood on Trial. 1980: Echoes.*

### Barbara Stanwyck

*1927: Broadway Nights. 1929: The Locked Door. Mexicali Rose. *The Voice of Hollywood. 1930: Ladies of Leisure. 1931: Illicit. Ten cents a Dance. Miracle Woman. *Screen Snapshots No. 4. Night Nurse. 1932: Forbidden. Shopworn. So Big. The Purchase Price. 1933: Baby Face/Baby Face Harrington. The Bitter Tea of General Yen. Ladies They Talk About. Ever in My Heart. 1934: A Lost Lady (GB: Courageous). Gambling Lady. The Secret Bride (GB: Concealment). 1935: Red Salute (GB: Arms and the Girl). The Woman in Red. Annie Oakley. 1936: The Bride Walks Out. A Message to Garcia. The Plough and the Stars. His Brother's Wife. Banjo on My Knee. 1937: Internes Can't Take Money (GB: You Can't Take Money). This is My Affair (GB: His Affair). Stella Dallas. Breakfast for Two. 1938: The Mad Miss Manton. Always Goodbye. 1939: Union Pacific. Golden Boy. Remember the Night. 1941: You Belong to Me. Ball of Fire. The Lady Eve. Meet John Doe. 1942: The Gay Sisters. The Great Man's Lady. 1943: Lady of Burlesque (GB: Striptease Lady). Flesh and Fantasy. 1944: Hollywood Canteen. Double Indemnity. My Reputation (released*

*1946). 1945: *Hollywood Victory Caravan. Christmas in Connecticut (GB: Indiscretion). 1946: The Bride Wore Boots. California. The Strange Love of Martha Ivers. 1947: The Two Mrs Carrolls. Variety Girl. The Other Love. Cry Wolf. 1948: BF's Daughter (GB: Polly Fulton). Sorry, Wrong Number. 1949: Thelma Jordon (GB: The File on Thelma Jordon). East Side, West Side. The Lady Gambles. *Eyes of Hollywood. 1950: To Please a Lady. The Furies. No Man of Her Own. 1951: The Man with a Cloak. 1952: Clash by Night. 1953: All I Desire. Titanic. Jeopardy. The Moonlighter. Blowing Wild. 1954: Witness to Murder. Executive Suite. Cattle Queen of Montana. The Violent Men (GB: Rough Company). 1955: Escape to Burma. 1956: The Maverick Queen. These Wilder Years. There's Always Tomorrow. 1957: Crime of Passion. Forty Guns. Trooper Hook. 1962: A Walk on the Wild Side. 1964: Roustabout. 1965: The Night Walker. 1970: The House That Wouldn't Die (TV). 1971: A Taste of Evil (TV). 1972: The Letters (TV).*

### Barbara Steele

*1958: Bachelor of Hearts. Houseboat. 1959: Sapphire. The 39 Steps. Upstairs and Downstairs. Your Money or Your Wife. 1960: Mask of the Demon (GB: Black Sunday). 1961: The Iron Captain. The Pit and the Pendulum. 1962: Revenge of the Mercenaries. 8½. L'orribile segreto del Dr Hichcock (GB: The Terror of Dr Hichcock. US: The Horrible Dr Hitchcock). Le coup. Amour sans lendemain. Danse macabre (GB and US: Castle of Blood). 1963: The Spectre (US: The Ghost). Hours of Love. Un tentativo sentimentale. Le voci bianche. Les baisers. 1964: Le sexe des anges. I maniaci (US: The Maniacs). The Long Hair of Death. Amore facile. Le monocle rit jaune. El ataco (US: The Road to Violence). 1965: I soldi. L'armata Brancaleone. Cinque tombe per un medium (GB and US: Terror-Creatures from the Grave). Gli amanti d'oltre tomba (GB: The Faceless Monster. US: Nightmare Castle). La sorella di Satana (GB: Revenge of the Blood Beast. US: The She Beast). 1966: Young Törless. Un angelo per Satan/An Angel for Satan. For Love and Gold. 1967: Fermato il mondo ... voglio scendere. 1968: Handicap. Curse of the Crimson Altar (US: Crimson Cult). 1969: Honeymoon with a Stranger (TV). 1974: The Parasite Murders (GB: Shivers. US: They Came from Within). Caged Heat. 1977: I Never Promised You a Rose Garden. 1978: Piranha. Pretty Baby. La clé sur la porte. The Space Watch Murders (TV). 1979: The Silent Scream.*

### Meryl Streep

*1976: Julia. 1977: The Deadliest Season (TV). 1978: The Deer Hunter. 1979: Manhattan. The Seduction of Joe Tynan. Kramer vs Kramer. 1981: The French Lieutenant's Woman. 1982: Still of the Night. Sophie's Choice. Alice at the Palace (TV). 1983: Silkwood. 1984: In Our Hands. Falling in Love. 1985: Plenty. Out of Africa. 1986: Heartburn. Directed by William Wyler. 1987:* Evil Angels. Ironweed.

### Claire Trevor

*1933: Life in the Raw. Jimmy and Sally. The Last Trail. The Mad Game. 1934: Hold That Girl. Baby Take a Bow. Elinore Norton. Wild Gold. 1935: Dante's Inferno. Spring Tonic. Navy Wife. Black Sheep. 1936: Human Cargo. My Marriage. The Song and Dance Man. To Mary – with Love. 15 Maiden Lane. Career Woman. Star for a Night. 1937: One Mile from Heaven. Time Out for Romance. Second Honeymoon. Big Town Girl. Dead End. King of Gamblers. 1938: The Amazing Dr Clitterhouse. Walking Down Broadway. Valley of the Giants. Two of a Kind. 1939: I Stole a Million. Stagecoach. Allegheny Uprising (GB: The First Rebel). 1940: The Dark Command. 1941: Texas. Honky Tonk. 1942: Street of Chance. The Adventures of Martin Eden. Crossroads. 1943: Woman of the Town. The Desperadoes. Good Luck, Mr Yates. 1945: Murder, My Sweet (GB: Farewell, My Lovely). Johnny Angel. 1946: Crack-Up. The Bachelor's Daughters (GB: Bachelor Girls). 1947: Born to Kill (GB: Lady of Deceit). 1948: The Velvet Touch. Raw Deal. Key Largo. The Babe Ruth Story. 1949: The Lucky Stiff. 1950: Borderline. 1951: Hard, Fast and Beautiful. Best of the Badmen. Hoodlum Empire. 1952: My Man and I. Stop, You're Killing Me. 1953: The Stranger Wore a Gun. 1954: The High and the Mighty. 1955: Man without a Star. Lucy Gallant. 1956: The Mountain. 1957: If You Knew Elizabeth (TV). 1958: Marjorie Morningstar. 1962: Two Weeks in Another Town. The Stripper (GB: Woman of Summer). 1965: How to Murder Your Wife. 1967: The Cape Town Affair. 1982: Kiss Me Goodbye.*

### Lana Turner

*1937: A Star is Born. Topper. The Great Garrick. They Won't Forget. 1938. †The Chaser. Four's a Crowd. The Adventures of Marco Polo. Dramatic School. Love Finds Andy Hardy. Rich Man, Poor Girl. 1939: Dancing Co-Ed (GB: Every Other Inch a Lady). Calling Dr Kildare. These Glamour Girls. 1940: Two Girls on Broadway (GB: Change Your Partners). We Who Are Young. 1941: Dr Jekyll and Mr Hyde. Ziegfeld Girl. Johnny Eager. Honky Tonk. 1942: Somewhere I'll Find You. 1943: *Show Business At War. Slightly Dangerous. DuBarry Was a Lady. The Youngest Profession. 1944: Marriage is a Private Affair. 1945: Weekend at the Waldorf. Keep Your Powder Dry. 1946: The Postman Always Rings Twice. 1947: Green Dolphin Street. Cass Timberlane. 1948: Homecoming. The Three Musketeers. 1950: A Life of Her Own. Mr Imperium (GB: You Belong to My Heart). 1952: The Merry Widow. The Bad and the Beautiful. 1953: Latin Lovers. 1954: Flame and the Flesh. Betrayed. 1955: The Prodigal. The Sea Chase. Diane. The Rains of Ranchipur. 1957: Peyton Place. 1958: The Lady Takes a Flyer. Another Time, Another Place. 1959: Imitation of Life. 1960: Portrait in Black. 1961: Bachelor in Paradise. By Love Possessed. 1962: Who's Got the Action? 1964: Love Has Many Faces. 1966: Madame X. 1969: The Big Cube. 1974: Persecution. 1976: Bittersweet Love. 1978: Witches' Brew (released 1985).*

†Most scenes deleted from final release print.

### Mae West

*Night after Night. 1933: She Done Him Wrong. I'm No Angel. 1934: Belle of the Nineties. 1935: Goin' to Town. 1936: Klondike Annie. Go West, Young Man. 1938: Every Day's a Holiday. 1940: My Little Chickadee. 1943: The Heat's On (GB: Tropicana). 1970: Myra Breckinridge. 1977: Sextette.*

### Marie Windsor

*1941: All American Co-Ed. 1942: *The Lady or the Tiger. Parachute Nurse. Call Out the Marines. George Washington Slept Here. The Big Street. Smart Alecks. Eyes in the Night. 1943: Let's Face It. Chatterbox. Three Hearts for Julia. Pilot No. 5. 1947: Song of the Thin Man. The Hucksters. The Romance of Rosy Ridge. The Unfinished Dance. *I Love My Wife, But! 1948: On an Island with You. The Kissing Bandit. The Three Musketeers. Force of Evil. 1949: The Beautiful Blonde from Bashful Bend. Outpost in Morocco. The Fighting Kentuckian. Hellfire. 1950: Dakota Lil. The Showdown. Double Deal. Frenchie. 1951: Little Big Horn (GB: The Fighting Seventh). Two Dollar Bettor (GB: Beginner's Luck). Hurricane Island. The Narrow Margin. 1952: Japanese War Bride. The Jungle. The Sniper. Outlaw Women. 1953: The Tall Texan. City That Never Sleeps. Trouble along the Way. The Eddie Cantor Story. So This is Love (GB: The Grace Moore Story). Cat Women of the Moon. 1954: Hell's Half Acre. The Bounty Hunter. The Silver Star. 1955: Abbott and Costello Meet the Mummy. Stories of the Century No. 1 – Belle Starr. No Man's Woman. Two-Gun Lady. 1956: The Killing. Swamp Women. The Unholy Wife. 1957: The Girl in Black Stockings. The Story of Mankind. The Parson and the Outlaw. 1958: Day of the Bad Man. Island Women. 1962: Paradise Alley. 1963: Critic's Choice. The Day Mars Invaded Earth. Mail Order Bride (GB: West of Montana). 1964: Bedtime Story. 1966: Chamber of Horrors. 1969: The Good Guys and the Bad Guys. 1970: Wild Women (TV). 1971: Support Your Local Gunfighter. One More Train to Rob. 1973: Cahill: United States Marshal (GB: Cahill). The Outfit. Manhunter (TV). 1974: The Apple Dumpling Gang. 1975: Hearts of the West (GB: Hollywood Cowboy). 1976: Freaky Friday. Stranded (TV). 1983: Lovely But Deadly. 1985: JOE and the Colonel (TV). 1987: Commando Squad.*

### Googie Withers

*1934: The Girl in the Crowd. The Love Test. 1935: All at Sea. Windfall. Dark World. Her Last Affaire. 1936: She Knew What She Wanted. Crown v Stevens. Crime over London. King of Hearts. Accused. 1937: Action for Slander. Pearls Bring Tears. Paradise for Two (US: The Gaiety Girls). The Green Cockatoo. 1938: Kate Plus Ten. Paid in Error. Convict 99. You're the Doctor. If I Were Boss. Strange Boarders. The Lady Vanishes. Murder in Soho (US: Murder in the Night). 1939: Dead Men Are Dangerous. She Couldn't Say No. Trouble Brewing. The Gang's All Here (US: The Amazing Mr Forrest). 1940: Bulldog Sees It Through. Busman's Honeymoon (US: Haunted Honeymoon). 1941: Jeannie. 1942: One of Our Aircraft is Missing. Back Room Boy. 1943: The Silver Fleet. 1944: On Approval. They Came to a City. Natasha (dubbed voice only). 1945: Dead of Night. Pink String and Sealing Wax. 1947: The Loves of Joanna Godden. It Always Rains on Sunday. 1948: Miranda. 1949: Once Upon a Dream. Traveller's Joy. 1950: Night and the City. 1951: White Corridors. The Magic Box. Lady Godiva Rides Again. 1952: Derby Day (US: Four Against Fate). 1954: Devil on Horseback. 1955: Port of Escape. 1970: The Nickel Queen. 1985: Time After Time (TV). Hôtel du Lac (TV). 1987: Northanger Abbey (TV).*

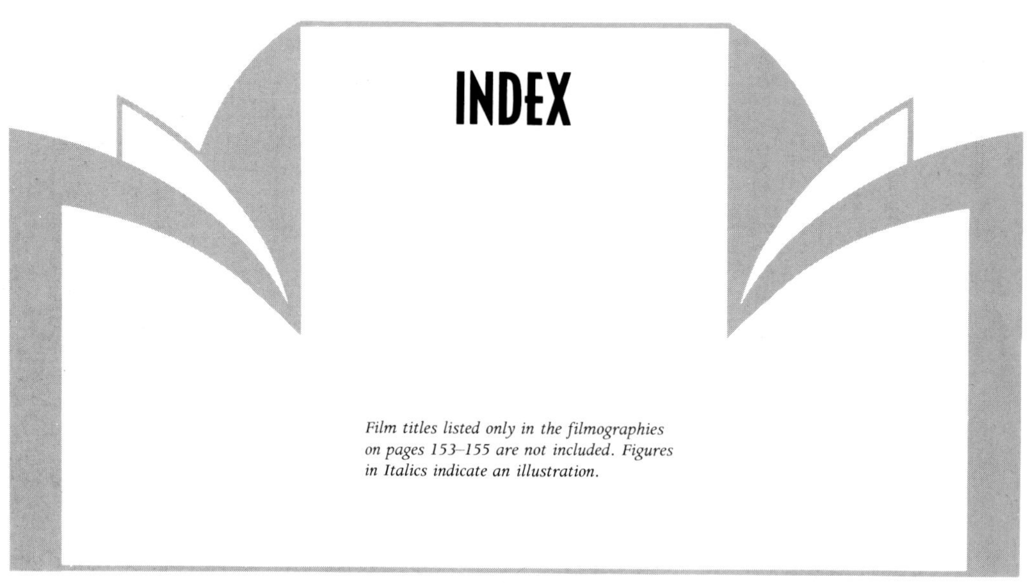


*Film titles listed only in the filmographies on pages 153–155 are not included. Figures in Italics indicate an illustration.*